MW00786804

TOO FAST TO LIVE

TOO YOUNG TO DIE

First published in the United Kingdom in 2020 by

Pavilion
43 Great Ormond Street
London
WC1N 3HZ

ISBN 978-1-91164-136-0

A CIP catalogue record for this book is available from the British Library.

10 9 8 7 6 5 4 3 2 1

Reproduction by Rival Colour Ltd, UK

Printed in Singapore

www.pavilionbooks.com

ACKNOWLEDGMENTS

Several people provided guidance and emotional support over the five years it took to bring this book to fruition. Firstly, thanks to Steven Kasher and Kat Jones, who took a 'flyer' on me at the Kasher Gallery on West 23rd Street in New York City when they agreed to present Rude and Reckless in July 2011, my first exhibition. I will always be grateful for their support, patience and enthusiasm. Rude and Reckless led me to Kaytie Johnson (chief curator of The Galleries at Moore College in Philadelphia at the time) and her colleague Gabrielle Lavin, who in January 2014 curated what I believe was the first museum exhibition of punk and post-punk graphic design (as opposed to memorabilia) in the US: Pretty Vacant: The Graphic Language of Punk.

More recently, Andrew Blauvelt, director of Cranbrook Art Museum in Bloomfield Hills, Michigan (a brilliant curator) and Chris Scoates, the brave director of the Museum of Arts and Design ('MAD') in New York City, who made Too Fast To Live, Too Young To Die: Punk Graphics, 1976–1986 his first exhibition there, have been critically important in bringing my collection to a wider audience. Collaborating with them was an exciting and challenging experience.

I have to thank the esteemed individuals who have contributed to this book: Russ Bestley, Art Chantry, Sebastian Conran, Glen Cummings, Malcolm Garrett, Steven Heller, Adam Michaels, Rick Poynor and Michael Wilde. Having Malcolm Garrett and Peter Saville design the front and back covers for this book is a dream come true. (Thanks to the fantastic Sheila Rock, for introducing me to Malcolm.)

I'm grateful to editor Mal Peachey, designer Barbara Doherty, and Katie Cowan at Pavilion for understanding that punk and post-punk graphics represent a design category worthy of a book of this scale and critical scholarship.

Thanks to my friend and fellow traveller Craig Kallman, whose shared zeal for these materials boosted my morale when it was flagging (he has what is unquestionably the greatest collection of vinyl on the planet).

Last but not least, thanks to my cousin John Krivine for introducing me to the rather menacing, tatty world of punk rock in London over four decades ago. Without punk, I am not sure how I would have survived those years of teen angst and alienation.

The high quality of many of the scans seen in the book is due in no small part to the archival mounting and restoration work of Ian Wright, a personal friend and owner of M&W Graphics based in New York. Many posters which might have been written off as total losses were saved by his conservation work.

Andrew Krivine, 2019

This book is dedicated to Dolly Frankel, Ruth Krivine and Shelagh Krivine.

TOO FAST TO LIVE
TOO YOUNG TO DIE

ANDREW KRIVINE

PAVILION

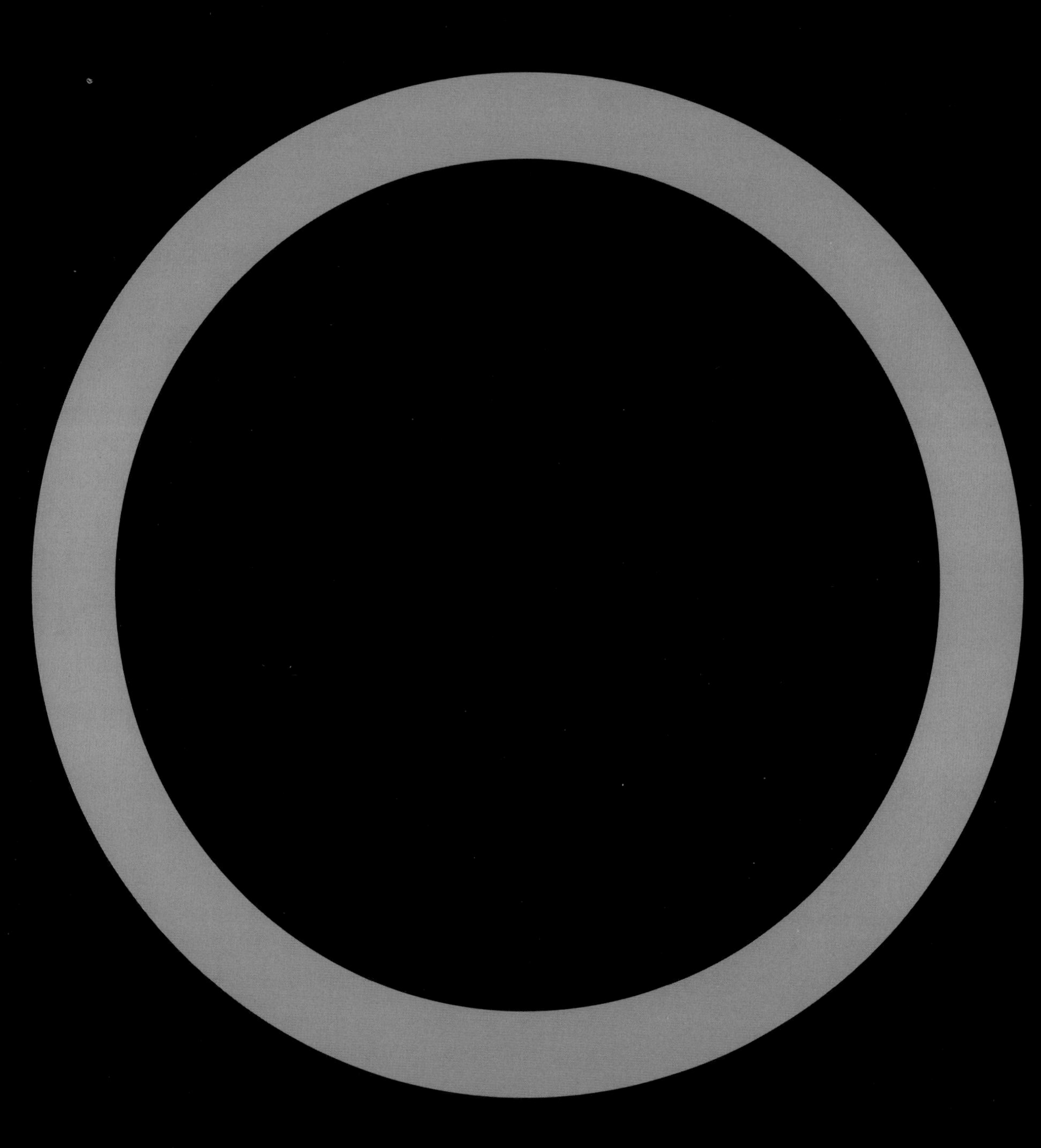

NO ELVIS, BEATLES OR ROLLING STONES: A COLLECTOR'S JOURNEY

The summer of 1977 was one of the formative periods of my life. From my first encounter with punk rock, the music, the posters and fashion immediately struck me. Mainstream popular culture of the mid-1970s held zero interest for me. I detested the pretensions of prog-rock – that often shapeless, indulgent music which dominated the airwaves then. With the exception of The Who, I had no music to call my own. Hearing the first Clash record in June 1977 flipped a switch in my brain and my musical world was transformed.

My father's family lived in London, and every summer during my teens I would visit relatives for several weeks. My first cousin, John Krivine, was immersed in punk fashion, having founded the King's Road shop Acme Attractions with Steph Raynor in the early 1970s, followed by BOY in 1977. BOY was one of a handful of punk clothing stores in London at the time. I spent several days in the shop that July, and while John conducted BOY business I would observe the exotic (in some instances, rather scary) punk patrons in the shop. Many afternoons I would walk up and down the King's Road, going to record shops and, with trepidation, step through the entrance of Seditionaries, the ground zero for punk fashion[1]. For a sixteen-year-old who was lacking in self-confidence and an ocean away from his suburban environs, Seditionaries was an awesome and menacing place.

By the time I returned to my hometown of Briarcliff Manor (within NYC's commuter belt) in early September 1977, I had become a devout proselytizer for punk and had begun to form what is now a vast collection of punk-related memorabilia and art. Kitted out with oxblood DMs along with blue suede brothel creepers, several BOY and Seditionaries shirts and bondage zipper trousers, I was convinced that within weeks, punk was going to sweep America and

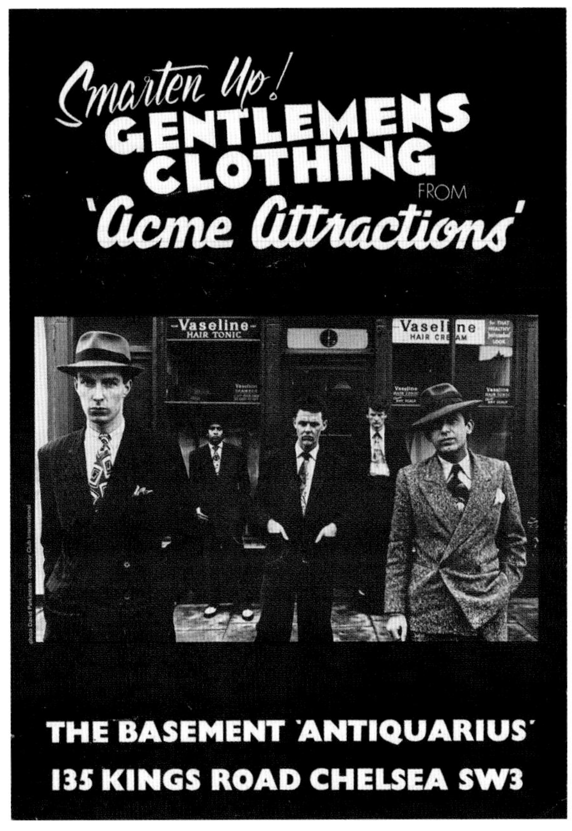

1

j.j. krivine's
ACME Attractions
FASHIONWARE, WHOLESALE, RETAIL, FOR SALE & HIRE
THE BASEMENT, 135a, KINGS ROAD, LONDON, S.W.3, ENGLAND
telephone 01-351 0638 & 01-582 0932

2

3

ACME ATTRACTIONS: 1 1976 poster, **David Parkinson** photography, courtesy of *Club International* magazine; **2** Acme Attractions letterhead, John Jason Krivine (1976); **3** 20th Century Antiques, John Krivine's first shop in Brixton (1975)

[1] Prior to the opening of Seditionaries at 430 King's Road in December 1976, Malcolm McLaren and Vivienne Westwood created three other boutique concepts at the same location, beginning with Let It Rock in 1972, followed by Too Fast To Live Too Young To Die (hence the book title, I gladly admit) in 1973, and then SEX in 1974.

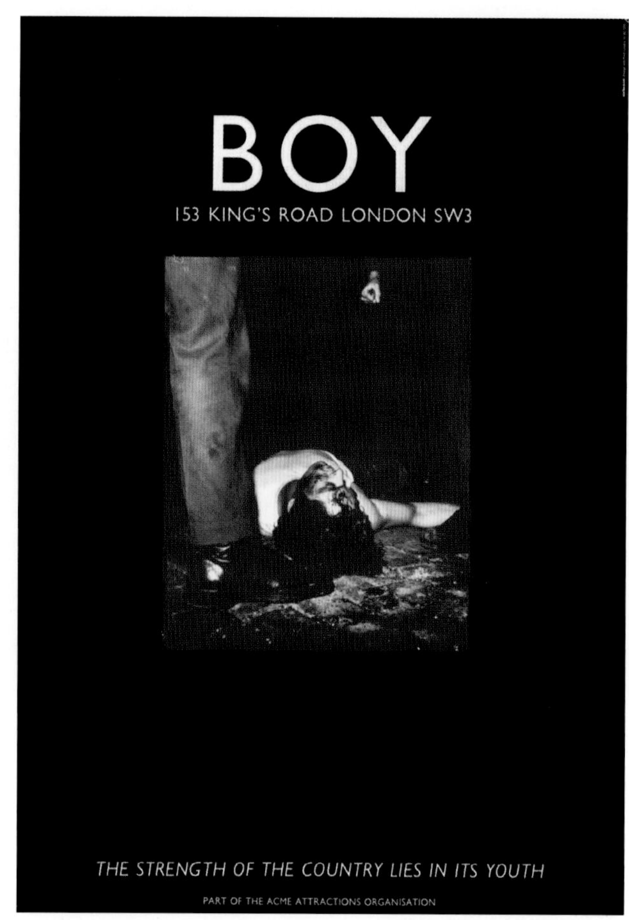

ABOVE: (left) fanzine ad for ACME Attractrions, sited at what would become the HQ of BOY (1977); (right) BOY poster (1977), **Peter Christopherson** and **John Harewood** design

LEFT: photo of the Monads, just prior to High School talent show performance (April 1978)

ABOVE: The walls of my suburban bedroom, Briarcliff Manor, NY (1977)

I would be credited for being the cool 'first mover' in Briarcliff. How much more deluded could I have been? I don't know what I was thinking. Fortunately, because I had lived in Briarcliff since birth and the school had a small, closely knit group of kids, I wasn't immediately beaten to a pulp. My classmates were bemused and made a few sarcastic comments but basically tolerated my obsession with punk.

The geographical arc of my late teens and university years helped shape my collection. During my senior year in high school I would often take the Metro-North train into Manhattan with friends and go to such clubs as Hurrah, Max's Kansas City and, of course, CBGB. We were all huge fans of The Cramps and the Dead Boys. A few of us formed a punk band called the Monads and we had several rehearsals but only played in public twice – once at the annual high school talent show and then at the home of a hapless fellow student, who unwisely allowed us to perform at a party while his parents were away. If memory serves correctly, the police arrived at some point during the evening. Destruction of property resulted, which was never intended and I regret to this day. One of our songs, 'V2 Rocket', shamelessly stole Steve Jones' riff from 'Submission'. In the end, my bandmates and I followed the punk lifestyle to its logical conclusion: our drummer, Michael Azerrad, went on to fame and glory in the world of rock journalism; our semi-dreadlocked bassist Peter Brown became a highly respected gynecologist; our scorching lead guitarist Charlie Briggs is a professor of medieval history at the University of Vermont and Fellow of the Royal Historical Society; our mildly terrifying lead singer, Michael O'Clair, is a thriving litigator in Seattle; and I work in commercial banking for the only progressive bank in the United States.

During the years 1977–80 (which were my senior year in high school and first few years at Northwestern University in Evanston, Illinois), I continued to add to my punk collection. On subsequent visits to London I

ABOVE: Polaroid of Monads in rehearsal (March 1978)

RIGHT: leaning on the window of Stiff Records shop/offices, 32 Alexander Street, London W2 (1978)

scoured record shops (including Rough Trade's first outlet in Ladbroke Grove) and Better Badges for fanzines, badges and other ephemera. I also trekked to the headquarters of some labels – notably Virgin and Stiff Records – trolling for any promotional materials they cared to part with. I went to many of the venues where punk bands were allowed to play – the Vortex, 100 Club, Dingwalls, Marquee and Music Machine – and was very lucky to be subjected to waves of snarling feedback, standing a few feet from many of the greats. Possibly as a result, I am now partially deaf in my left ear (no small achievement).

My mother moved to San Diego in 1978 and on holiday breaks with her I would see such British bands as 999, The Only Ones and Penetration at the local venues, which were within spitting distance of the Pacific Ocean, which was an odd juxtaposition. Back in Evanston, I would take the L train to Wax Trax! Records (near the infamous Biograph Theatre, site of John Dillinger's ambush by federal agents in July 1934) to see bands at the Aragon Ballroom, Park West, Club C.O.D. and O'Banion's.

A junior year spent at the University of East Anglia in Norwich, England, was one of the happiest

periods of my life. I saw almost every British post-punk band to pass through Norwich, either at the student union or in local clubs such as The Gala Ballroom and Jacquard Club. UEA was part of the university touring circuit that crisscrossed the Isles. Evenings were spent going to some extraordinary performances, including a Cure concert in Norwich's St Andrews Hall, an imposing flint structure dating back to the fifteenth century, during their Faith tour (an immersive, gothic experience). Other bands to appear included a very young U2, Altered Images, the Au Pairs, Echo & The Bunnymen, The Jam, Madness and The Skids. While in Norwich I focused my collecting compulsion on post-punk bands, including the Au Pairs, Gang Of Four, Echo & The Bunnymen, Joy Division, Orchestral Manoeuvres In The Dark, A Certain Ratio, Wah! Heat and The Teardrop Explodes. Looking back, I am grateful to have come of age during a time of such musical creativity.

In my travels, I continued to add to the collection, having developed a love for the materials and what I now recognize to have been a subconscious appreciation of the artistry of countless punk and post-punk poster designs.

BELOW: set of promotional badges for the *Norwich – A Fine City* compilation LP, Romans In Britain Records (1981)

In subsequent years I scoured record fairs, went to going-out-of-business sales at failing record shops and, later, discovered rarities on the web, relentlessly adding materials. As this endeavour became more consuming, I had to ask myself: What compelled me to devote so much time and effort over the expanse of decades? What was it, exactly, that drew me to punk and post-punk, sustaining my interest for nearly four decades?

The fashion, graphic designs, the intense irritation punk provoked in the older generation and, of course, the music of the period all fuelled my passion. Punk sonically pulsates; it has velocity, aggression and humour. Punk rejects hypocrisy and pretense. There is no hierarchy with narcissistic performers demanding 'tribute', or barriers to prevent you from joining a band and making a racket. Rudimentary command of guitar, drumming or even singing is simply not an issue (as I can well attest: I was a dreadful guitarist, but that didn't stop me; two chords was a challenge I welcomed).

My preoccupation with all things punk and post-punk led me to research the era and learn more about the creators responsible for these extraordinary designs. The body of published works devoted to punk rock history and art is extensive and growing. I knew from the start that punk was distinct from prior youth movements, yet how it evolved remains a subject of fascination.

Punk and post-punk design broke decisively from the Aubrey Beardsley and Alphonse Mucha-infused psychedelic design aesthetic of the dominant rock-poster artists from the 1960s (e.g., Wes Wilson, David Byrd, Stanley Mouse, Rick Griffin, Victor Moscoso, Nigel Waymouth and Michael English) – though punk and post-punk graphic designers were by no means contemptuous of the past. Elements from several twentieth-century movements – Bauhaus, Futurism, Vorticism, expressionism, De Stijl, Soviet contructivism and surrealism – all are represented in the collection. I see, too, the extent to which many of these artists embraced Dadaism and pop art with gusto.

Readers will quickly see that the selection from my collection gathered in this book teems with pop art-influenced works (referencing Blake, Hamilton, Lichtenstein, Paolozzi, Rauschenberg, Warhol and others). Many punk and post-punk posters could (ironically) be considered 'applied pop art', using visually compelling, engaging imagery designed to convince the public to attend commercial venues and buy the product. Regarding Dada, John Heartfield and Hannah Höch (one of the few female Dadaists and earliest practitioners of assemblage) were huge influences.[2] The Dadaists were provocateurs whose impulses meshed perfectly with strands within punk, and were also a galvanizing influence on anarcho-punk graphic design.[3]

LEFT: me in Waveney Terrace dorm room UEA, Norwich, UK (1981)

BELOW: at Electric Lady Studios NY, with friend David Butner and Joe Strummer (spring 1980)

[2] Of note, in 1977 the Institute of Contemporary Art in London mounted an exhibition of Heartfield's work, John Heartfield: Photomontage (compiled by the Elephanten Press Galerie, Berlin). The exhibition ran from late July to mid-September, which curiously coincides with the British punk scene at its height. Who knows who might have found inspiration?

[3] The most culturally potent manifestation of the Situationist International occurred during the student riots in Paris, 1968. The SI was a movement embraced by Malcolm McLaren, Jamie Reid and Tony Wilson during their formative student years.

ABOVE: (top) with Bloody Hell, performing at the Gala Ballroom, Norwich (May 1981); (bottom) with friend Peter Samuel, rehearsing at the UEA practice space for students, Norwich (December 1980)

Heartfield and Höch employed visual elements and techniques that can be seen throughout the collection. Using advertising materials from news and glamour weeklies in the twenties and thirties, they would appropriate and splice fragments of fractured images, body parts, faces, soldiers, politicians and movie stars to create surreal, often disturbing collages. While a contributor to the communist, pro-Soviet *Arbeiter-Illustrierte-Zeitung*, Heartfield created photomontages that lampooned the Nazi hierarchy and predicted the cataclysm to come, creating 240 covers for the *AIZ* over several years – a political sensibility that permeates countless punk and post-punk flyers and posters. The Dadaist artistic legacy is reflected in many of the works by, among others, Linder Sterling, Winston Smith, Adam Ant (specifically, his earliest Antz gig flyers) and Gee Vaucher, included herein.

In contrast to the 1960s, graphic design and music in the punk era were more closely fused, particularly in Britain. Musicians such as Viv Albertine, Adam Ant, Ian Dury, John Foxx, Mick Jones, Glen Matlock and Paul Simonon all attended art schools before forming bands. The widely accepted narrative of punk's spontaneous, untutored DIY impulse – as was the case with the music – is, in my opinion, largely inaccurate regarding the designs. An art school foundation underscores much of the work in this book.

Fashion always figured prominently in rock; almost all the pop icons of the 1960s were keenly attuned to it, and The Beatles notoriously went so far as to squander a fortune on their fashion folly, the Apple Boutique on Baker Street, which lasted barely eight months and was shuttered in July 1968. Yet the relationship between mediums took on a radically different character and tone with the birth of punk.

These punk and post-punk designs were not created in a vacuum. The young Britons who would become designers or join bands came up

through institutions that had been transformed. The Labour government emerged from World War II with a mandate from voters to reshape Britain into a less stratified, more inclusive and equitable society. Along with housing and universal access to health care, education had become a priority for the Attlee government; and indeed, during the fifties and sixties, art schools across the United Kingdom were direct beneficiaries of this public policy. These institutions spawned a pool of talent that would make their mark in the media, advertising and pop music industries, as well as the arts. The British graphical works in this book are a legacy of well-funded policies and programmes implemented over three decades after the war, based on the conviction that art and art history enriched society. Because in both America and Britain today, arts programmes are under siege and our respective cultures relentlessly starved of resources, the need for preservation is more pressing than ever.

The relation of art colleges to punk is a central reason why its fashion was inherently graphic. Certain bands explicitly referenced art schools, most notably The Jam in the first song on *In The City* (1977), entitled 'Art School'. The T-shirts and trousers stocked by King's Road punk fashion purveyors BOY and Seditionaries and, as importantly, the gear created by the bands themselves, were embossed with slogans, patches, typography and symbols. During this period, Vivienne Westwood created several T-shirts which juxtaposed lyrics from Sex Pistols songs with images in a fusion of music and graphics (saturation marketing in action). The effect of these hand-stencilled articles was incendiary. Before punk, such graphics were found exclusively in poster art but never really crossed over into other mediums. For the first time in popular youth culture, graphic design, fashion and music had merged. The effect was potent: punk clothes *were* prêt-à-porter graphic design.

ABOVE: with my friend Chris Dawes in Waveney Terrace dorm room, UEA, Norwich (April 1981)

For example, thanks to Julien Temple's foresight back in December 1976, we have an early video record of The Clash customizing their own boiler suits and shirts in a dank London taxi repair garage, using stencils and spray-paint guns. The results can be seen on the gear worn by the band for the cover photo on the single 'White Riot'. Gesamtkunstwerk, a creation that synthesizes the musical, theatrical and visual arts, is a term best used with caution; The Clash, though, embraced the idea. In Julien's film *The Clash: New Year's Day '77*, we see how the band's music (the inaugural gig at the Roxy), graphic art (Paul Simonon's mural on the wall of their Rehearsal Rehearsals practice studio in Camden Town), the venue as backdrop and their clothing all fused seamlessly.

Others created distinct looks as well, like Poly Styrene (neon plastic dresses, US Army helmet with goggles), Buzzcocks (Piet Mondrian designs on button-down shirts), Siouxsie Sioux (who practically invented goth fashion) and Generation X (who, along with The Jam, were really unreconstructed mods born ten years too late, with Tony James' stencils used to emblazon their T-shirts with pop art symbols). During the first wave of punk, the fashion had vitality and immediacy from multiple, cross-pollinating sources: clothing designers, the bands and the kids who went to the clubs.

While cataloguing the collection, the extent to which so many British punk, new wave and post-punk musicians forged enduring partnerships with graphic designers and art directors became apparent. The periods covered here coincided with the rise of independent designers, in a departure from the 1950s and 60s, when record labels had salaried design staff expected to create covers almost on a piecework basis, with minimal focus on a specific genre or performer.

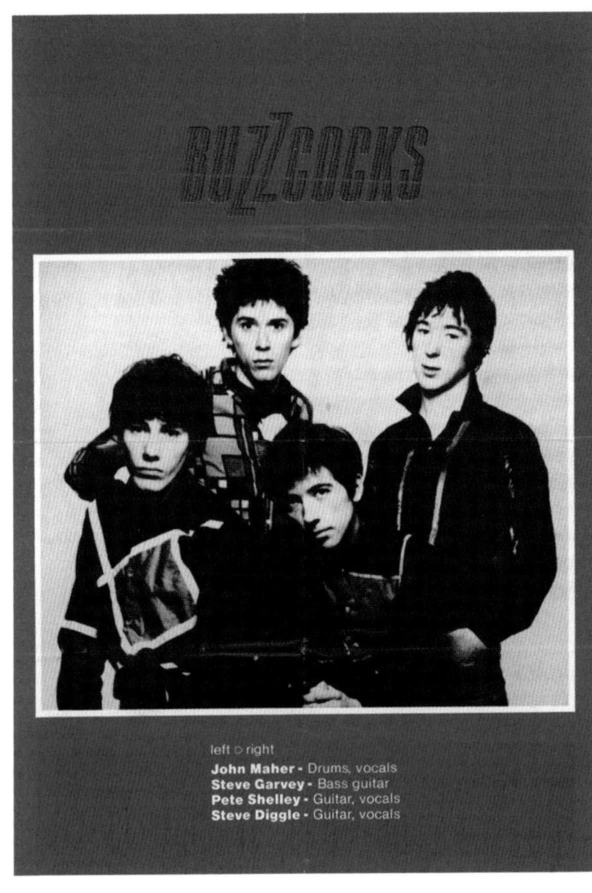

ABOVE: The Clash 'White Riot' – 45 front cover, CBS Records (1977), **Sebastian Conran** design, **Caroline Coon** photography

RIGHT: Buzzcocks two-sided promotional flyer, UA Records (March 1978)

Examples of such collaborations throughout this work include the following (a sampling by no means complete):

Martyn Atkins – Echo & The Bunnymen, The Teardrop Explodes
Barney Bubbles – The Damned, Hawkwind
Mike Coles – Killing Joke
Sebastian Conran – The Clash
Malcolm Garrett – Buzzcocks, 999, Magazine
Paul Henry – 999, The Stranglers
Russell Mills – Penetration
Rob O'Connor (Styrolounge Design Studio) – Siouxsie and The Banshees
Jamie Reid – Sex Pistols
Rocking Russian (Alex McDowell) – Rich Kids, Siouxsie and The Banshees
Peter Saville – Joy Division, New Order, OMD, Ultravox
Jo Slee, David Storey and Caryn Gough – who, collectively, collaborated with Morrissey to create a series of distinct portraits of kitchen-sink realism, seen on virtually every single sleeve and LP cover of The Smiths
Bill Smith – The Jam
George Snow – 999
Gee Vaucher and Dave King – Crass
Andy Vella and Porl Thompson – The Cure

With rare exceptions (most notably the brilliant artists Raymond Pettibon for Black Flag and Winston Smith[4] for Dead Kennedys), this kind of joint effort was not as common in the United States. Yet there were a number of US groups (including The Cramps and Devo) who created most of their own sleeves and poster designs. And, of course, Talking Heads, who famously met at the Rhode Island School of Design; David Byrne himself was responsible for a number of their early singles covers.

In conjunction with the designers and art directors, many talented photographers made critical contributions to designs. The list is long and includes: Roberta Bayley, Janette Beckman, Adrian Boot, Anton Corbijn, Kevin Cummins, Chalkie Davies, Ian Dickson, Brian Duffy, Erica Echenberg, Jill Furmanovsky, Chris Gabrin, Brian Griffin, David Godlis, Peter 'Kodick' Gravelle, Bob Gruen, Trevor Key, Laura Levine, Gered Mankowitz, Dennis Morris, Keith Morris, Marcia Resnick, Mick Rock, Sheila Rock, Kate Simon, Pennie Smith and Ray Stevenson. Their images were essential, vital elements that enhance the artistry of many of the posters in this book.

The intersection of music, visual arts and fashion continues to fascinate. No popular youth movement of the past five decades has fused the three mediums so perfectly, and I hope the book inspires neo-punk revivalists in the decades to come. I am convinced that the artists represented in this book produced many of the finest postmodern graphic designs of the twentieth century. Often, they would mash together elements of high and low art, with exuberance and superb effect. If readers experience even a fraction of the exhilaration and joy these posters and artifacts have given and continue to give me, this magnificent obsession will not have been in vain.

Andrew Krivine, 2019

---

[4] Winston conceived of the Alternative Tentacles record label logo, the DK logo and six record sleeves for Dead Kennedys, and while at Alternative Tentacles he was responsible for an entire range of promotional materials. James Patrick Morey (his real name) uses the handle Winston Smith for his artworks in a tip o' the hat to Orwell's novel, ***1984***. Winston also created designs for a number of other bands, including the Butthole Surfers, Cheetah Chrome's Motherfuckers, Jello Biafra with D.O.A., and Green Day.

BOY

Dear Andrew,

as a result of a meeting of the board, we have decided to offer you a position with this company on a temporary non-paid basis for the purpose of installing a computer to handle the administration of the company.

Despite numerous applications from America Business School Graduates, we offer you this valued position in the knowledge that you are the Man for the Job.

With love

John 21-9-83

Acme Attractions Limited
Registered in England 1376232
Directors: J. Krivine S. Raynor
Est. 1972

Shop: 153 King's Road London SW3 *Telephone:* 01-351 1115
Wholesale: 4th floor Quadrant House 250 Kennington Lane London SE11 England
Telephone: 01-735 3852

ABOVE: Job offer letter from John Kirvine, owner of BOY, to cousin Andrew Kirvine, September 1983.

[EDITOR'S NOTE]

This book is not intended to be a comprehensive history of punk and post-punk music, but is rather a visual examination of the graphic art which the music inspired. Remarkably, it represents just a part of arguably the largest collection of punk and post-punk graphic art in the world, all owned by the author. Due to limitations of space in this volume, it was not possible to include representations of all the punk and post-punk bands whose graphic art are a part of the author's collection of more than 3000 images.

POSTSCRIPT

During the course of this mammoth undertaking, every effort has been made to identify and credit the legions of art directors, designers and photographers responsible for the hundreds of posters and flyers contained herein. For any omission, we humbly and sincerely apologize and if you contact us we'll correct any mistakes or omissions in future printings.

WITH LOVE AND HATE FROM NEW YORK

by Steven Heller

Punk graphic style comprises the clichéd and unique. It is not solely an aggressively untutored do-it-yourself mashup of types and images that has been copied by graphic designers all over the world, but it's got plenty of that aesthetic. Punk styles and methods changed from locale to locale, band to band, and album to album. In the United States, East Coast punk differed from West Coast; Northwest grunge differed from California edge. American punk was distinct from British, which had a raunchy personality all its own and in contrast to French and Italian, which were a bit tamer but no less exuberant. Punk in the German Democratic Republic (GDR) was unlike any, since rebellion did not altogether suit the government's agenda. Various social, cultural and political distinctions existed between working-class England and middle-class United States, though each had left wings, right wings and apolitical wings too. This book proves that there is more to punk than meets the myopic eye.

Branding played a role in punk. The Sex Pistols' record covers were distinct from those of The Clash, which was nothing like Television or Blondie, and so on. Most bands, while adhering to a generalized punk aesthetic, expressed it in their own visual dialects and through their own particular lenses. Zines, a great source of punk typography, also varied widely from deliberately raucous to naively ratty. Some punk scenes were more into cut 'n' paste flyers than others who could afford to print more ambitious silkscreen posters. Some were glam and others retro. Some copied historical design icons – Jamie Reid's *Never Mind The Bollocks...* (1977) for instance is clearly inspired by the first edition of Wyndham Lewis' 1914 vorticist magazine *Blast*, while The Skids' sophomore album release *Days*

ABOVE: The Skids' *Days In Europa* poster (1979) **Mick Brownfield** illustration, **Pearce Marchbanks** design, allegedly withdrawn by Virgin due to complaints regarding its use of Ludwig Hohlwein's designs for Nazi Germany's 1936 Berlin Olympics as the basis for the artwork

In Europe (1979, see previous page) borrows a Nazi-era Ludwig Hohlwein magazine cover. Yet the one common denominator with all punk printed matter is the rejection of hippie psychedelics and underground aesthetics that prevailed during the late 1960s.

Every movement needs an enemy to declare war upon; but the spoils were rarely the same. Referring to both the sound and look of New York punk music and graphics, Jon Holmstrom, founding editor and designer of *Punk* magazine, once told me, 'There was a concerted effort by bands like Suicide, the Ramones and Talking Heads to follow the aesthetic that "less is more" and to strip music down to its core ... After all, most of the bands at CBGB's had gone to art school or were aware of the art scene of the time ...We were also going for minimalism and simplicity at *Punk* magazine.'

If words like minimal and simplicity contradict the emblematically messy DIY punk style-image, it explains why not every shred of punk paper was made up of ransom notes, collage and marker scribbles. Holmstrom, for example – a student in 1974 of the legendary *MAD Magazine* editor Harvey Kurtzman at New York's School of Visual Arts – charted a different course. He was a huge fan of comics and splash panel hand-lettering that characterized his magazine's punk sensibility. He further filled *Punk* with grainy high-contrast photos and limited (though hardly subdued) layouts. 'We couldn't afford four-colour printing or expensive typesetting, so we didn't mind if a page looked handmade, or if the lettering looked like a demented criminal had scrawled on a page. What I always tried to do was express a concept,' Holmstrom explained. 'If we couldn't get around budget limitations, we'd throw it out and think of something else.'

Punk graphic style was often a more or less intuitive, improvisational response to music that was rooted in nasty guitar and percussion. 'All early punk rockers were ex-hippies who got sick and tired of following their stupid rules,' Holmstrom points out. 'We wanted to wipe out all music made after 1966. We wanted to bring back cool-looking clothes and never see another pair of bell-bottoms. We wanted to destroy disco music and turn everyone onto the Ramones.'

As the late sixties was about sex, drugs and rock and roll, the seventies fostered punk's hard-edged beats and low-rent lyrics. Sex, drugs and rock and roll was still in the mix but the so-called uniforms of alienation changed along with the graphic stuff that telegraphed punk to the world. Later, with the advent of post-punk and bands like The Flying Lizards, the style was influenced by professional designers, photographers and illustrators.

Hilly Krystal's storied CBGB in New York's East Village evoked the surge of graphic energy that promoted the music. The dark and dingy Bowery club was awash with stickers, graffiti and all forms of graphic detritus from floor to ceiling. Being there was like entering into a life-size Google search for 'punk band graphics'. Logos, illos and photos were everywhere the eye could see in the cramped space.

Yet to truly appreciate punk's visual styles, it is necessary to drill deep into those layers stuck on Hilly's walls and embrace the printed matter that poured from offset presses, copy machines and more. While some pieces were meant to last as artifacts, others were made to be tomorrow's trash. The canon of punk design includes icons such as Jamie Reid's 1977 Sex Pistols' 'God Save The Queen' record sleeve, Malcolm Garrett and Linder Sterling's 1977 Buzzcocks 'Orgasm Addict' poster and Gary Panter's 'Screamers' illustration. Some punk design, like Gene Greif's 1978 work for The Clash's *Give 'Em Enough Rope* sleeve wasn't even done by a committed punk but rather a well-tutored graphic designer who captured the aesthetic of the moment.

Andrew Krivine's documentation and his first New York exhibition, Rude and Reckless: Punk/Post-Punk Graphics 1976–82 in July 2011, followed in January 2014 by Pretty Vacant at the

Sniffin' Glue: Issue 7, New York Outrageous (February 1977)

Galleries at Moore College in Philadelphia, did more to stake out the scene that became a movement and is now a historic manifestation. This book reveals how rude and crude became stylish and fashionable yet at the same time how rebellion was expressed by design both low and high. Punk left a large mark through its varied mark makers. Today, decades later, we can appreciate punk's influence on film, art, fashion and so much more. Jon Holmstrom told me, 'I was always hoping I'd see the next art or music movement that would wipe out punk the way we destroyed hippie culture. I wanted to see something more interesting and outrageous than punk rock take over the world and introduce new ideas and make punk seem like an outdated concept. But it hasn't happened yet.' Looking through this collection, whatever one feels about the importance of maintaining the professional niceties of type and image, a collective, enthusiastic fervency comes through that defined a movement, generation and culture.

1

2

3

THE VELVET UNDERGROUND: 1 poster, **Wes Wilson** and **Bellmer Wright** design, likely an authorized British print, *c.*1969, on textured paper stock; **2** reprint poster for 1968 gig printed by the V.U. Appreciation Society (1985) image from the LP *White Light/White Heat*, Verve Records (1968), **Andy Warhol** concept, **Acy R. Lehman** cover design, **Billy Name** photography; **3** poster for concert at the Avalon Ballroom, San Francisco, CA (July 1968), **Paul Kagan** design featuring the 128th image from the Family Dog series

THE VELVET UNDERGROUND: (right) poster for initial UK release of the Andy Warhol/Paul Morrissey movie, artwork **Alan Aldridge** (1970); (above) US promotional disc for the movie (1966)

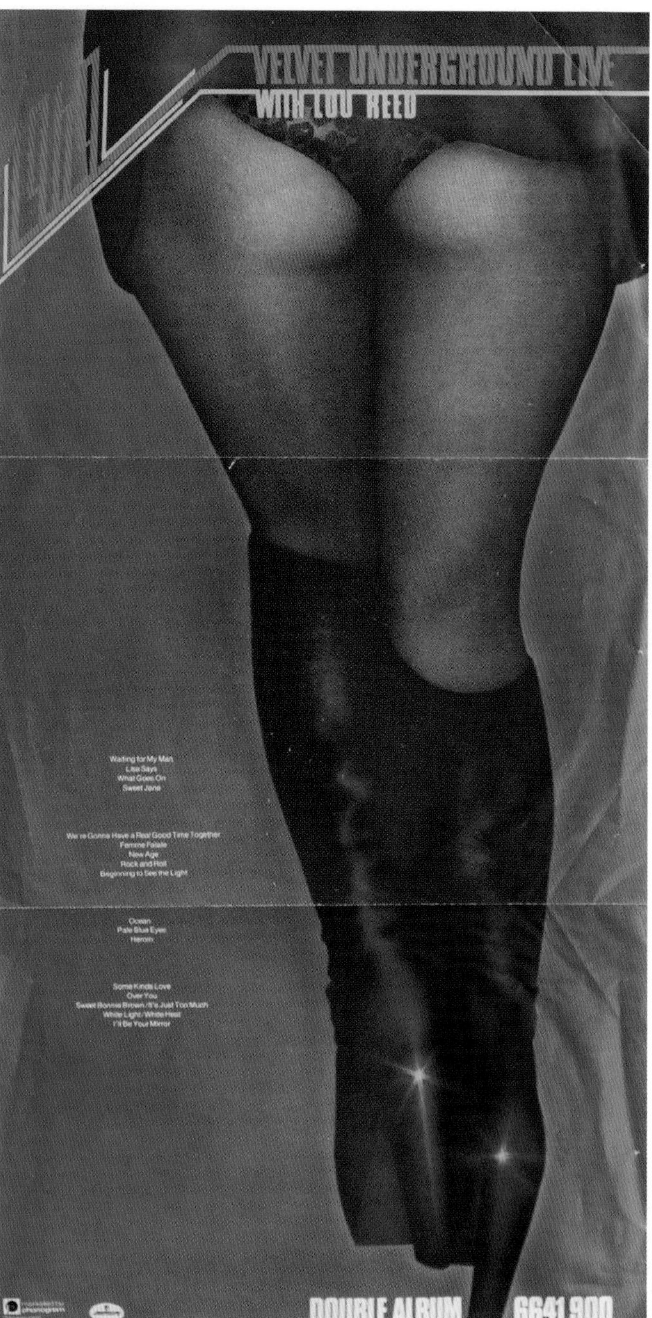

THE VELVET UNDERGROUND: (left) *Velvet Underground Live* LP poster, Mercury Records (1974), **Ernst Thormalen** design; (below) poster for concert with Doug Yule at Max's Kansas City, NYC, NY (1970), **Steve Nelson** design, courtesy of Steven Kasher

LOU REED: *Lou Reed* – LP poster, RCA (1972), **Ronn Campisi** photography

LOU REED: *Rock N Roll Animal* LP poster, RCA Records (1974), **Acy R. Lehman** art direction; **DeWayne Dalrymple** photography

Lou Reed's *Rock N Roll Animal* was recorded live on 21 December 1973 at Howard Stein's Academy of Music in NYC. Superb photo of a proto-punk, swaggering Lou.

Andrew Krivine

LOU REED: (left) cover of *Let It Rock* magazine, London, John Pidgeon, editor (1974); (below, top) *Coney Island Baby* cover of promotional booklet, RCA Records (1975); (bottom, both) *Coney Island Baby* insert from promotional booklet (1975)

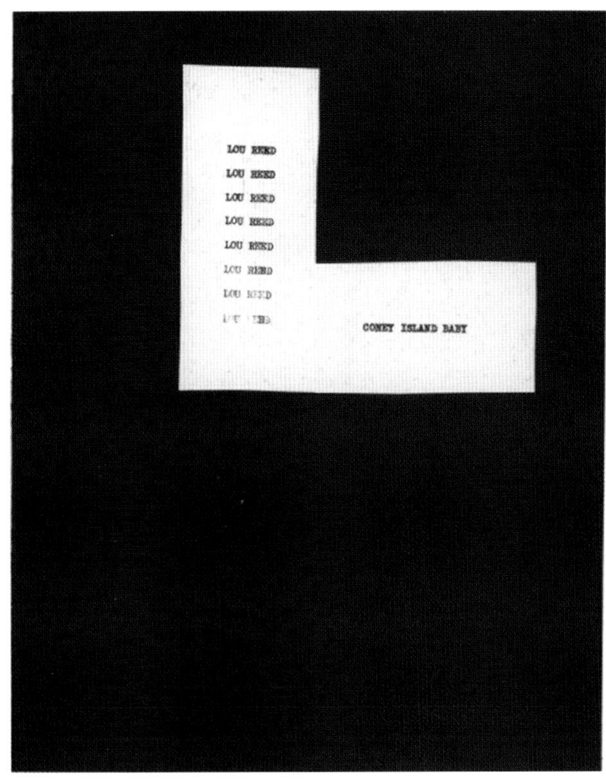

"THE MOST
IMPORTANT WRITER
IN ROCK AND ROLL."

<u>DAVID BOWIE</u>

"A PARTICULARLY LOATHSOME
EXAMPLE OF THE DUES WE MUST PAY
IN ORDER TO SUPPORT ARTISTIC
FREEDOM, LOU REED STRETCHES
THE LIMITS OF TOLERANCE EVEN
IN THOSE DEDICATED TO IT."

<u>RALPH J. GLEASON</u>

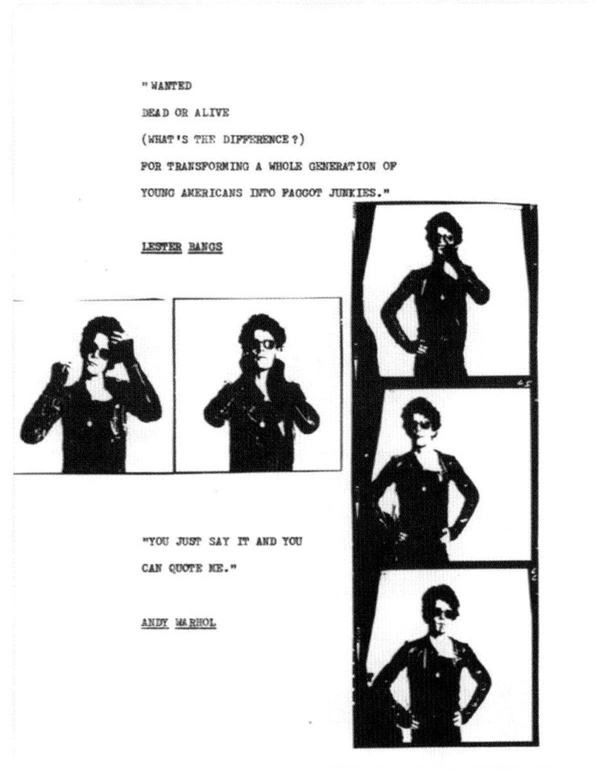

"WANTED
DEAD OR ALIVE
(WHAT'S THE DIFFERENCE?)
FOR TRANSFORMING A WHOLE GENERATION OF
YOUNG AMERICANS INTO FAGGOT JUNKIES."

<u>LESTER BANGS</u>

"YOU JUST SAY IT AND YOU
CAN QUOTE ME."

<u>ANDY WARHOL</u>

JOHN CALE: (above) *Slow Dazzle* LP poster, Island Records (1975), **Michael Wade** design, **Keith Morris** photography; (right) *Guts* LP poster, Island/ Antilles Records (1977), **Bloomfield/Travis** design; **Michael Beal** art direction and photography

The hockey mask in this image preceded the use by serial killer Jason in John Carpenter's horror classic, *Halloween*, by one year. The *Guts* album was a compilation of outtakes from various recording sessions, featuring a stellar cast of musicians including Brian Eno, Chris Spedding, Phil Manzanera, Andy Mackay and Phil Collins, and radical cover versions of 'Heartbreak Hotel' and Jonathan Richman and The Modern Lovers' classic 'Pablo Picasso'. The former Velvet Underground guitarist (and producer of The Stooges' debut album in 1969) immersed himself in the punk scene in the late 70s and produced several punk/ new wave bands – including Sham 69, Menace, Patti Smith, The Modern Lovers and Squeeze.

Russ Bestley

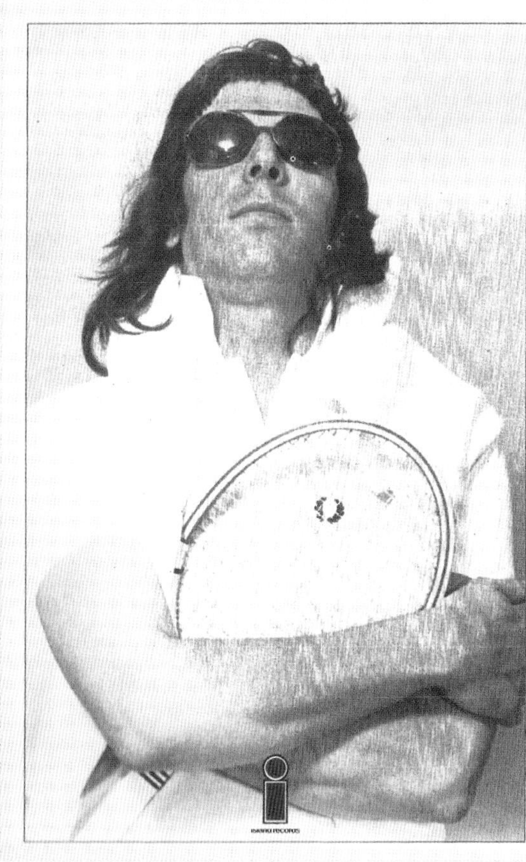

JOHN CALE
SLOW DAZZLE ILPS 9317
Mr Wilson – Taking it all Away – Dirtyass Rock 'n' Roll – Darling I Need You – Rollaroll – Heartbreak Hotel – Ski Patrol – I'm Not The Loving Kind

JOHN CALE
FEAR ILPS 9301
Fear Is A Man's Best Friend – Buffalo Ballet – Barracuda – Emily – Ship Of Fools – Gun – The Man Who Couldn't Afford To Orgy – You Know More Than I Know – Momamma Scuba

Also available on cassettes & cartridges.

AT CRYSTAL PALACE

JOHN CALE: *Slow Dazzle* – flyer for performance at Crystal Palace, London, Island Records (1975)

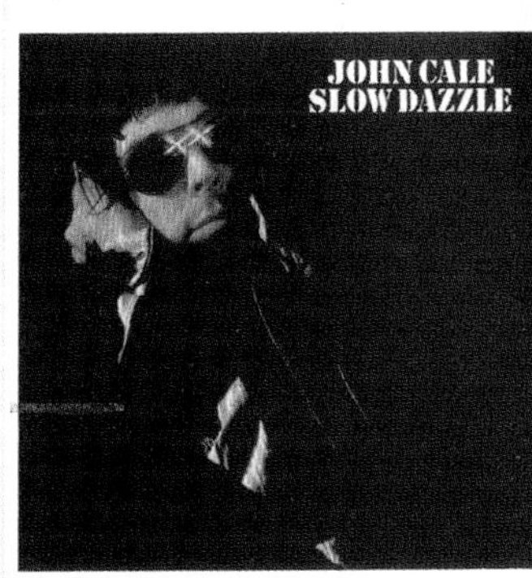

"By mixing art and atrocity in odd doses Cale has kept his reputation intact."
THE GUARDIAN

"The first track on John Cale's SLOW DAZZLE is so excellent that I played it eight times before I could bring myself to continue. Fortunately the rest of the album is of a uniformly high standard."
NEW MUSICAL EXPRESS

"Making no bones about it, this is intelligent, attractive music that deserves to give Cale his first top twenty album as a solo artist. I think it will. This is his time."
MELODY MAKER

"SLOW DAZZLE is John Cale's most complete album yet."
SOUNDS

"SLOW DAZZLE proves beyond doubt that he is master of many styles, some acceptable, some that drain the listener completely. Now more than ever Cale is mining a rich vein of personal honesty that transcends almost all of his potential competitors."
NEW MUSICAL EXPRESS

NEW YORK DOLLS: (above) *New York Dolls* LP poster for debut album, Mercury Records (July 1973), **Toshi** photography; (right) cassette insert for Lipstick Killers (ROIR, 1981), **Bob Gruen** photography, **Scott Kempner** typography

Tues. Wed. Thurs. Sept. 4 5 6 8:00 pm
at Matrix 412 Broadway 434 2444

It's the S.F. debut of the

New York Dolls

with the Tubes

also Pristine Condition and Naomi Ruth Eisenburg

$ 2.50 all ages welcome adults no minimum, people under 21 - 2 drink minimum
coming to Matrix Sept 7 8 Papa John Creach + Zulu also Steelwind

NEW YORK DOLLS: (above) flyer for first appearance in San Francisco, CA (1973) **Matrix** design; (left) promotional stickers, Mercury Records (1973)

NEW YORK DOLLS: front cover of *Rock Scene* magazine, Lisa Robinson editor (March 1974)

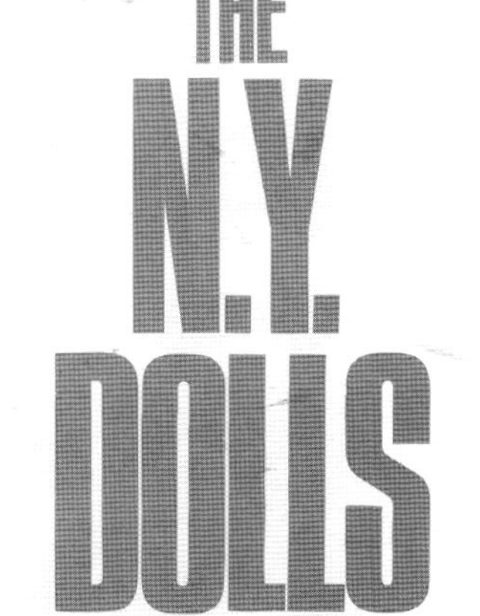

NEW YORK DOLLS: (left) flyer for gigs in NYC during February–March 1975 at the dinner theatre/cabaret space The Little Hippodrome; this brief residency marked a pivotal moment – the end of the proto-punk era and the emergence of punk, courtesy Roberta Bayley; (right) poster for first performance in Detroit, Michigan (22 September 1973) **Dennis Loren** design

THE HEARTBREAKERS: flyer for radio station KPFA in Berkeley, CA (1975), **Roberta Bayley** photography

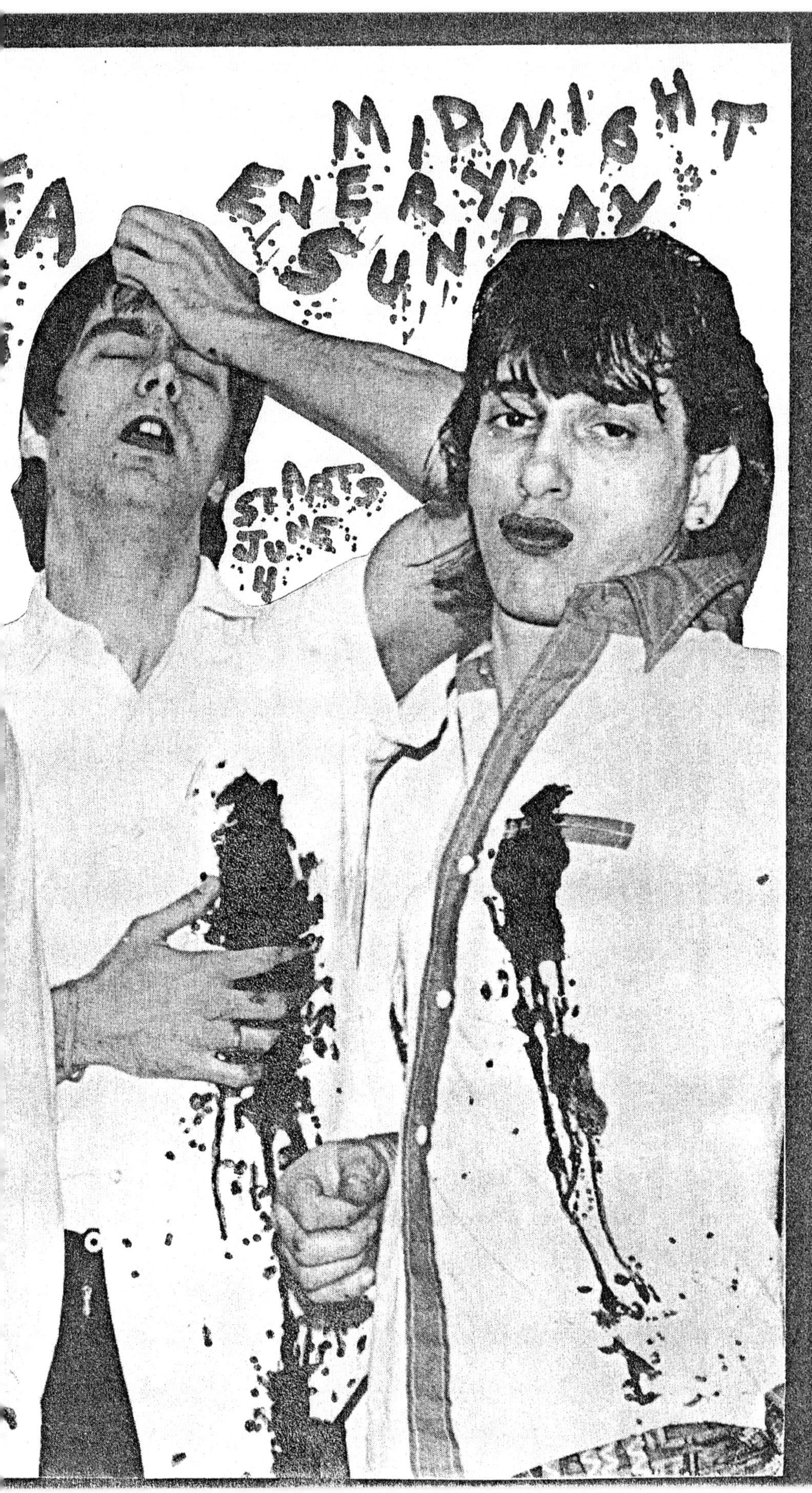

This photograph features the first line-up of The Heartbreakers with Richard Hell (2nd left) who, in May 1975, founded the band with Jerry Nolan and Johnny Thunders. Hell was a Heartbreaker for less than one year, before going off to form Richard Hell & The Voidoids with guitar god Robert Quine, Ivan Julian and Marc Bell in early 1976.

Andrew Krivine

1

2

THE HEARTBREAKERS

THE RAMONES

Wayne County DJ

New Year's Eve Champagne Party

refreshments provided $7.50 (includes everything) at THE SEA OF CLOUDS club 5 E. 16th St. 5th fl. continuous music doors open at 11 PM call 255-5931

3

THE HEARTBREAKERS:
1 UK badge sheet, Track Records (1976); **2** flyer for concert at Max's Kansas City, New York City, NY (July 1976); **3** poster for concert with the Ramones at The Sea of Clouds Club, New York (New Year's Eve, 1976)

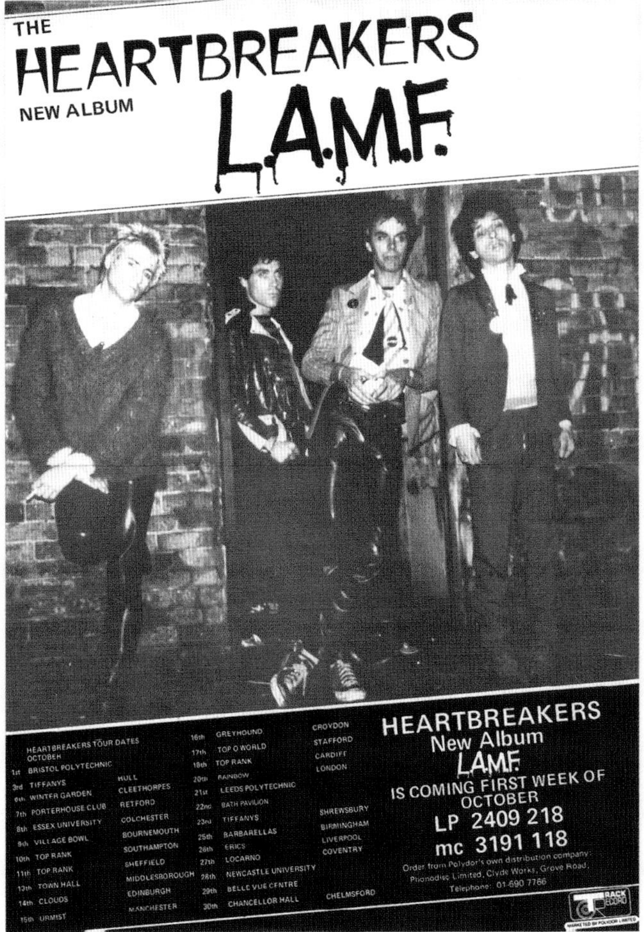

THE HEARTBREAKERS: (above) UK poster, Jungle Records (1977), **Barry Jones** design; (left) *L.A.M.F.* UK LP/tour flyer, Track Records (September 1977)

IGGY AND THE STOOGES: *Metallic K.O.* LP poster, Skydog Records (1976), **Michael Beal** design

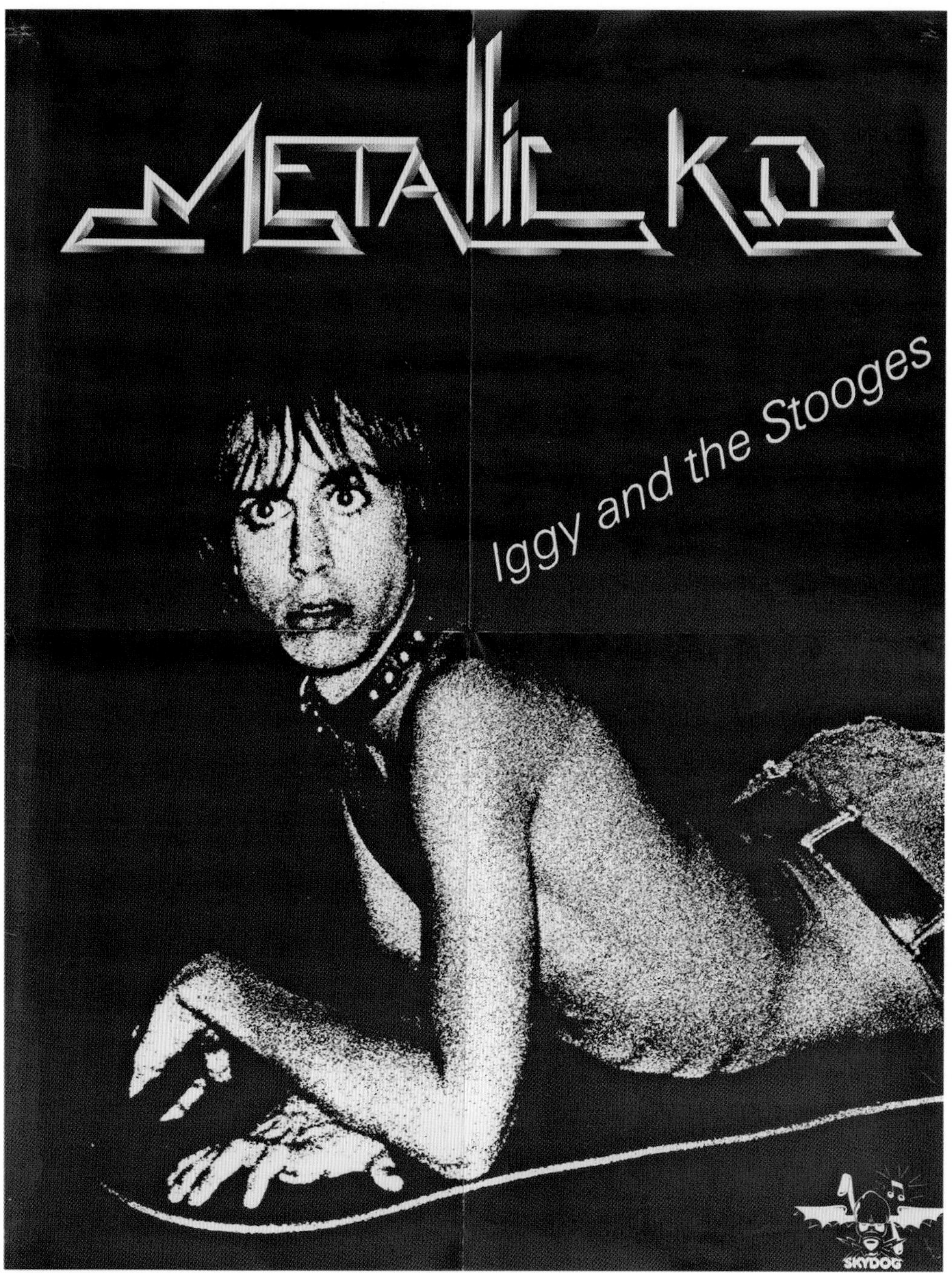

The final, riotous, live show by Iggy and The Stooges, at Michigan Palace, Detroit, on 9 February 1974, was recorded on a reel-to-reel tape machine by Michael Tipton. The band faced a hostile audience of local bikers, known as the Scorpions, and their confrontational approach and refusal to back down in the face of intimidation only fuelled more trouble. Part of the show was released as a semi-official live album by Marc Zermati's influential Skydog label in 1976 – although, in fact, side one of the album was taken from a previous concert at the same venue on 6 October 1973. Designed by Michael Beal, who would go on to work with Count Bishops, Eddie and The Hot Rods, The Heartbreakers and The Only Ones.

Russ Bestley

1

2

3

4

IGGY POP: 1 cover of *ZigZag* magazine; Leighton Buzzard, **Kris Needs** editor (March 1977); **2** advertisement for European fan club (September 1977); **3** Cover of *TB Sheets* 'zine, (November 1977), **Andrew Kent** photography; **4** *TV Eye* album promo badges RCA Records (1978)

IGGY POP: flyer for concert at The Palladium, New York City, NY (6 October 1977)

IGGY POP: (left) *The Idiot* – debut LP poster, RCA Records (1977); (right) *Lust For Life* advertisement, RCA Records (1977)

IGGY POP: (left) cover star of *Raw Power* magazine (1976); (right) *I Wanna Be Your Dog* fanzine, **Gilles Scheps** editor, Paris (1977)

poetic proto-punkers

book-rockers

Patti Smith: up top, romantic, wistful, of the ages, is that a Mapplethorpe photo?

Television: a sassy, undernourished boy band below, in more anonymous photo style (albeit w/ credited photo)

see the Television member holding a Television(!) but nothing's on TV – it's Blank(!)

see the shift in tonal range and the halo behind the right side of Patti's head * the degraded image, a xerograph, two steps from its photographic master

duplicated at a copy shop, handed out, left on tables, taped, pasted, stapled to any visible surface in August 1978

'white bond' office paper, now warped by humidity and yellowed by its acid content

this copy spared the telephone pole, w/ no noticeable wounds, held by a hoarder

chartpak? letraset? type applied with skill

typographic hierarchy via all caps vs. upper and lowercase setting in medium-scale sans serif vs. micro-level typewriter typesetting

configuration careful if shaky

an after-hours professional effort despite amateur affect?

Glen Cummings / Adam Michaels

PATTI SMITH AND TELEVISION: (above, left) poster for one-week residency at Max's Kansas City, New York City (August/September 1974), **Richard Hell** design

PATTI SMITH (above, right) band-aid decorated poster for Patti Smith Group concert in Finney Chapel at Oberlin College, Ohio (February 1978)

PATTI SMITH: *Horses* – LP poster, Arista Records (1975), **Robert L. Heimall** design, **Robert Mapplethorpe** photography

The cover for the *Horses* LP was designed by Robert L. Heimall, who is also credited with designing the sleeves for the MC5's *Kick Out the Jams* LP and *The Stooges* LP (both records were released by Elektra Records in 1969). The photograph was taken by Patti's close friend and renowned photographer, Robert Mapplethorpe.

Andrew Krivine

PATTI SMITH: *Punk* magazine #2 (March 1976), **John Holmstrom** artwork and design, **Guillemette Barbet** photography

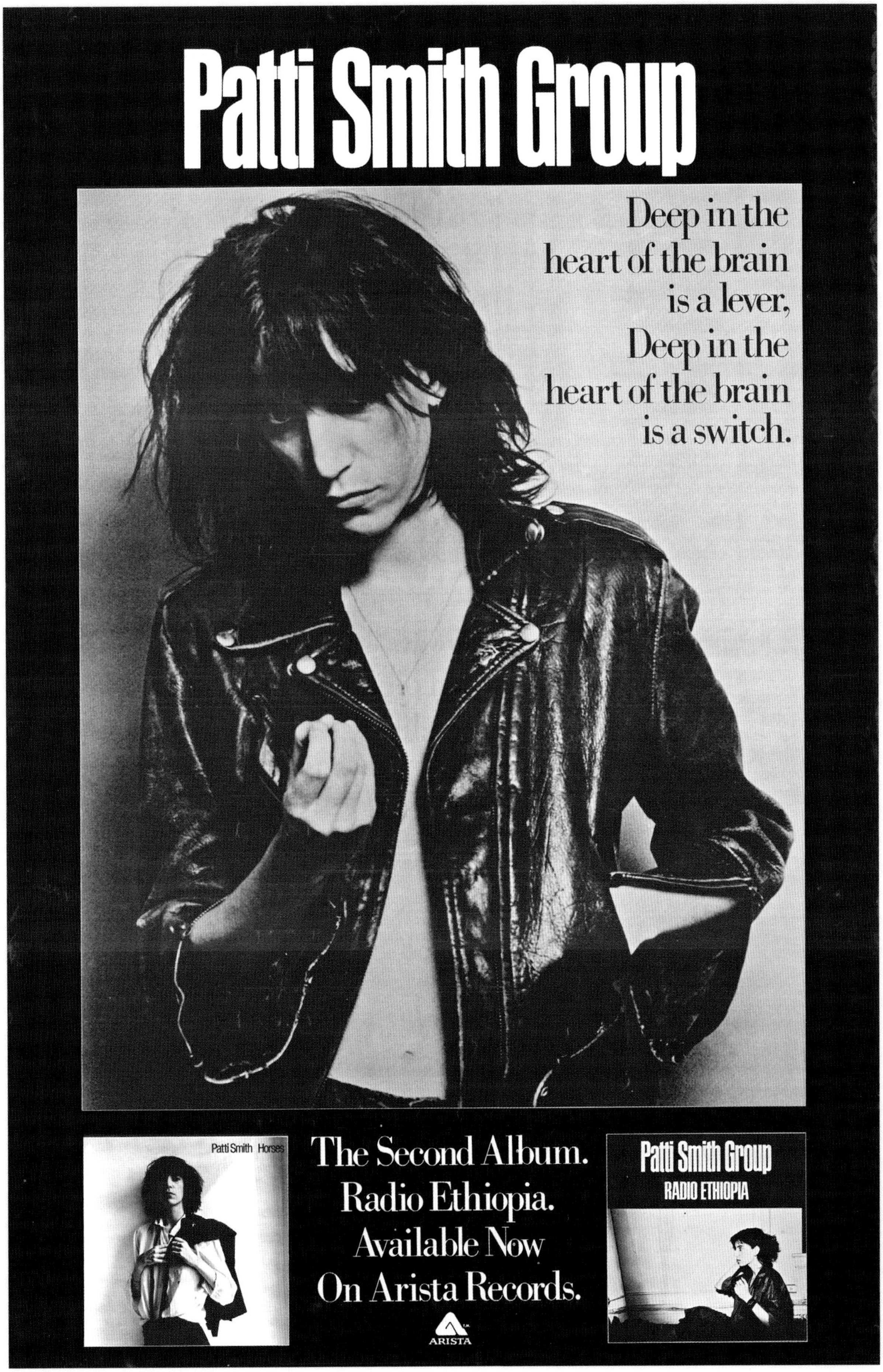

Patti Smith Group

Deep in the
heart of the brain
is a lever,
Deep in the
heart of the brain
is a switch.

The Second Album.
Radio Ethiopia.
Available Now
On Arista Records.

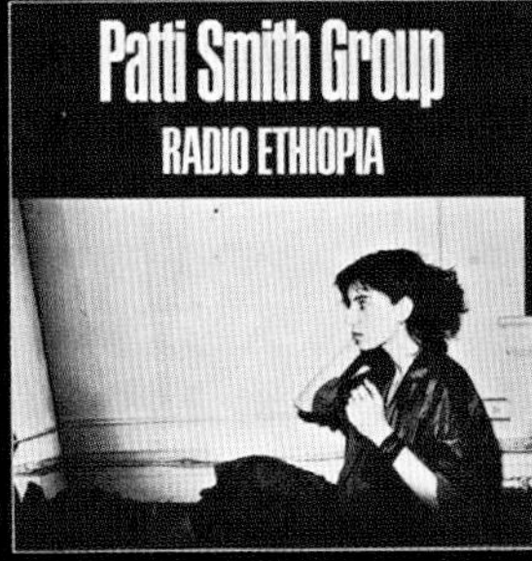

PATTI SMITH: *Radio Ethiopia* LP poster, Arista Records (1976) **Lynn Goldsmith** and **Robert Mapplethorpe** photography

1

2

3

4

TELEVISION: 1 concert handbill for The Truck & Warehouse Theatre (22 November 1974), **Bob Gruen** photography; **2** CBGB flyer showing joint residency dates for Television and Talking Heads (June 1978); **3** European tour programme front cover (1977); **4** Tom Verlaine self-portrait from the European tour programme (1977)

TELEVISION: (above) European tour programme back cover (1977) signed by the band; (below) *Adventure* LP poster, Elektra Records (1978), **Paul Jansen** art direction, **Johnny Lee** design, **Gerrit Van Der Meer** photography

RICHARD HELL & THE VOIDOIDS: *The Blank Generation* LP poster, Sire/Stiff Records (1977)

RICHARD HELL & THE VOIDOIDS: UK tour (supporting The Clash) poster, Sire/Phonogram Records (1977)

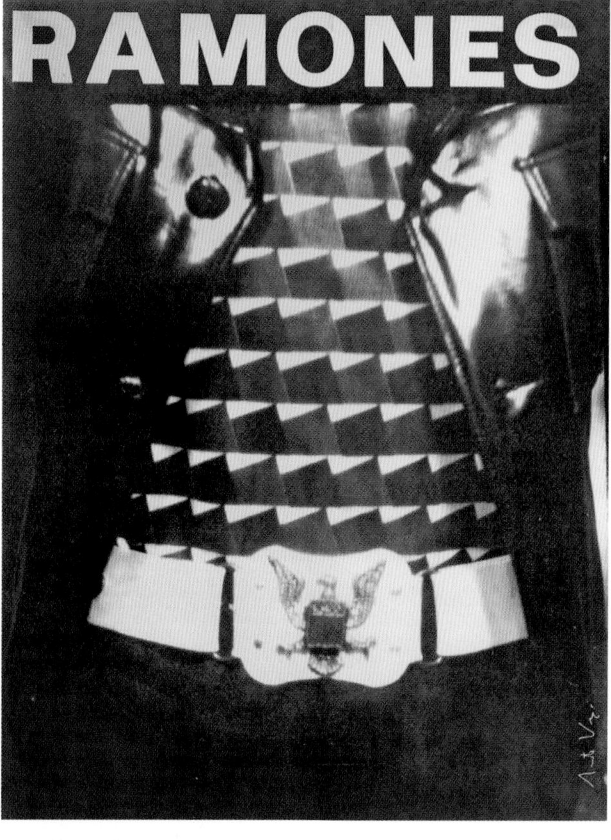

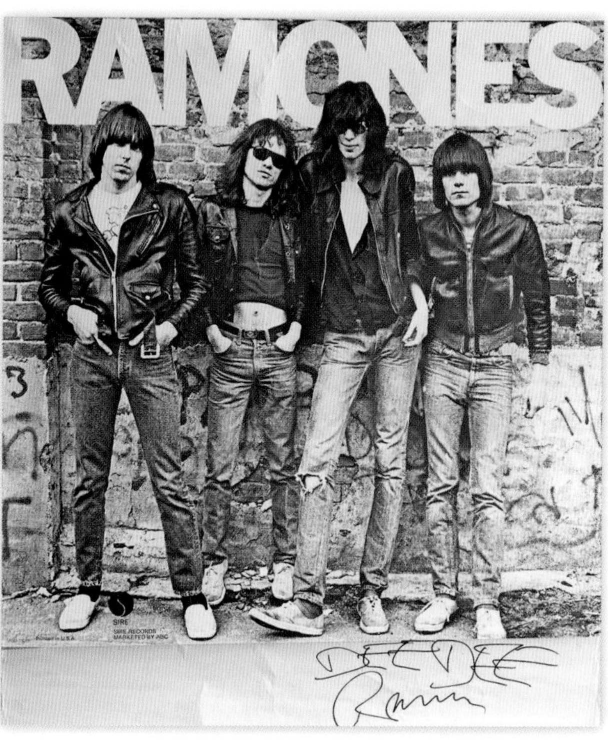

RAMONES: (above, left) showcase poster used to promote the band during an Unsigned Bands Contest held at CBGB's (1975), **Arturo Vega** design; (above, right) *Ramones* debut LP poster, Sire Records (1976), **Roberta Bayley** photography, signed by Dee Dee

This debut album was initially marketed by ABC Records Inc. in 1976. Roberta Bayley (effectively the staff photographer for *Punk* Magazine) is responsible for the most recognizable image of America's premier punk band. Several major punk musicians in England confirmed that this record was revelatory, including members ofThe Clash, The Damned and the Sex Pistols. On 4 July 1976 (the bicentennial weekend), the Ramones sold out the Roundhouse (3,000 tickets) and took London by storm. The *Ramones* LP was the detonator, triggering the punk rock explosion in the UK. This copy of the poster was signed by Dee Dee two years before his death and includes a perforated snipe at the bottom, which could be used to include local concert information.

Andrew Krivine

RAMONES: *Punk Magazine* #3 (1977), signed by the band

1

2

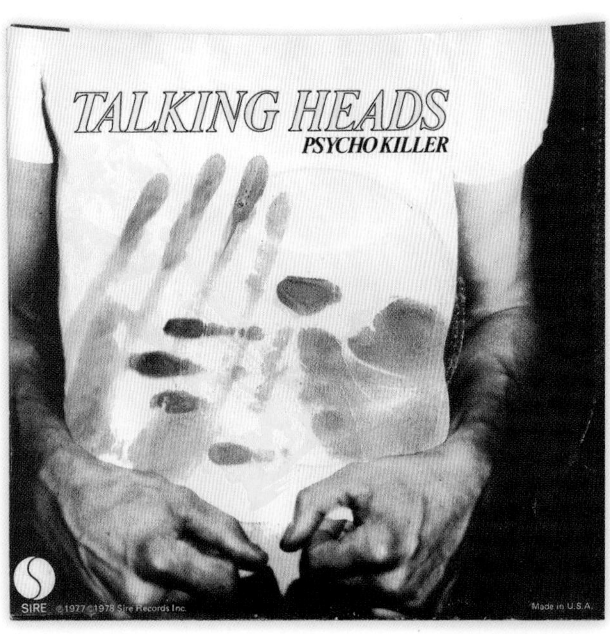

3

4

TALKING HEADS: 1 flyer for gig in Toronto (September 1977); **2** *77* UK debut LP poster, Sire Records (1977); **3** 'Psycho Killer' 45 front cover, Sire Records (1978); **4** concert flyer for series of gigs Keystone Club, Berkeley CA (7–10 December 1977)

TALKING HEADS: *Talking Heads 77* LP poster, Sire Records (1977), **David Byrne** and **Jerry Harrison** design, **Mick Rock** photography

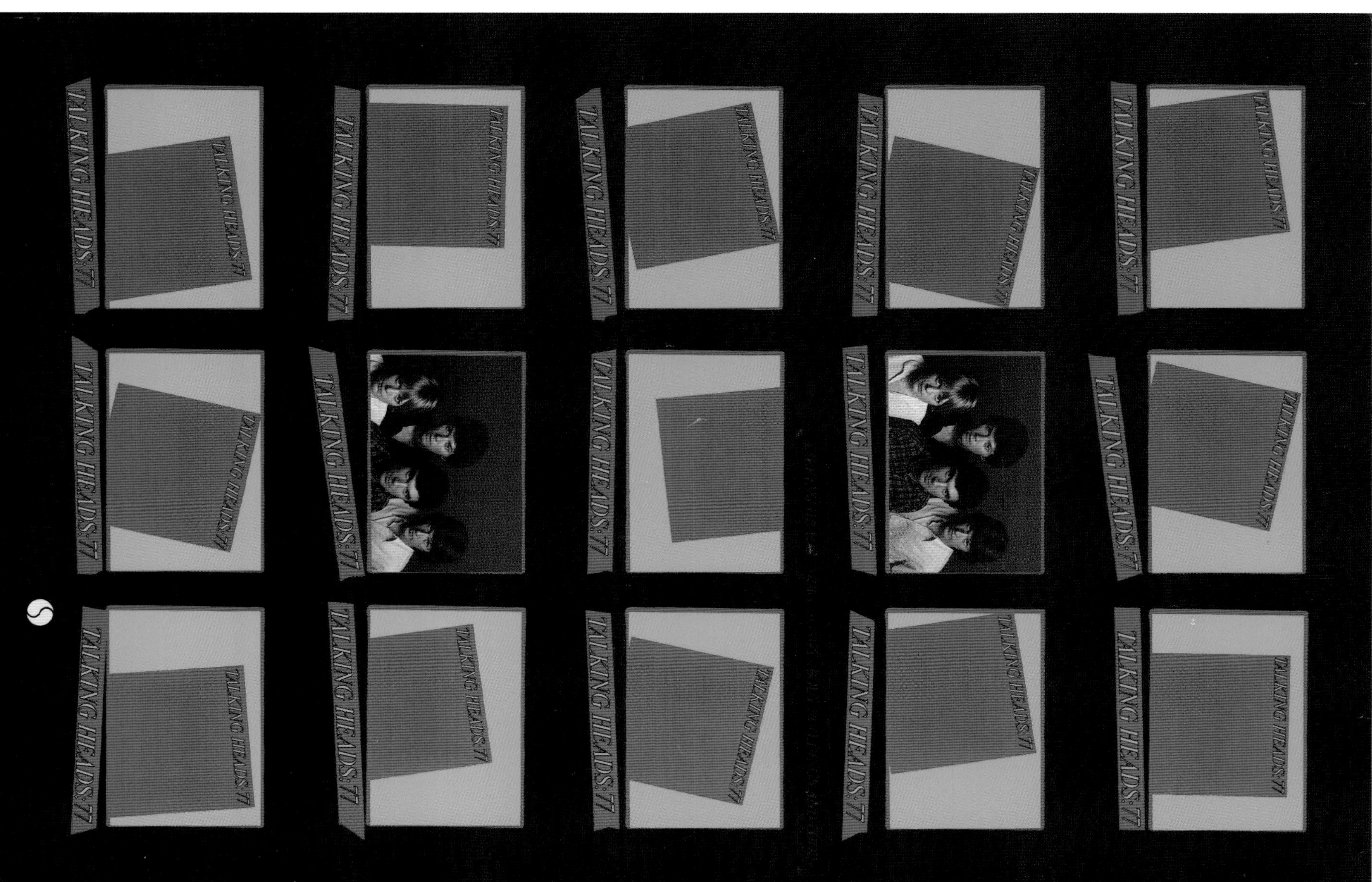

1

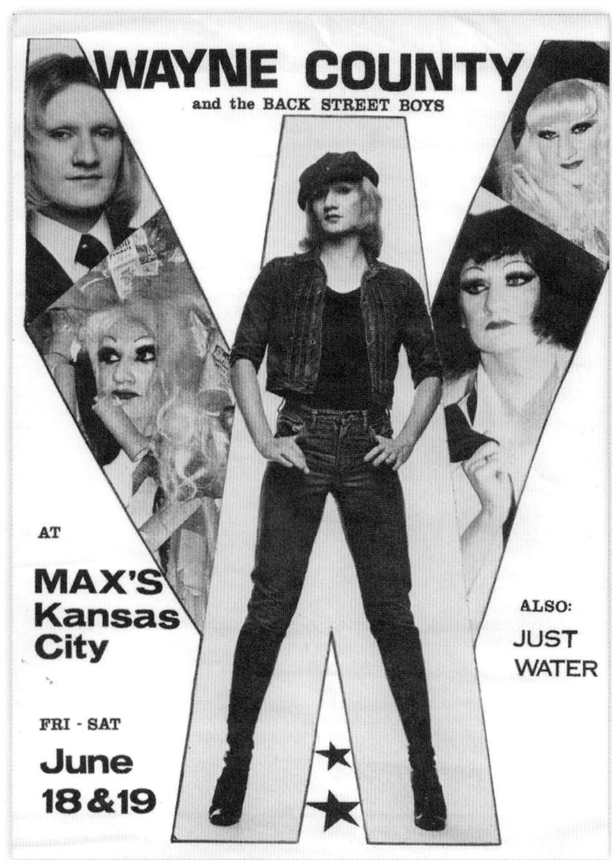

2

WAYNE COUNTY & THE BACKSTREET BOYS: 1 poster for concert at Max's Kansas City, NYC (1976); **2** ad for gig at Max's Kansas City (June 1976); **3** advertisement for *Fuck Off* 45rpm, S.F.A. Records (1977), photo by **Brian Aris**

3

WAYNE COUNTY: signed flyer for concert at The Roxy club, London (March 1977), design by **Barry Jones**

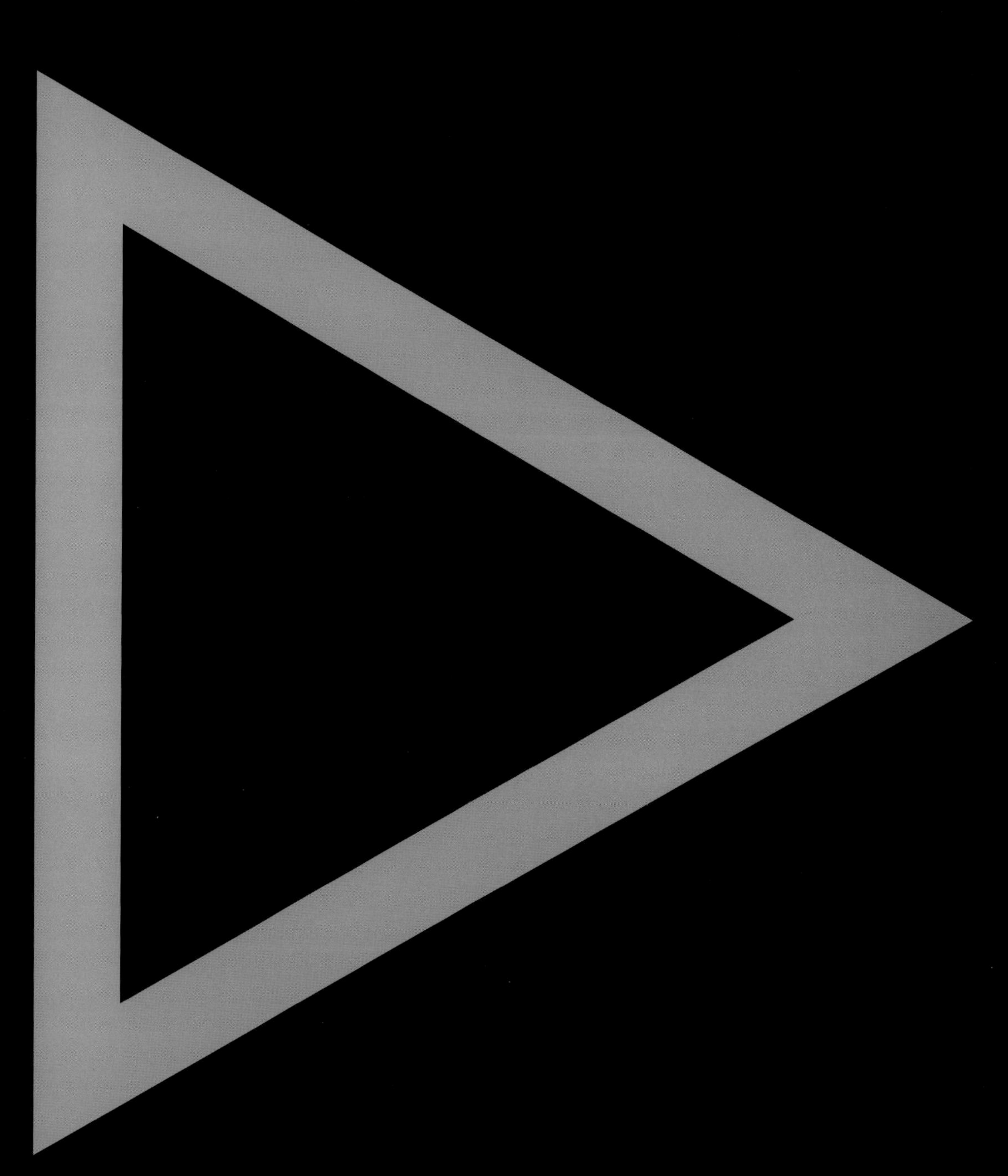

PUNK UNCOVERED: AN UNOFFICIAL HISTORY

by Russ Bestley and Ian Noble

Most visual histories of punk have emphasized the work of now-famous graphic designers, such as Malcolm Garrett, Peter Saville, Barney Bubbles, Russell Mills and Jamie Reid. Yet the greater impact of punk on the hearts, minds and attitudes of the youth at that time was through a provincial second wave, or the beginnings of the 'punk diaspora' as Jon Savage has called it, more related to the suburbs and towns of Britain. Provoked by the received view of punk via the sensationalized reporting of the mainstream press, local scenes grew up across the nation, each with highly individual interpretations of the music and variations in attitude and approach.

Far from the metropolitan/London axis, this provincial interpretation of punk, as fashion, as music and as graphic output, adopted a range of individual approaches based on the part played by the music press – in particular the *NME* [*New Musical Express*] – the airplay given by Radio One DJ John Peel, the national press and local cultural history and aspirations.

The mainstream press, almost entirely opposed to the movement, played a large part

Poster advertising the Newsreel Collective's documentary about the Rock Against Racism movement in London (1978)

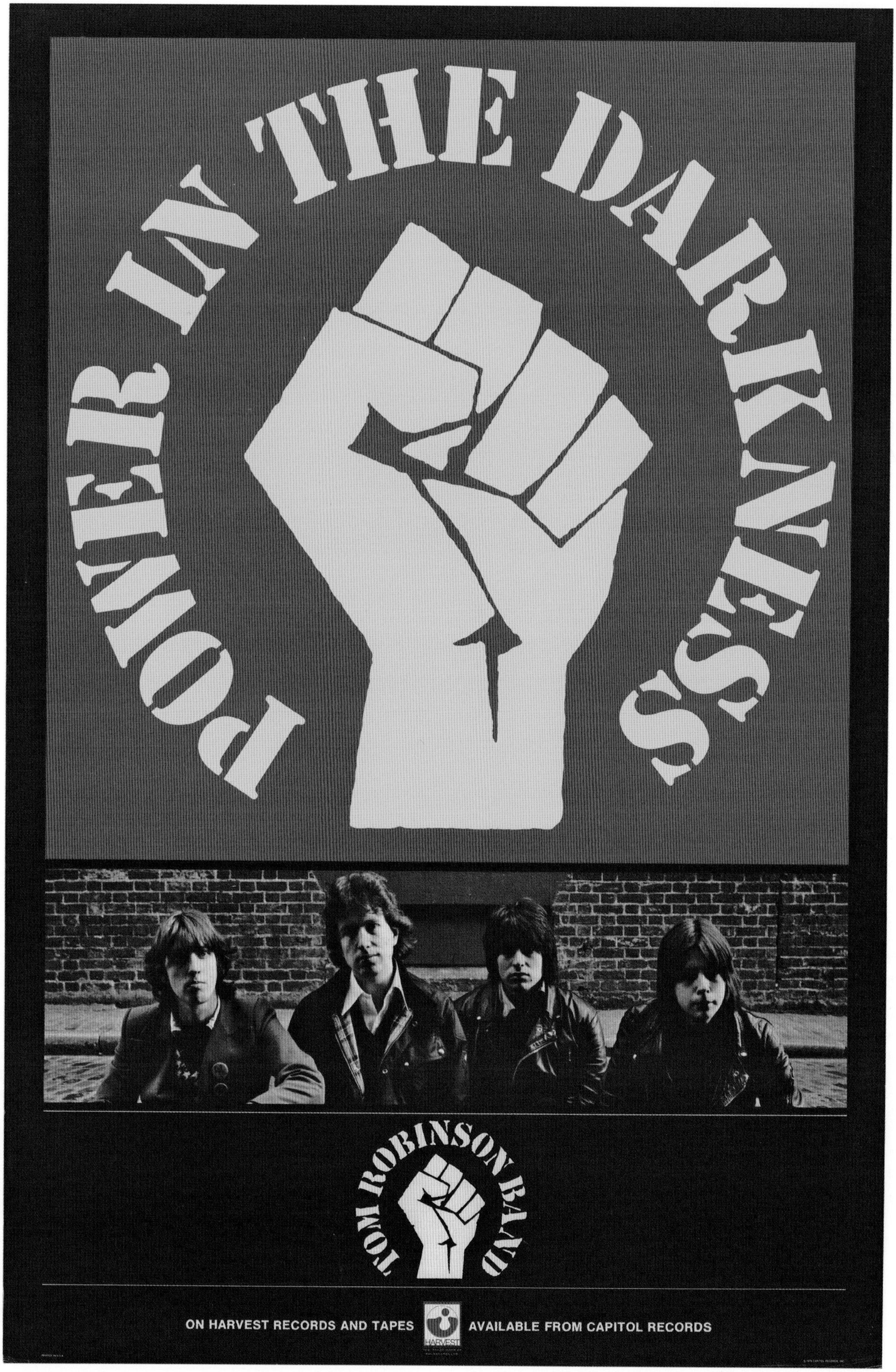

POWER IN THE DARKNESS

ON HARVEST RECORDS AND TAPES 

AVAILABLE FROM CAPITOL RECORDS

in the way punk was to be adopted and reinterpreted in regions geographically too distant from the major cities to have a direct connection or a word-of-mouth familiarity. More difficult to define, but no less significant, were those deep-seated feelings of frustration and rebellion reflected in the local culture – a regional fan base was established which took a distinctively parochial reading of the genre. This is significant, for local history, provincial attitudes and a distinctly popular culture played an equal part in the construction of this 'second wave', as did the suggested ('serious' or 'arthouse') influences of the official history of the genre (The Velvet Underground, Stooges, etc.). Outside the larger metropolitan areas of the big cities, deep-seated conservative attitudes were rife – following the recession of the mid-1970s and a failed Labour administration, Margaret Thatcher was elected prime minister and soon created a far-right government. In smaller communities across Britain, this reflected a return to more hardline Victorian values. Though punk was becoming a fashion cliché in London, being a provincial punk was a political statement, a 'leap of faith'.

For punk to have survived, it needed to react to a particular social and political climate. Worsening unemployment, Northern Ireland, Reagan, Thatcher, the nuclear threat and the resurgence of CND [the Campaign for Nuclear Disarmament], the emergence of gay rights, the undermining of the trade unions and later the jingoism of the Falklands War all contributed to the climate of engagement. Some bands became identified with single issues, such as TRB [the Tom Robinson Band], whose 'Glad To Be Gay' (EMI, 1978) became an anthem for gay liberation. Au Pairs, comprising two men and two women, became associated with a newly defined approach to the concerns of women and the feminist movement, particularly with the release of the single 'Diet/It's Obvious' (021 Records, 1980). Though the group achieved some success in the post-punk independent market, they were to be defined by this early approach in all their later work. The Slits and The Raincoats established a new position for women in the male-dominated rock music scene. The period also marked a new range of interpretations of punk's employment of shock tactics, challenging middle-class norms and values. The earlier knowing dumbness of, for instance, the wearing of swastikas by Sid Vicious and Siouxsie Sioux had been balanced by the proactive movements within the scene: Rock Against Racism and the Anti-Nazi League.

TOM ROBINSON BAND: logo for Harvest Records poster (1977), **Roger Huddle** design
AU PAIRS: badge for'Diet/ It's Obvious' 021 Records (1980)

THE MO-DETTES: (right) 'White Mice' / 'Masochistic Opposite' 45, Rough Trade Records (1979), **June Miles-Kingston** design

With the right wing appeased by a sympathetic government, the more political sections within the scene were forced to fragment their activities to address specific issues. A range of tactics were adopted by the new generation of oppositional groups, and the employment of visual codes became more critically targeted.

The geography of the UK meant that punk spread quickly and found a sympathetic audience already inclined toward the feelings of rejection and alienation that characterized much of the music. More local aspirations and interpretations of the punk ethos were played out in smaller towns and cities across the country, deeply affecting many of the people involved – bands, fans, designers. This led to a resurgence of the cottage industry, the skills-building of independent businesses and many new innovations in marketing and production. This significant but largely undocumented influence spawned a large number of smaller-league bands, labels and networks of activity. Bands from these towns were part of extended local networks and often toured together to other towns, pooling resources and equipment. In this way an alternative version of punk was propagated, and local exchanges were built up.

The look of much of this recorded work in the form of 12-inch LP and seven-inch single and EP sleeves, and echoed in fanzines, advertisements and flyers, was often anonymous or uncredited and a celebration of the low-cost production values of necessity. The output of many of the untrained or non-professional artworkers – band members or friends of the band (often at local art colleges) – produced unusual collaborations. The Human League's line-up involved at least one band member who did not have a musical role: Adrian Wright originally provided slide projections on stage, an integral part of the Human League's early live appeal. This also reflected an attempt to create multi-disciplinary live performances in the true punk spirit – filmmaker Mick

SCRITTI POLITTI: 'Skank Bloc Bolgna' / 'In And Ought The Western World' / '28 / 8 / 78' 45, St Pancras Records (1978)

1

2

Duffield provided projected backdrops for live performances by the band Crass. Many other groups (notably Wire) incorporated poetry and performance art into their live shows.

The grassroots approach centered on the relationship between the audience and the groups – often the fans were the bands, and the bands were the fans. The spirit of 'everyone can be in a band' grew into 'everyone can release their own record' and 'everyone can have their own label' and this extended to the production of the sleeve artwork. The (initial) rejection of the large or major record labels as possible benefactors is exemplified in the impossibly uncommercial nature of the record sleeves.

This activity involved design strategies that, although based on limited budgets, were in many cases inventive, sophisticated and engaged in deliberate decisions concerning the 'hard-edged' employment of particular images, anti-typography and production processes. These attempts to capture, and communicate, the aggressive or discordant tone of the lyrics and music position much of the work as important examples of how a surface may indeed capture the experience or emotion of a

3

1 ATV: *Love Lies Limp* flexi-disc, S.G. Records (September 1977); **2 STIFF RECORDS:** badges (1977/8); **3 SEDITIONARIES:** double-sided catalogue/mail-order form for the Malcolm McLaren/Vivienne Westwood shop of that name (1977), **Vivienne Westwood** design

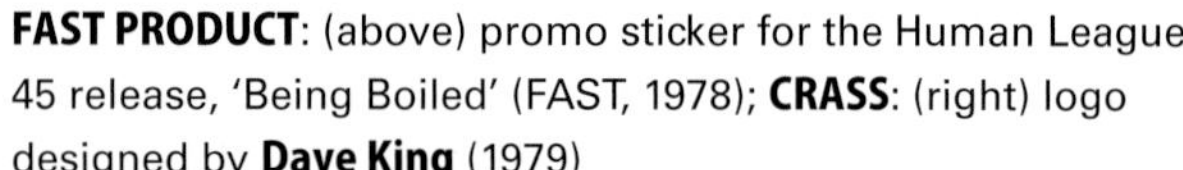
FAST PRODUCT: (above) promo sticker for the Human League 45 release, 'Being Boiled' (FAST, 1978); **CRASS**: (right) logo designed by **Dave King** (1979)

musical form. Importantly, these could not have been produced by anyone other than those directly involved in the scene.

The subcultural codes contained within the sleeves and band 'identities' acted as factors in defining the sense of belonging and membership both in a local and national sense. These codes often took the stereotypical devices of punk – hand-rendered and stencilled typefaces, ransom-note typography and photocopied imagery, often borrowed from newspaper stories of the day and related to the topical nature of the lyrics. In other cases, the look or feel was less deliberately DIY [do-it-yourself] and employed images of local significance and genuine low-tech production such as the use of typewritten text and crudely rendered images. This approach exemplified a persistent refusal to engage in sophisticated design values despite subsequent commercial success. These designers and artists went on to produce work which refined the style of earlier production but maintained its raw disregard for more mainstream commercial aesthetic values.

Some independent labels became very successful, often making use of innovative marketing strategies and corporate styles. Early leaders in the independent sector, including Chiswick and Stiff, both born out of the pub-rock scene in London, were to figure less prominently as tastes changed rapidly in the late 1970s, and the search for a genuine 'alternative' scene exemplified by the likes of Rough Trade, Radar and Cherry Red Records in London, or by Factory in Manchester, FAST Product in Edinburgh, Zoo in Liverpool and Crass in Essex took hold.

By this time, many of the major record labels were heavily involved in marketing punk acts and fashions (and, in particular, what was to become defined as new wave). Demand soon outstripped supply, with labels scrambling to sign bands with some sign of 'street cred' and bands becoming 'punk' virtually overnight to cash in. Small independent labels were often subsidized – whether in terms of studio time, record manufacture or distribution – by larger production/distribution agencies. Several of the more proactive new labels (including FAST Product, Crass and Rough Trade), took distribution back into their roster of activities as this became a key defining factor in the independent scene.

The impact of available and affordable Xerox copies should not be underestimated as a design tool during the late 1970s, both in the art colleges and further beyond.

This unique period of activity documents a rare period of British social opposition to, and engagement in, the politics and values of the day. Punk's alternatives to the mainstream production of both music and design traces a connection to a canon of 'visual contrariness' that persists (and inspires) to this day.

I WANNA BE ME

Particularly after a deluge of books in 2016 (widely considered to be punk's fortieth anniversary), punk became probably the most extensively documented youth movement of the twentieth century. Many of the bands in the following pages are instantly recognizable. A brief introduction cannot do justice to this visually, sonically and socially exhilarating movement, and, consequently, there is no point in writing an extensive summary here. Without question, the definitive book on the subject is Jon Savage's scholarly and incisive *England's Dreaming* (Faber & Faber, 1991). For readers keen to understand the genesis of punk in the British Isles, see also Legs McNeil and Gillian McCain's *Please Kill Me: The Uncensored Oral History of Punk* (Grove Press, 1996), which is a superb, engaging chronicle of the beginnings of punk in New York.

What follows is an alphabetical compendium of graphic art made for and by the prime movers, performers and artists of the UK punk scene which began in 1976 and came into full bloom in the following year or two. There's no doubt that Malcolm McLaren and Vivienne Westwood's smart employment of Jamie Reid to oversee the creation of a Sex Pistols visual identity and their canny fashion business know-how made their band the slickest and best-structured on the punk scene, although at times it was difficult to see any difference in the Pistols' graphic presence and that of the major corporations and advertising practitioners that the scene was supposed to be disrupting and parodying.

The Clash, 999 and X-Ray Spex were extremely well 'designed' in terms of how they were presented to the general public well before they were signed by a record company, but once major record labels began signing bands whose only previous 'marketing' had been designed and presented by fanzine editors, there emerged a general graphic language of punk which you can see emerging in these pages.

Andrew Krivine

THE PIRATES
on tour
Out of their Skulls
AS8502
999
NINE NINE NINE
DEAD FINGERS TALK
ULU
TRUSS & BUCKET
CEILIDH BAND
Freshers Ball
Kebabs
3 Bars
DISCO
8pm-1am
15thOctober
£1.90
ULU, Malet St, London WC1

1

999: 1 gig poster for University of Central London, headlined by The Pirates, a former pre-Beatles-era backing band for Johnny Kidd (October 1977); **2** promotional poster (1978); **3** 'Emergency' 45 front cover, UA Records (1978), **George Snow** design

2

3

999: *999* debut LP poster, UA Records (March 1978), **Paul Henry** design, **Trevor Rogers** photography

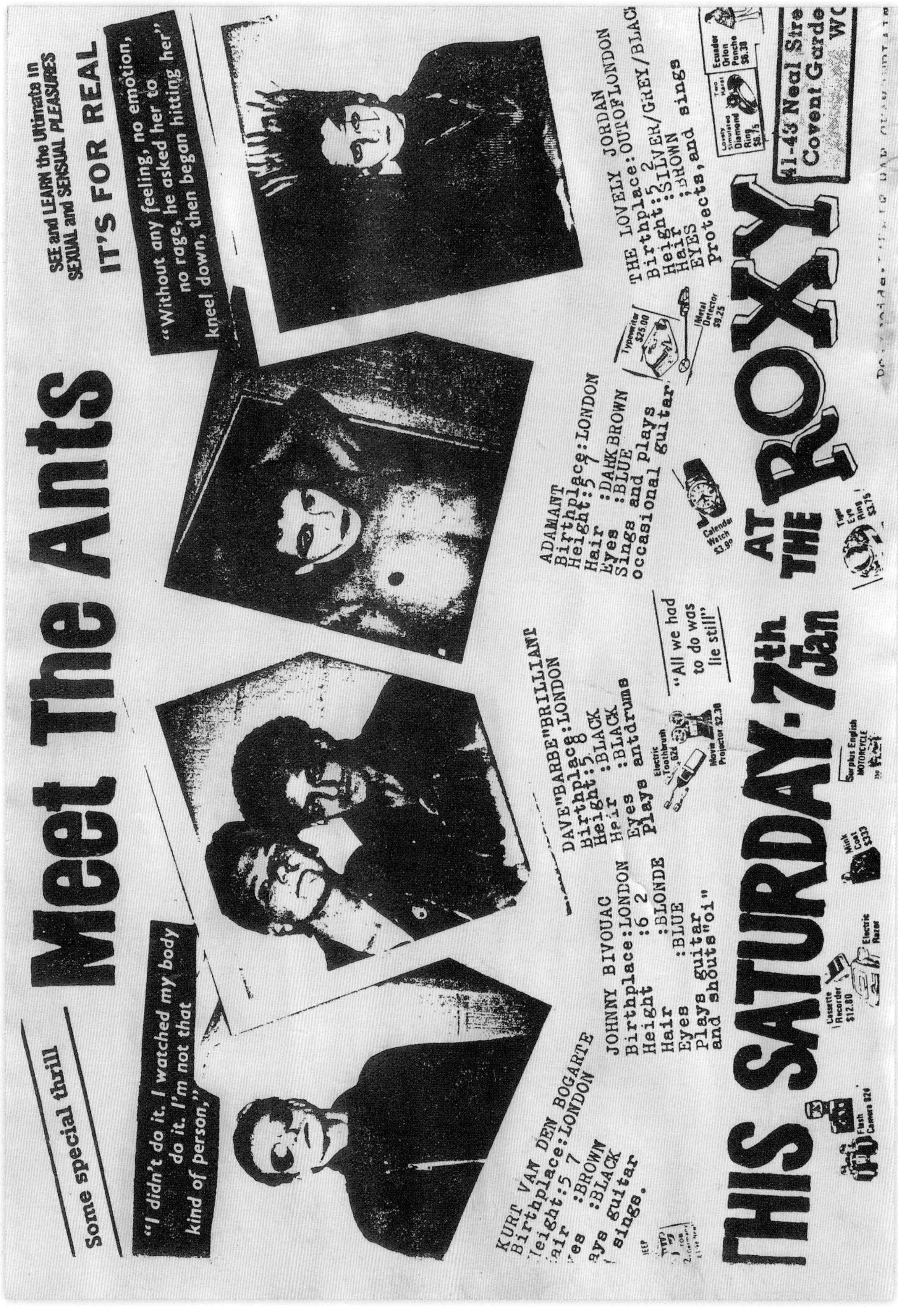

ADAM AND THE ANTS: concert flyer for gig at The Roxy, London (January 1978), limited edition reprint of 200 copies (*c.*1982), **Adam Ant** design

1

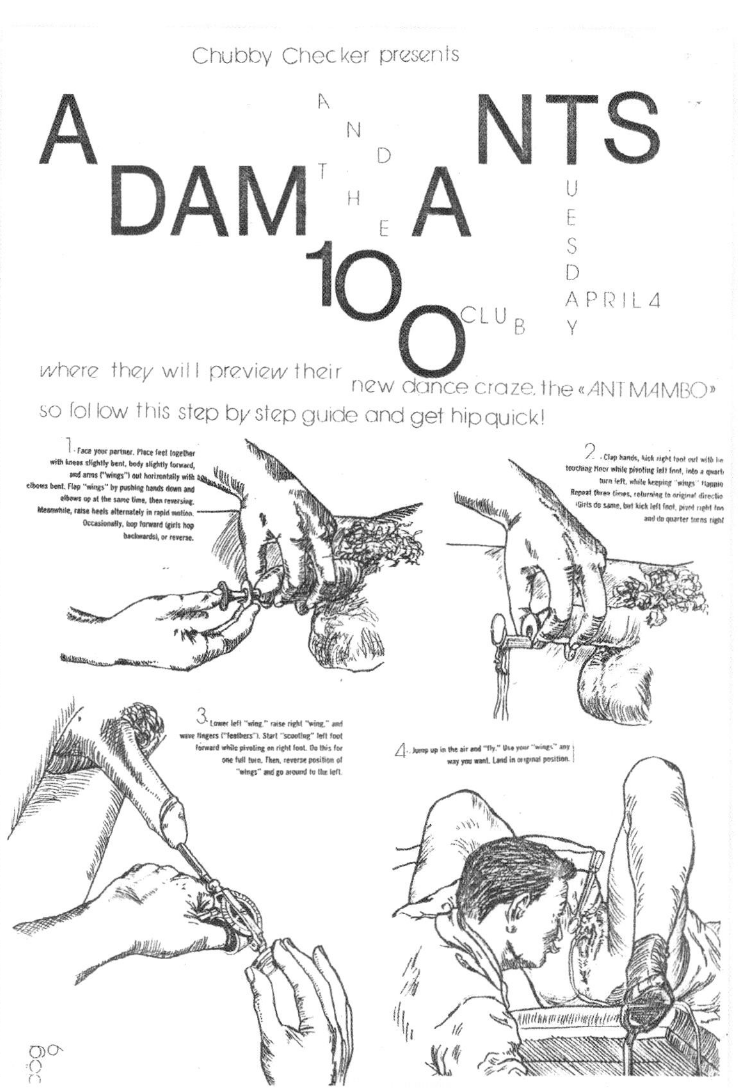

ADAM AND THE ANTS: 1 flyer for gig at the 100 Club, London (4 April 1978); **2** flyer for gig at The Vortex, London (19 September 1977); **3** *Dirk Wears White Sox* debut LP promotional badges, Do It Records (October 1978) and a *Stand And Deliver* era badge (1980)

3

2

ADAM AND THE ANTS: concert flyer for Moonlight Club, West Hampstead, London (July 1978), **Adam Ant** design

1

ADAM AND THE ANTS:
1 'Young Parisians' 45 newsprint advertisement, Decca Records (October 1978); **2** 'Zerox' 45 tour blank poster, Do It Records (July 1979); **3** *Dirk Wears White Sox* flyer for the UK tour (April 1980), limited edition reprint of 200 copies (*c.*1982), **Adam Ant** design

2

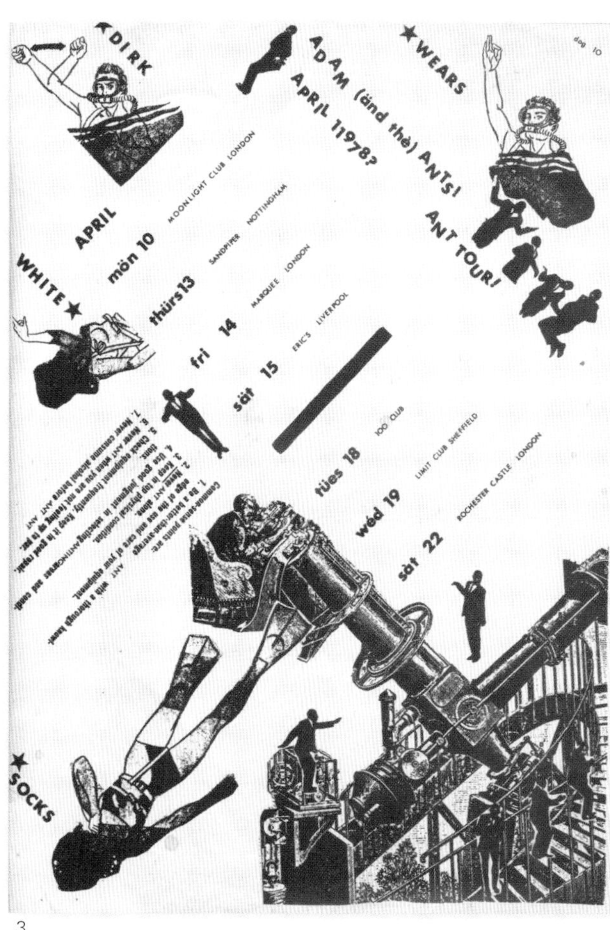

3

THE ADVERTS: 'One Chord Wonder' 45 poster, Stiff Records (1977), **Barney Bubbles** design

Poster promoting the release of the debut single by The Adverts, 'One Chord Wonders' mistitled on the record cover, and again here, as 'One Chord Wonder' by Stiff Records in April 1977. The poster features a photograph of the group from the same session as the reverse of the record sleeve along with bold, distressed sans serif typography in keeping with punk's lo-tech, do-it-yourself pronouncements at the time. Stiff Records had already scored a major punk victory in releasing the first UK punk single, The Damned's 'New Rose', in October 1976, and album, *Damned, Damned, Damned*, in February 1977. Both bands toured the UK together in May and June that year under the promotional motto, 'The Damned can now play three chords. The Adverts can play one. Hear all four of them at...'

Russ Bestley

THE ADVERTS: flyer for concert at Vortex, London (25 July 1977)

THE ADVERTS

GARY GILMORE'S EYES

BORED TEENAGERS

NEW SINGLE

AVAILABLE NOW

ANC 1043

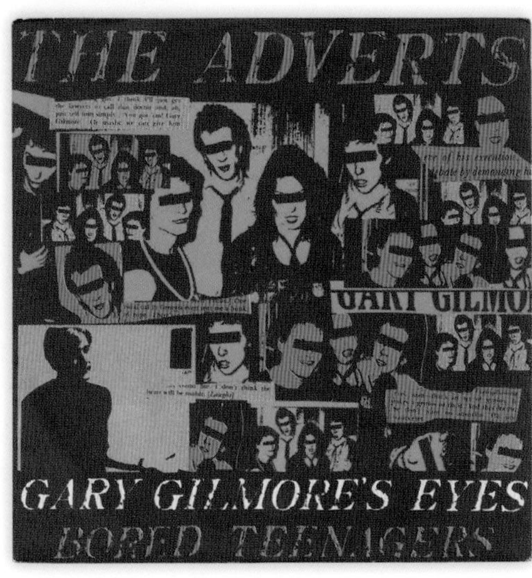

THE ADVERTS: (above) 'Gary Gilmore's Eyes' 45 poster, Anchor Records (1977), **Nicholas De Ville** design; (right) 'Gary Gilmore's Eyes' 45 front cover, Anchor Records (1977)

ALTERNATIVE TV: *The Image Has Cracked* LP poster, Deptford Fun City Records (1978), artwork **X3 Posters, Bob Linney, Ken Maharg** design

This poster was designed by Bob Linney and Ken Maharg at X3 Studios, effectively the in-house atelier for the UK holding company Faulty Products, whose sub-labels included Illegal and Deptford Fun City Records. Miles Copeland III, the brother of Police drummer Stewart, founded Faulty Products in 1977. ATV was led by Mark Perry who was also responsible for publishing the seminal British punk fanzine, Sniffin' Glue. X3 Studios designed posters for several acts managed by Miles, including The Cortinas, Chelsea, The Cramps, Lords of the New Church and The Police. Scant information on X3 Studios is available, but they were outstanding designers who were masterful in their use of screenprinted saturated, neon colours and were quite prolific during this period.

Andrew Krivine

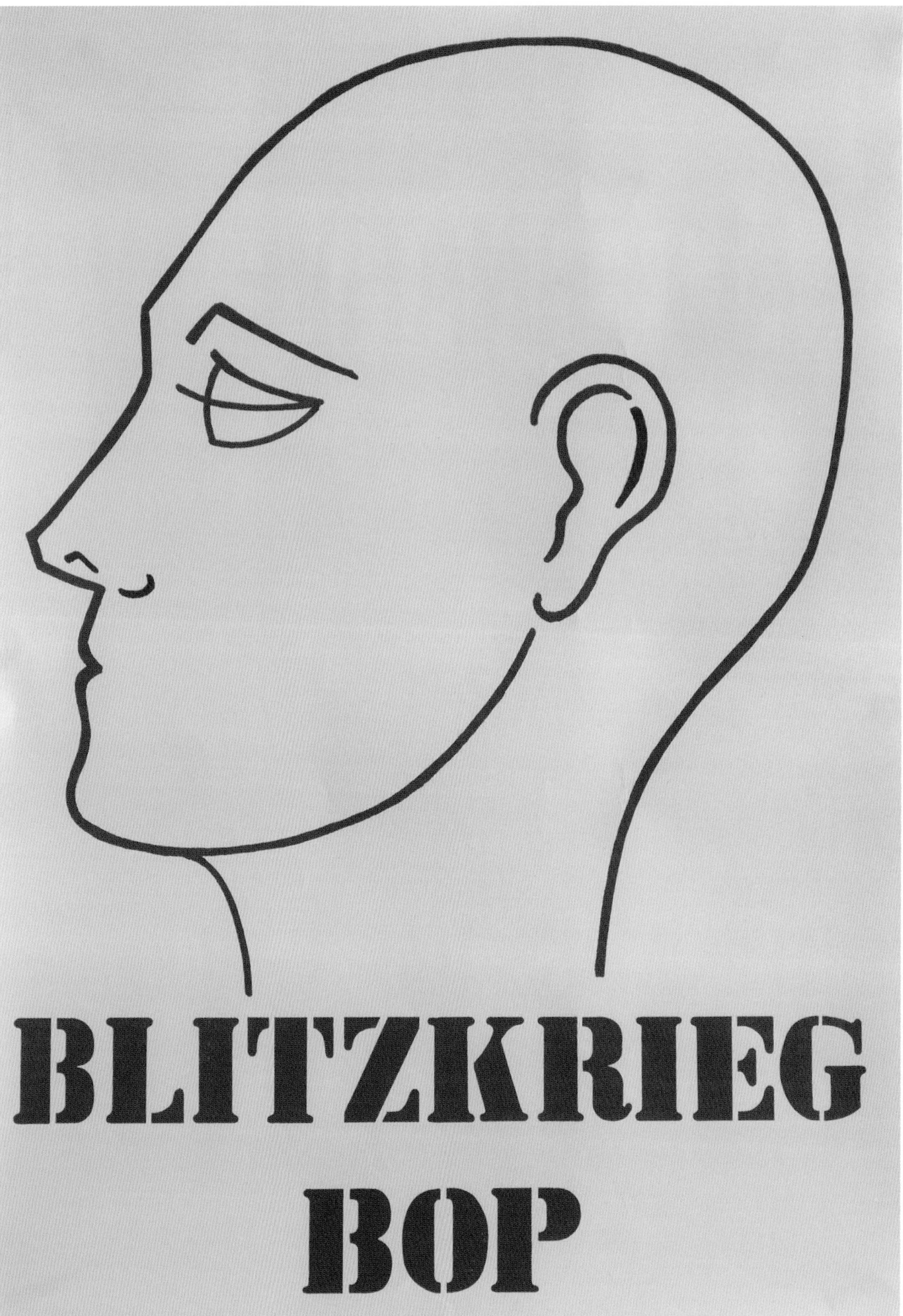

BLITZKRIEG BOP: promotional poster (1977); Blitzkrieg Bop was a British punk band from Teesside. The short-lived but noteworthy band produced just one self-released EP, followed by a single released on Lightning Records (1978)

THE BOYS: 'First Time' 45 front cover, NEMS Records (1977)

A DIFFERENT KIND OF KITCHEN

Malcolm Garrett

I am fortunate that my introduction to designing for music was with a band as extraordinary as Buzzcocks. They were lyrically incisive, with a musicality that embraced an existential warmth, yet with a disarmingly unassuming aggression. Their potency emerged from an almost naïve willingness to just get on with it. As a designer, I was informed as much by my own naïveté as that of the band's, and also by a shared energy and desire to simply do what was needed *for ourselves*. The relationship we developed was one that allowed for the exploration of new musical and graphic territory which, as history has shown, was at a pivotal point for the entire music industry.

BACK TO FRONT

From the start, I began to think about more than making record sleeves. Looking beyond the production of two-dimensional imagery, what was very important to me were the ways in which a family of complementary graphic components could be brought together to tell a complex visual story in a bold, compelling and memorable way.

Acceptance that the front of a record sleeve should be the single focus of interest was something that I questioned early on. I was never satisfied by presenting an LP as a kind of mini canvas, as it so often is when featuring a photo or illustration. To me, a record sleeve is better considered as a flat box, where the reverse, inner bag and disc label are facets of a whole package, each having equal importance in the telling of a bigger visual story. I'm less concerned with the sleeve's iconography than with its physicality and spatial presence. I often like the back more than the front.

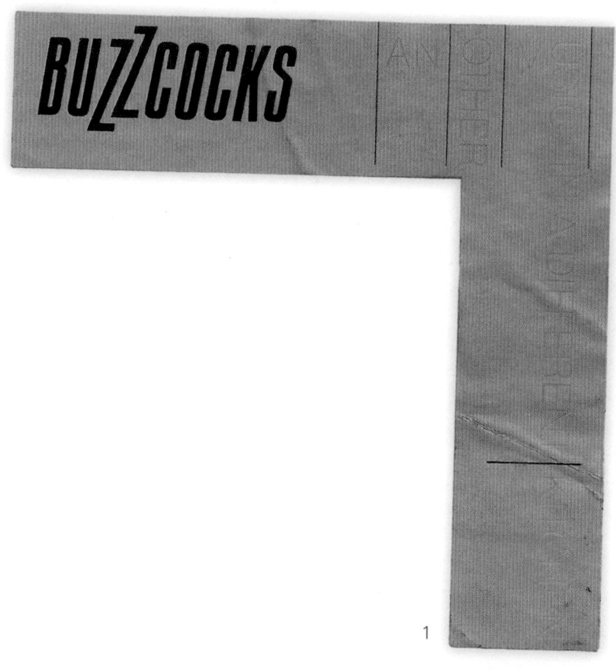

1

2

3

BUZZCOCKS: 1 promotional sticker printed on silver for *Another Music in a Different Kitchen*, United Artists Records (1978); **2** sticker in yellow (1978); **3** badge (1978), **Malcolm Garrett** design

FREE YOUR MIND

Of course, before punk and before Buzzcocks I was already absorbing influences and ideas from all around me: the late-sixties counterculture and music scenes found on both coasts of the USA; and, especially important to me, the electronic 'kosmische musik' scenes emerging from cities across the whole of West Germany at the turn of the decade.

One figure central to all that inspired me was the designer Barney Bubbles and his role within the group Hawkwind. His work, across all aspects of their presentation, fused many of these ideas into a cognitive whole and had a great effect on the visual sensibility of the teenage Malcolm Garrett. This singularly English, psychedelic, futuristic view of contemporary sociopolitics, taken alongside the pop-art infused avant-garde of the Velvet Underground and the 'conceptual continuity' of Frank Zappa's Mothers of Invention, shaped my conception of what a music-led life should look like.

It was into this volatile arena that the Sex Pistols, The Clash and the whole punk cavalcade thrust itself. For me, the fuse had already been primed and I was ready to do battle. The incendiary challenges and call-to-arms graphics espoused by Malcolm McLaren, Jamie Reid, Vivienne Westwood, Mark Perry and the whole London rabble simply ignited that fuse. Unbeknownst to me the mysterious Barney Bubbles, who never credited his work, was similarly ignited and his work soon found outlet on the nascent Stiff Records, which had just released the first punk record, The Damned's 'New Rose'.

With Buzzcocks at the forefront, Manchester quickly created its own response. This was not merely a 'version' of punk but the beginning of a new aesthetic framework that The Fall, Joy Division, Magazine and countless others on the scene or who followed each helped construct.

KRAFTWERK: (left) cardboard display for the *Radio-Activity* LP, Capitol Records (1975), **Emil Schult** graphics; **HAWKWIND:** (above) *Doremi Fasol Latido* LP poster included with record, United Artists Records (1972), **Barney Bubbles** design

A NEW HORMONES BY-PRODUCT

It was a natural step for me to contribute, integrating the influence of those countercultural tenets and graphic motifs from earlier times. All of the visual components pertaining to Buzzcocks and its products – including advertising, clothes and stage sets, merchandising, as well as the records and sleeves themselves, of course – were a strategically considered and essential part of the band's overall graphic persona.

From the start, Buzzcocks' manager and New Hormones label founder Richard Boon took a guiding role, producing the photo and layout for the 'Spiral Scratch' EP and early handbills. Having been introduced to him and the band early in 1977 by art college friend Linder Sterling, I was invited to design a poster for early live gigs. This featured the logo in use to this day, and was the start of a collaboration that has continued throughout the whole of the band's career. The pairing of Richard and me, with input from a perceptive group, ensured evocation of ideas and attention to detail unmatched in the music industry at that time.

The first record sleeve I produced was later in the year for the single 'Orgasm Addict', their first on signing to United Artists. Its abrasive combination of feminist imagery and vivid colour with a distinct typographic sensibility set it apart from both the mainstream and emerging punk style. It set a new marker for the new wave and challenged our own abilities to maintain the standard we set.

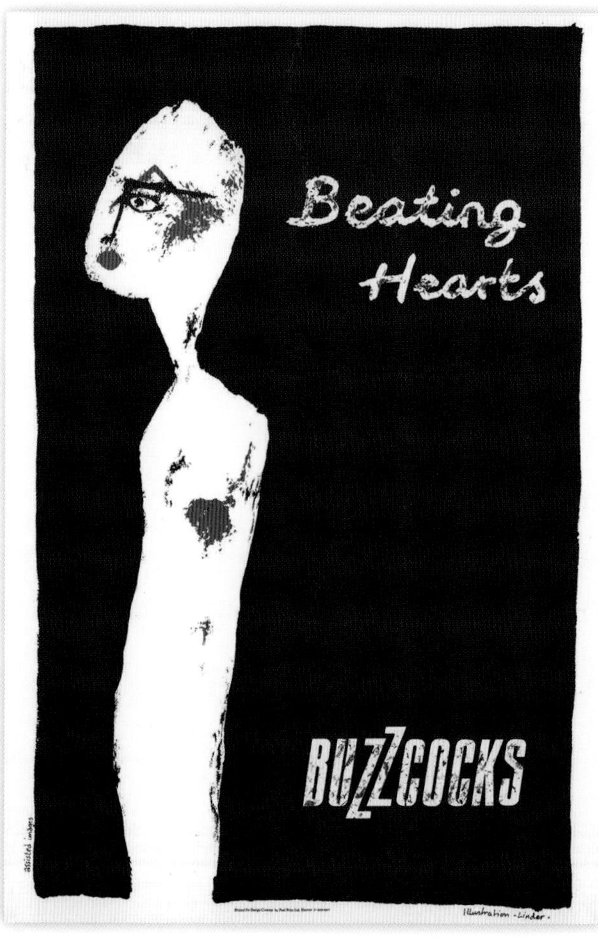

BUZZCOCKS: (left) *Beating Hearts* UK tour poster (1978) **Linder Sterling** artwork; **MAGAZINE:** (right) *The Correct Use of Soap* LP poster, Virgin Records (1980), **Malcolm Garrett** design

MAGAZINE: *Magic, Murder and the Weather* LP poster, IRS (1981), **Malcolm Garrett** design

AFTER THE ARTEFACT

A number of themes permeate the graphic design throughout the sequence of record releases until the band first split in 1981, the most notable being the variety of fine art references that govern the look of many items. The spirits of Kazimir Malevich, John Heartfield, Marcel Duchamp, René Magritte, Alexander Rodchenko, Piet Mondrian, Dada, the Bauhaus, De Stijl, Jan Tschichold, Andy Warhol, Peter Phillips, Ad Reinhardt and others were surreptitiously invoked as covert or indirect virtual collaborators. My work was referred to as 'pop constructivist' for a time.

Many details too were informed by a subliminal Beatles subtext, including the reference to the 'White Album' (*The Beatles*, 1968) in the blind embossing on *Love Bites*; and the layout of the back of *Singles Going Steady* (originally planned as the front) bore a more than passing resemblance in form and concept to *Let It Be* (1970). A later 'best of' four-track EP was even knowingly titled *The Fab Four.*

It is clear from early visuals that Buzzcocks had a seeming fixation with kitchens and household appliances, at once both ironic celebration and subversion of the normality of the homely northern working-class backgrounds they sought to escape. The title of the first album refers to a Howard Devoto lyric from an early song that speaks of stewing in one's own juice 'in another kitchen'. Many such lyrics provided inspiration to me as well as to Linder and Jon Savage, who produced a remarkable series of montages in classic Dada tradition. Only some found their way onto promotional material but many can be seen in their publication entitled *The Secret Public* (early 1978), the second New Hormones product.

THIS SINGLE OUT NOW. NEW SINGLE OUT SOON.

The lyrical potency of Pete Shelley, and Howard Devoto when he was with the band, provided a focus for many visuals and was further complemented by the evocative use of language in promotion and advertising. For example, naming of tours such as *entertaining friends, love bites* or *beating hearts* characterized the way Buzzcocks offered themselves to their public. 'Heart beats up love.'

They endeavoured to demystify advertising by tempting the audience to buy each subsequent 'product' offering with a clearly stated 'Marketing Ploy' or 'Sales Strategy'. Putting singles on albums was frowned upon as being counter to the punk ethic of value for money. Consequently, consumers were given 'Freedom of Choice' to consider purchase of the newest single advertised as appearing on the latest album, yet were offered 'No Choice' but to buy the album itself. Inherent in all this was a particular sense of fun, further enhanced by the marking of each stage in the project with a special badge. Record releases, tours and special moments were all registered, with twenty-eight official badges in all.

THROBBING GRISTLE: (above) 'United' 45 front cover, Industrial Records (1978); **WAH!:** (below) 'Somesay' 45 front cover, Eternal Records (1981)

ALL ART IS THEFT

BUZZCOCKS: 1 badge (1981); **2 ORCHESTRAL MANOEUVRES IN THE DARK:** *Dazzle Ships* tour programme cover, **P. Saville Associates** (1983); **3** *Dazzle Ships* tour programme interior showing original inspiration for the artwork and album title, **P. Saville Associates** (1983)

The visual presentation of all aspects of the band's activities was always seen as an exercise in a kind of post-corporate coordination, matched only by similar control exercised over such bands as the Sex Pistols and Throbbing Gristle. In subsequent years this became the norm in the music world with artists as diverse as Scraping Foetus Off The Wheel, New Order, Pop Will Eat Itself and Duran Duran all maintaining a personal interest in the development of their own graphic images.

None of this is an accident. Yet nothing is really new. All of the work you'll see and enjoy in this book is both fresh *and* reactionary, in that it is either a rejection or a response, negative or positive, to all that has preceded it. Either way, influence is inevitable.

1

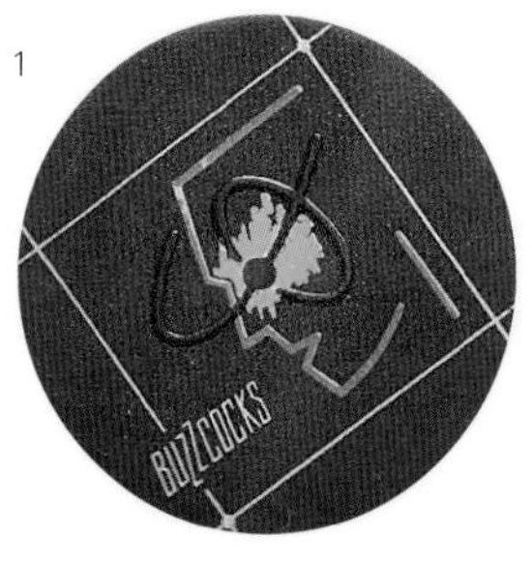

2

3

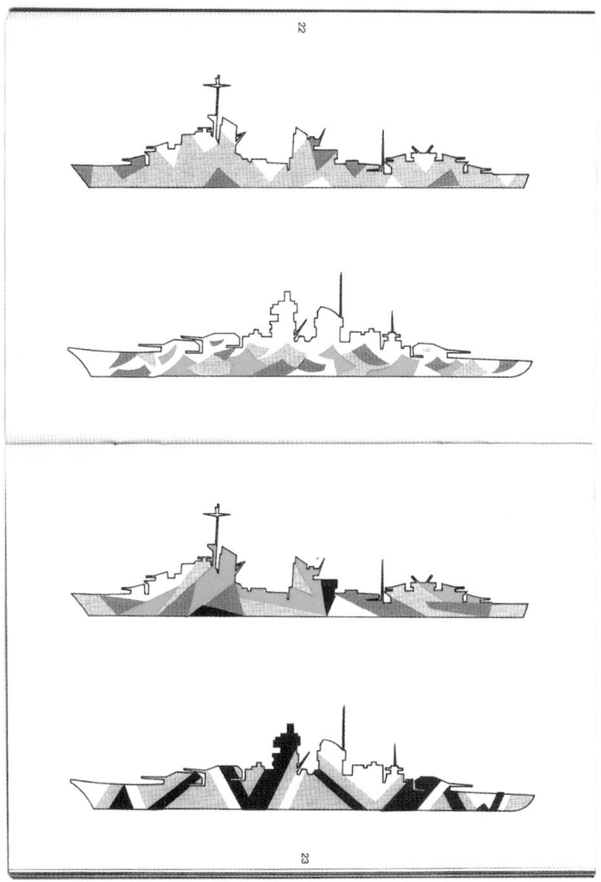

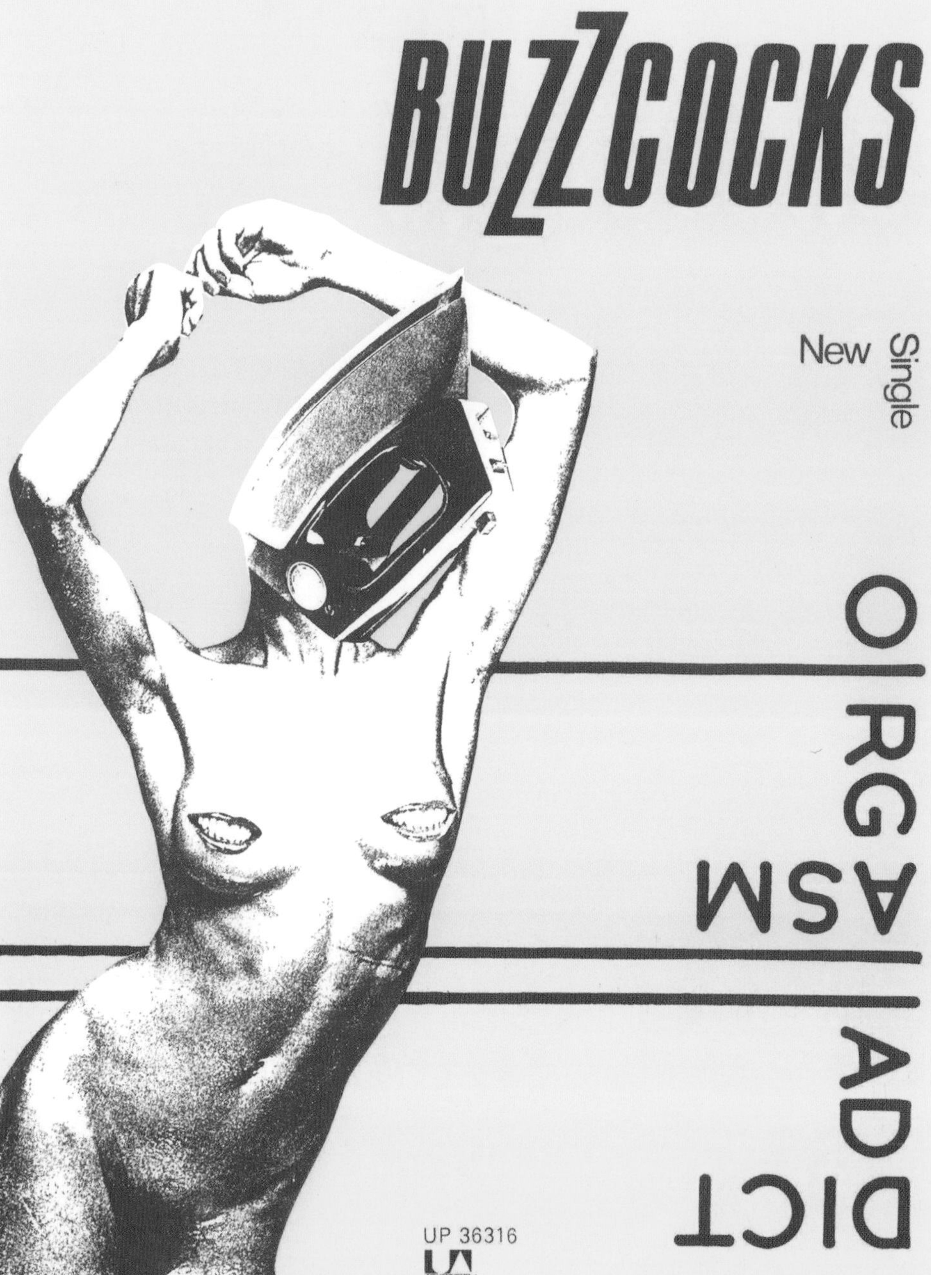

BUZZCOCKS: 'Orgasm Addict' 45 poster, United Artists Records (1977), **Linder Sterling** montage, which reflects the influence of German Dadaist, Hannah Höch, **Malcolm Garrett** logo design and typography

This poster (created in-house at UA) incorporates Linder Sterling's surreal photomontage of a naked female torso fused to a steam iron in lieu of a head, together with the distinctive band logo design, typography and layout by Malcolm Garrett. The collaboration of Malcolm, Richard Boon and Buzzcocks was one of the most prolific and visually sophisticated of the period (being post-punk two years before the emergence of post-punk), with Garrett essentially the in-house graphic designer for the band. The poster is the first to display one of the defining logos of the period, as instantly recognizable as those for The Clash, Crass and the Sex Pistols. Early in his career Garrett briefly worked with Barney Bubbles and is one of his more fervent admirers. Garrett went on to design sleeves and poster art for several major bands during the 1980s (including Magazine, Duran Duran, Simple Minds and Peter Gabriel) and has had a prolific career in design. He is currently the creative director of Images&Co in London.

Andrew Krivine

BUZZCOCKS: 1 poster for gig in Manchester (November 1976) signed by Pete Shelley and Howard Devoto; **2** 'Spiral Scratch' EP re-release poster, New Hormones Records (1979), **Buzzcocks/Richard Boon** design, **Richard Boon** photography (Polaroid); **3** front cover of first press kit issued by manager Richard Boon, New Hormones (c. early 1977); **4** songbook for *Another Music In A Different Kitchen*, Virgin Music Publishers (1978), **Malcolm Garrett** design

1

2

4

3

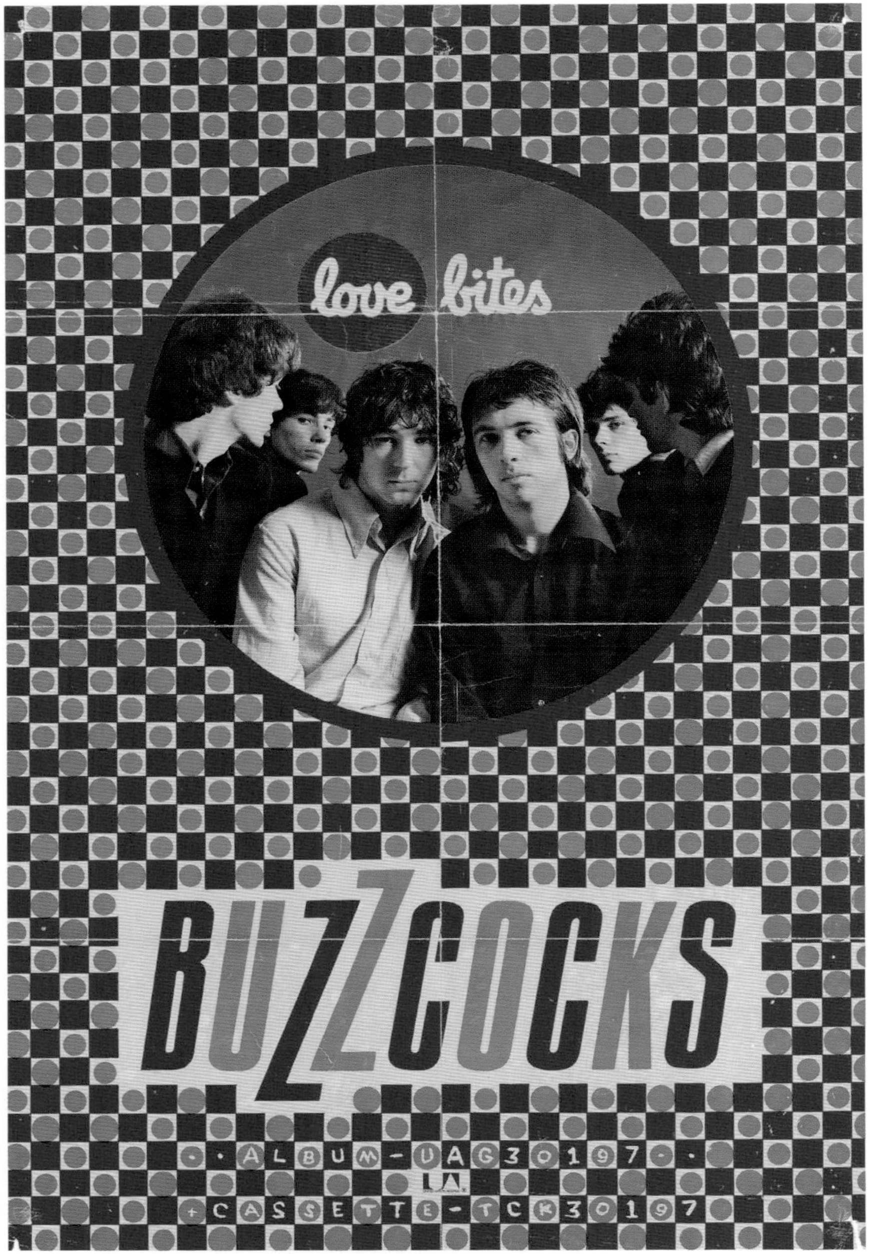

love bites
BUZZCOCKS
• ALBUM - UAG30197 •
CASSETTE - TCK30197

BUZZCOCKS: (below) *Love Bites* LP poster (alternate design), United Artists Records (1978), **Malcolm Garrett/Assorted Images** design, **Chris Gabrin** photography; (left) poster issued by The Secret Public (Buzzcocks UK fan club) (1980), **Malcolm Garrett/Assorted Images** design, **Adrian Boot** photography

1

2

3

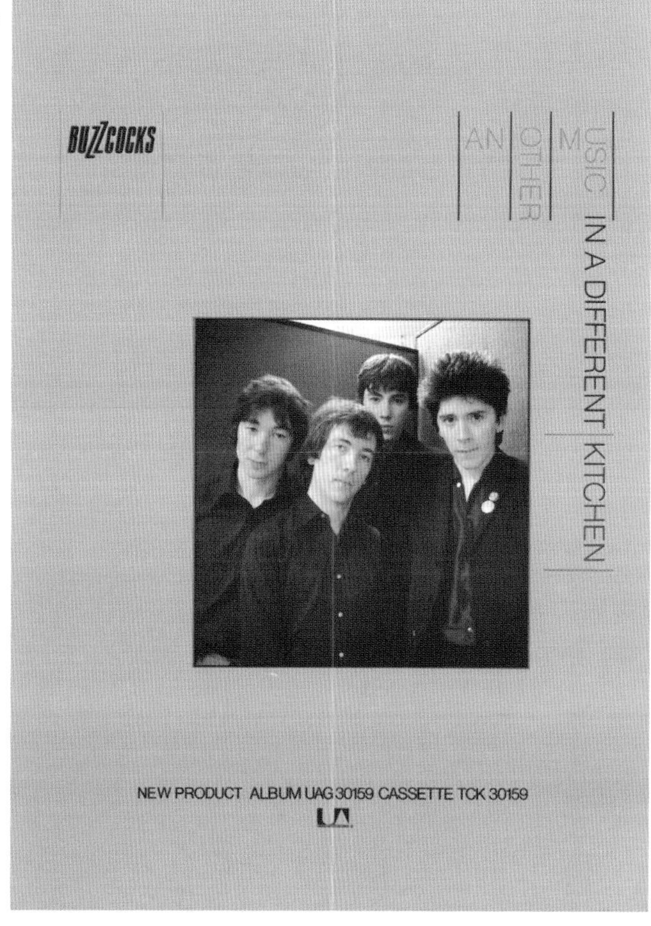

BUZZCOCKS: 1 'What Do I Get?' 45 sheet music, UA Records (1978); **2** promotional badges printed with lyrics to 'What Do I Get?', UA Records (1978); **3** *Another Music in a Different Kitchen* LP poster, UA Records (1978), **Malcolm Garrett/Assorted Images** design; **Jill Furmanovsky** photography

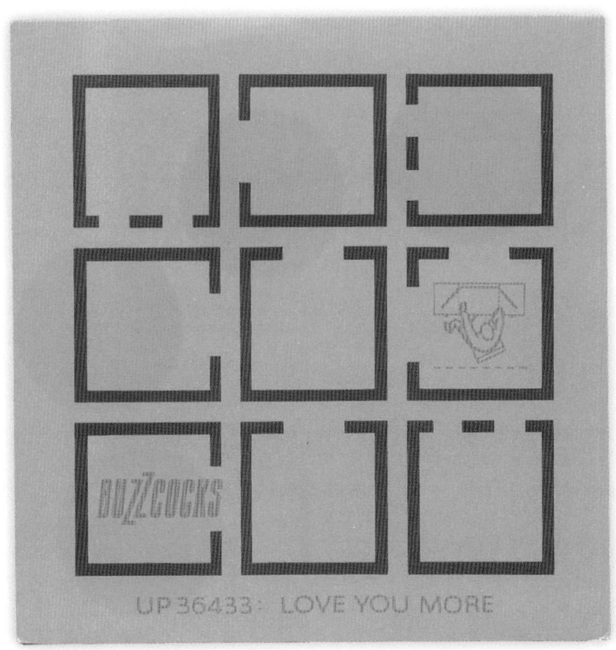

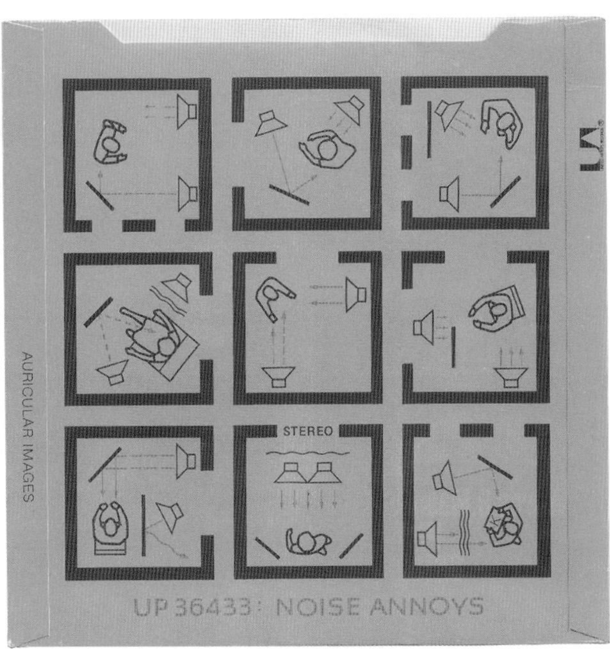

BUZZCOCKS: (above) 'Love You More' 45 front and back cover, UA Records (1978), **Malcolm Garrett/Auricular Images** design

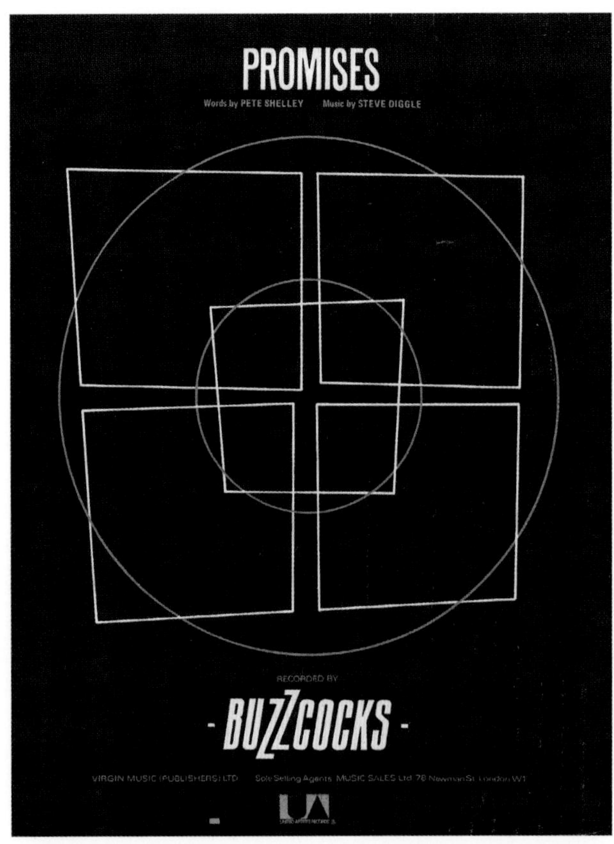

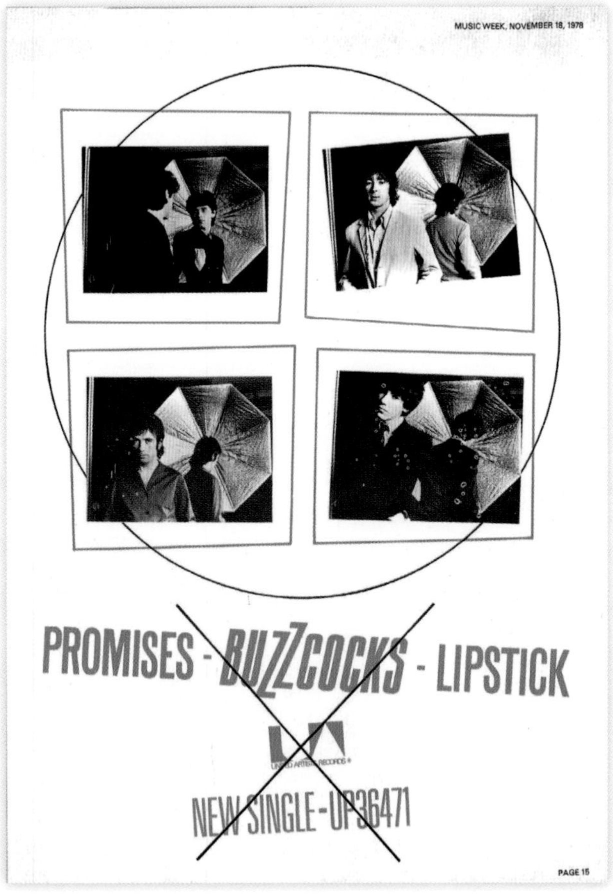

BUZZCOCKS: (above, left) 'Promises' 45 sheet music, UA Records (1978), **Malcolm Garrett/Altered Images** design; (above, right) 'Promises' / 'Lipstick' 45 advertisement from *Music Week*, UA Records (November 1978), **Malcolm Garrett/Altered Images** design

1

2

3

4

BUZZCOCKS: 1 *A Different Kind of Tension* LP poster, IRS Records (1979), from **Malcolm Garrett/Accompanying Images** design; **Jill Furmanovsky** photography; **2** *A Different Kind of Tension* LP poster, United Artists Records (1979), **Malcolm Garrett/Accompanying Images** design; **Jill Furmanovsky** photography; **3** promotional sticker, IRS Records (September 1979) **4** promotional sticker, UA Records (1979

the
BUZZCOCKS
are coming.

At 'Hotel Diplomat'
West 43rd St. off 6TH AVE.
Sat. Sept 15TH, 1979
8 30 pm

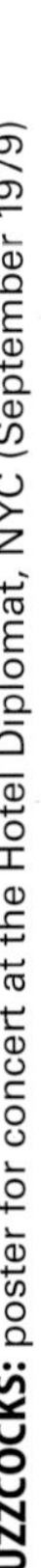

BUZZCOCKS: poster for concert at the Hotel Diplomat, NYC (September 1979)

CASH PUSSIES: '99% Is Shit' 45 cover, The Label (1979), **Joe Stevens** photography

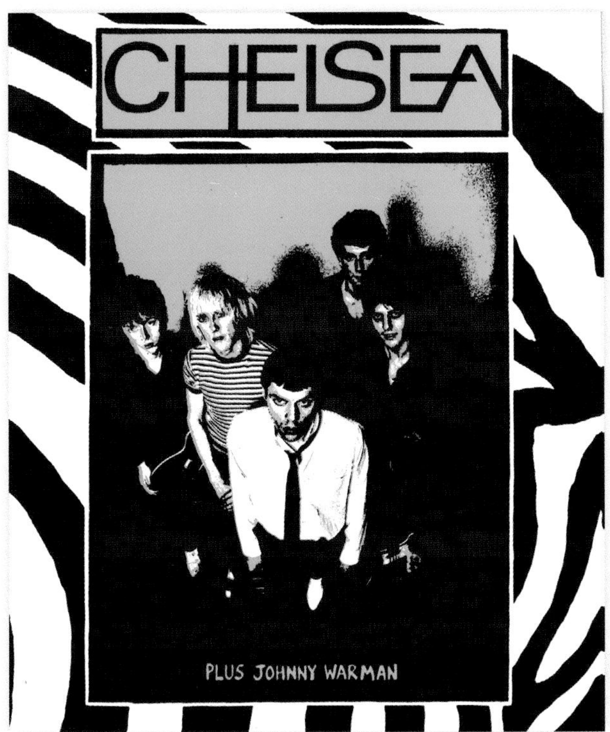

CHELSEA: (above) cropped gig poster (1978) **X3 Studios** design; (right) 'Right to Work' 45 poster, Step Forward Records (1977), **Peter Kodick** photography

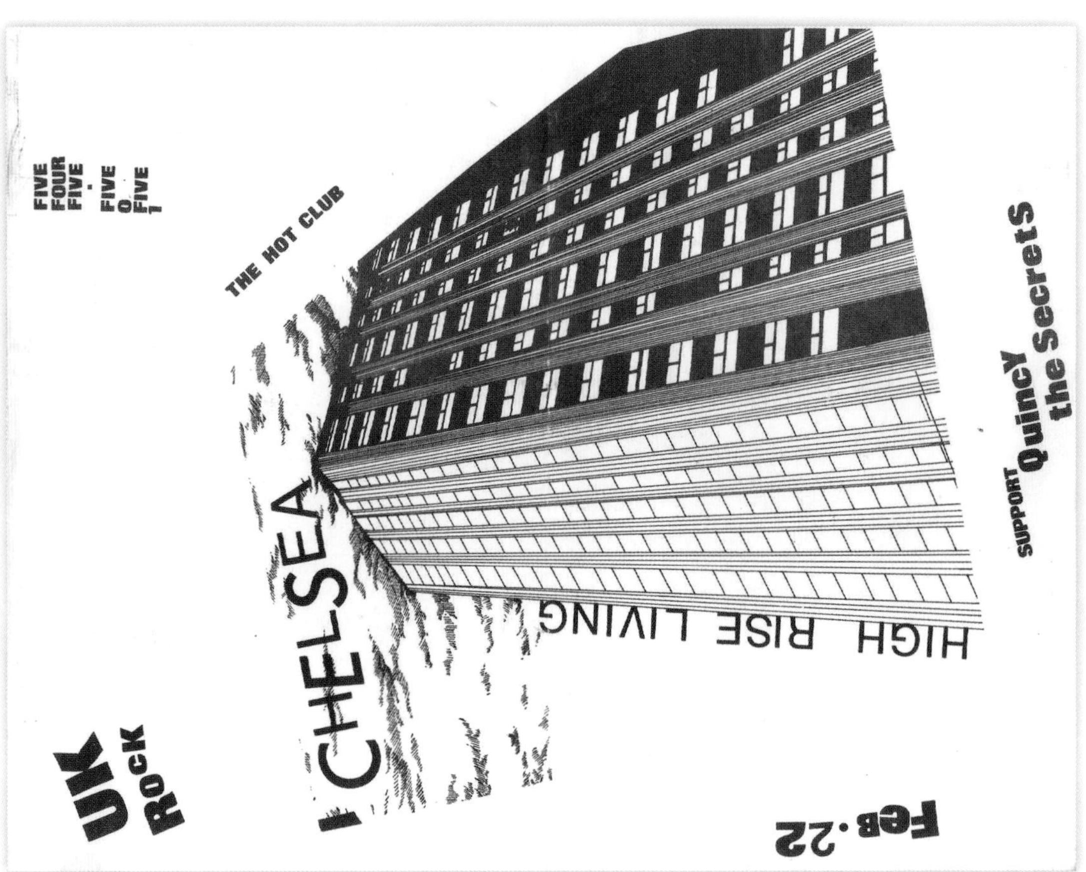

CHELSEA: (above, top) flyer for gig at The Hot Club, Philadelphia PA (c.1979); (above) *Chelsea*, debut US LP poster, IRS Records (1980), **Tony MacLean** design and photography

CHELSEA: 'Evacuate' 45 poster, Step Forward Records (198')

1977: YOU'RE ON THE NEVER-NEVER

A brief recollection by Sebastian Conran

By chance in November 1975, I gave the Sex Pistols their first actual booking, when I was treasurer of the Student Union at Central School of Art and Design; I was sitting in the Union office when two cool-looking guys, Paul Cook and Glen Matlock, strolled in, saying that they had a new band and were looking for a gig. I recall thinking 'Sex Pistols' was a bizarre name but they looked and sounded convincing, so I booked them for the following Thursday supporting the college band Brent Ford and The Nylons for a fee of £15; my good friend Alex McDowell however, the SU social secretary, took over from there. I recall enjoying the Sex Pistols' gig, which was pretty shambolic and consisted of Johnny Rotten blowing his nose into the microphone while the band played covers of Stooges, Monkees and Lou Reed numbers. Some students thought it was great but others thought it horrendous – which is always a good sign of successful provocation.

Meanwhile, I had already met The Clash's sound engineer Mickey Foote who'd moved in with Amy, one of my fellow housemates in the large run-down Decimus Burton house we shared in Regent's Park. This had been my family home before my father left to live in the country, but I took over the lease from the Crown and rented out rooms to fellow students. Eventually, both Joe Strummer and Mickey Foote came to live in the dilapidated mansion and we had all sorts of house guests, such as Johnny Thunders and The Heartbreakers. I first met Joe when his band The 101ers played at a party in the house, and Mickey introduced us. To me, Joe was really interesting on a personal level and we used to hang out, spending many evenings in the pub across the road (the Queen's Head & Artichoke) or going to gigs; his being twenty-five made him quite the mentor to a naive twenty-year-old like me.

Through Mickey and Joe I met The Clash, who were still nascent and had yet to play a gig. At the time they had Joe, Paul Simonon, Mick Jones,

Terry Chimes and Keith Levene (soon to be dropped) in the line-up. Being a practical and useful type, eventually I was roped in as a roadie-factotum by the manager Bernie Rhodes, supporting The Clash by setting up equipment and organizing such things as designing posters and flyers. I had helped Alex McDowell print T-shirts for Vivienne Westwood and put this experience to work for The Clash too, on my bedroom floor. Interested in photography, I had a darkroom in the house, which was useful for preparing artwork. The photographer Rocco Macauley also came to live in the house and he shot many of the images used on the posters and eventually the record sleeves, for which I designed and prepared the artwork.

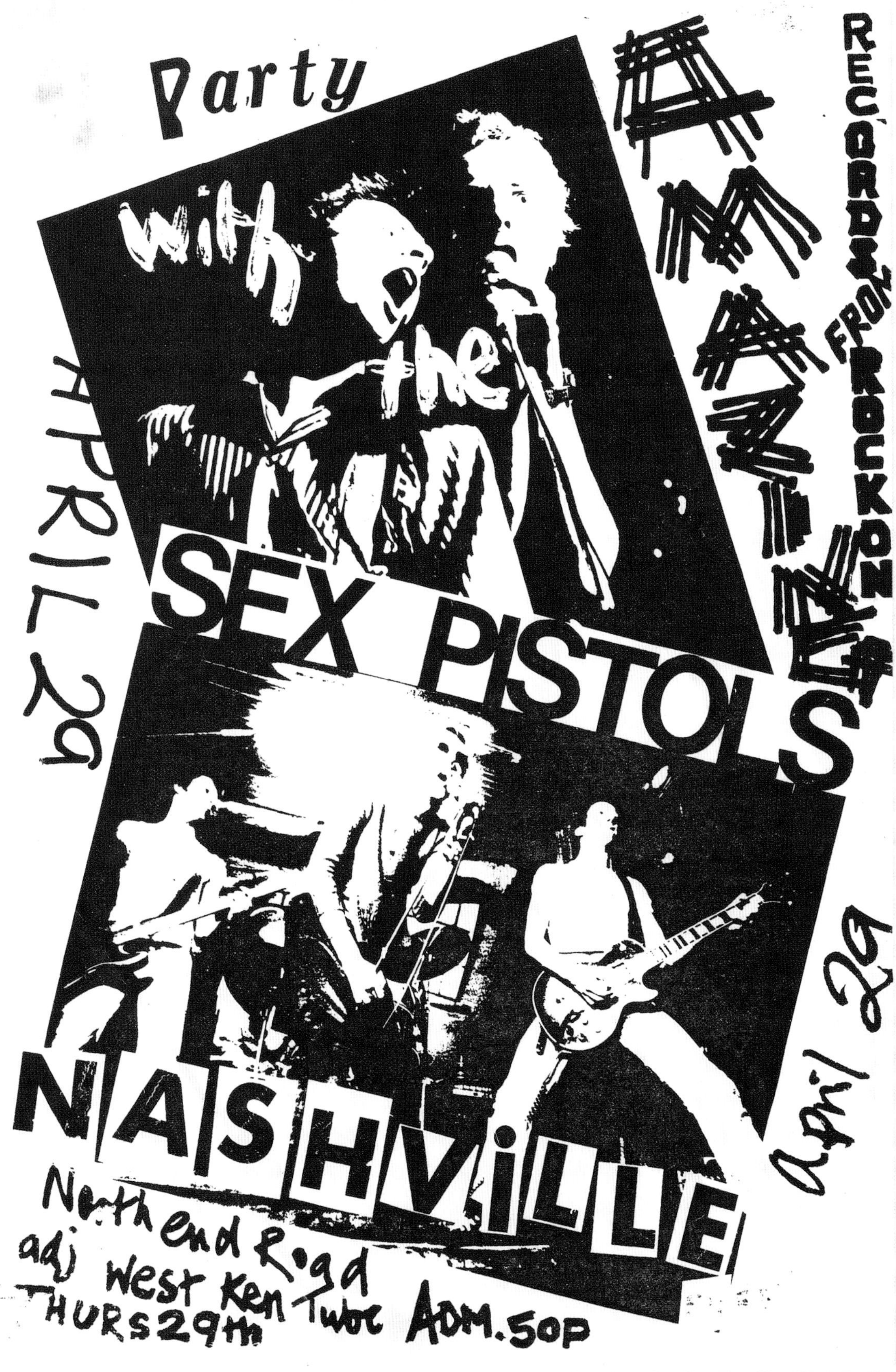

SEX PISTOLS: (left) flyer for cancelled gig at the Screen On The Green cinema, Islington, London (17 May 1976); (above) flyer for gig at The Nashville, London (29 April 1976)

THE CLASH: xeroxed flyer (1977), **Anya Phillips** photography; (opposite) 'White Riot' 45 back cover, CBS Records (1977), **Sebastian Conran** design

The Clash's first album cover was produced by the CBS in-house artwork department (but if you listen carefully, you can hear my feet stamping on the 'White Riot' track). I did, however, contribute to and design singles artwork for 'Complete Control' (my photo and the front), 'Capital Radio EP' (my photos), 'Remote Control' and 'Clash City Rockers' (photos by Rocco Macauley), in addition to all the associated posters and promotional material for gigs, et cetera. I was briefed on the design by Bernie and Paul Simonon, whose primary objective was to be sure they did not look too 'designed' or tasteful (which went maybe a little against my Conran genes).

I used my own and Rocco's photos, and would try to get the result to look a little raw by making the artwork very small so that errors were magnified when enlarged, which was especially effective on posters. I was a complete amateur, as required by the punk ethos; I had been studying industrial design engineering and only had a vague idea of what I was doing graphically, so the results were experimental and disruptive – which was the principle zeitgeist of early punk in the UK.

We started a company called Upstarts and marketed the clothes and T-shirts in the house: in a sewing room, consisting of Alex Michon and Christine, we designed and made clothes for The Clash musicians to wear onstage and in photos. I would take bales of cloth to South London to be cut to our patterns, then bring them back to be put into bundles, which I would take to the deeply unfashionable and decrepit fashion district of the East End to be made up in some Dickensian basement sweatshop. These would be given to the group and haphazardly sold by advertising them in the back of *Sounds* and *NME*.

When the band got bigger, their association with 'a privately educated millionaire's son' (I had no money at all) was drawn into question by the press, and Mick Jones wanted me to be disassociated; by then the feeling was pretty mutual, as fame can do horrible things to people. Chrissie Hynde suggested that I learn bass guitar and join her fledgling band, but I'd had enough of rock 'n' roll and wanted to get back to industrial design. Little did I think then that in forty years' time people would be vaguely interested in what I was doing...

THE CLASH: poster for concert with The Rockets and Subway Sect at the Royal College of Art in London, **Savage Pencil** artwork

This poster is a recent two-colour screen print of one of the rarest Clash posters, promoting the band's Night of Treason gig at the Royal College of Art in London on Guy Fawkes Night, 1976. Reproduced from the original artwork and signed by the artist 'Savage Pencil' (Edwin Pouncey). The print is signed, embossed and a numbered edition (no.5 of 150).

Andrew Krivine

THE CLASH: (bottom) tour blank, CBS Records (1977), poster uses the same **Roslaw Szaybo** design and **Kate Simon** photography from the band's debut LP; (top) Mont de Marsan Festival poster (August 1977), **Kate Simon** photography

THE CLASH: Get Out of Control tour blank posters (November 1977), **Sebastian Conran** design (courtesy of Sebastian Conran)

THE CLASH: flyer insert from fanzine *Ghast Up* #3 (May 1977), created with a typewriter repeating semicolons using a Roneo stencil. Image taken from a photograph by **Chalkie Davies**

THE CLASH: 'Clash City Rockers' c/w 'Jail Guitar Doors' 45 poster, CBS Records (1978), **Sebastian Conran** design

THE CLASH: Clash On Parole tour poster (July 1978), **Nick Egan** design, **Adrian Boot** photography

MUSIC MACHINE, J

THE CLASH: Clash On Parole tour flyer for concert at Music Machine, Camden, London (July 1978), **Adrian Boot** photography

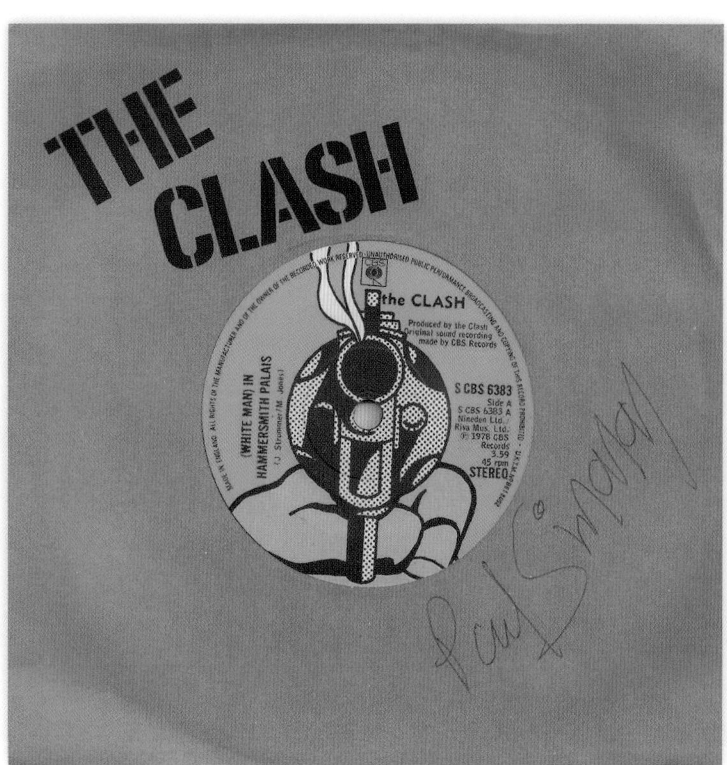

THE CLASH: (left) '(White Man) In Hammersmith Palais' 45 centrepiece and blue sleeve, CBS Records (1978), **Nick Egan** design, signed by Paul Simonon

THE CLASH: (right) '(White Man) In Hammersmith Palais' 45 poster, CBS Records (June 1978), **Nick Egan** design, graphics reflecting influences of Saul Bass and Roy Lichtenstein

THE CLASH: *Give 'Em Enough Rope* alternate US LP poster, Epic Records (1978), **Hugh Brown** and **Gene Greif** design

THE CLASH: (below) *Give 'Em Enough Rope* official Canadian LP poster, Epic Records (1978), **Hugh Brown** and **Gene Greif** design; (opposite) *Give 'Em Enough Rope* front and back of two-sided LP poster, CBS Records (1978)

The poster is also the record cover for the band's second LP, designed by Berkeley, California artist Hugh Brown (taken from his photo-collage End of the Trail for the Capitalist) and CBS sleeve designer Gene Greif (1977–80), who applied the flat, stark colours.

Andrew Krivine

GIVE 'EM ENOUGH ROPE THE CLASH GIVE 'EM ENOUGH ROPE THE CLASH GIVE 'EM ENOUGH ROPE THE CLASH

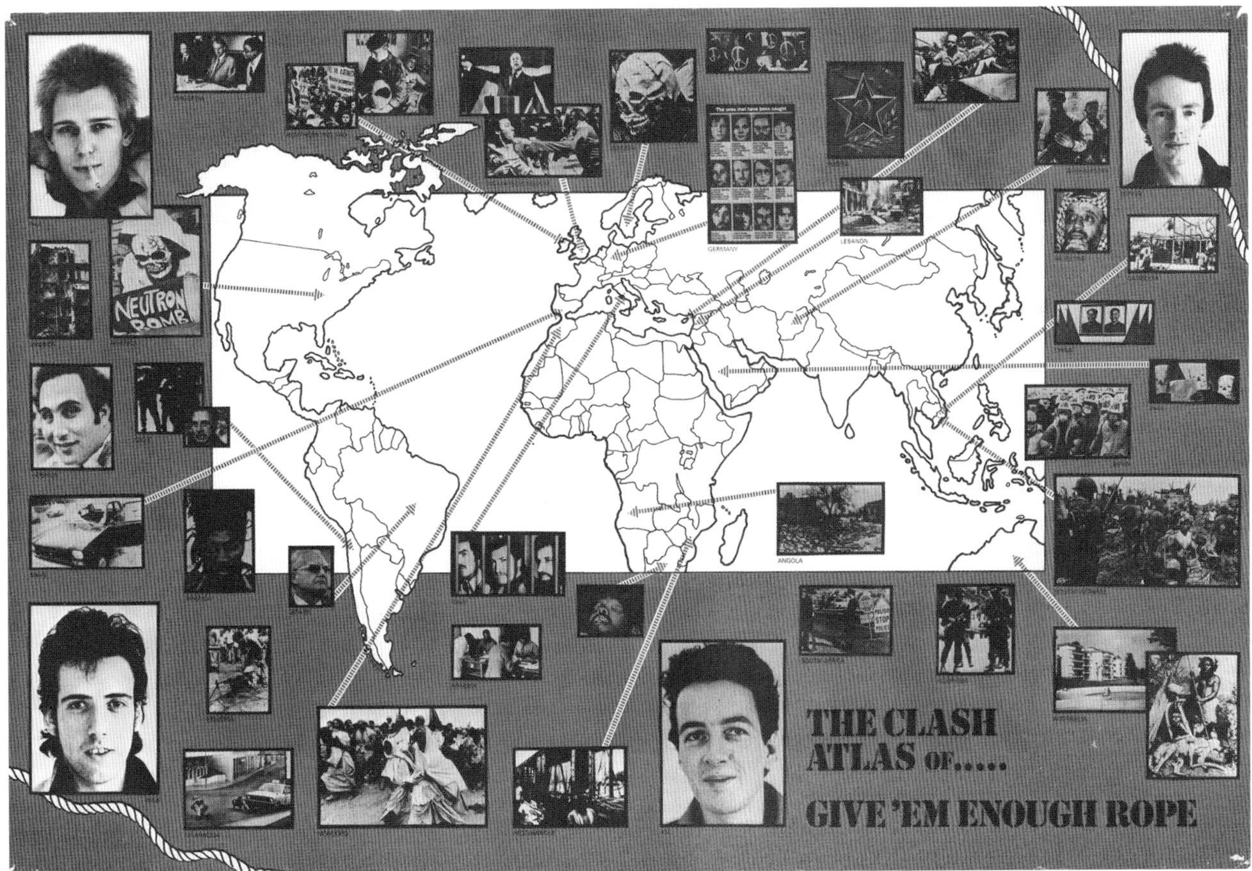
NEUTRON BOMB
GERMANY
LEBANON
ANGOLA
THE CLASH
ATLAS OF.....
GIVE 'EM ENOUGH ROPE

THE CLASH: US tour poster, Epic Records (1979)

This poster and flyer were created for a benefit show the band played for the organization New Youth in San Francisco. The venue was at 1839 Geary Street. The backstory of the gig is interesting; The Clash wanted to play the show but could not use their name because they were under contract with Bill Graham and he refused to grant his consent. The problem was solved by billing the band as 'THE BEST BAND EVER, DIRECT FROM ENGLAND' on the flyer for the concert, and 'THE WHITE RIOT!' on the poster.

Andrew Krivine

THE CLASH: (above) poster and (right) flyer for the New Youth benefit concert, San Francisco, CA (February 1979)

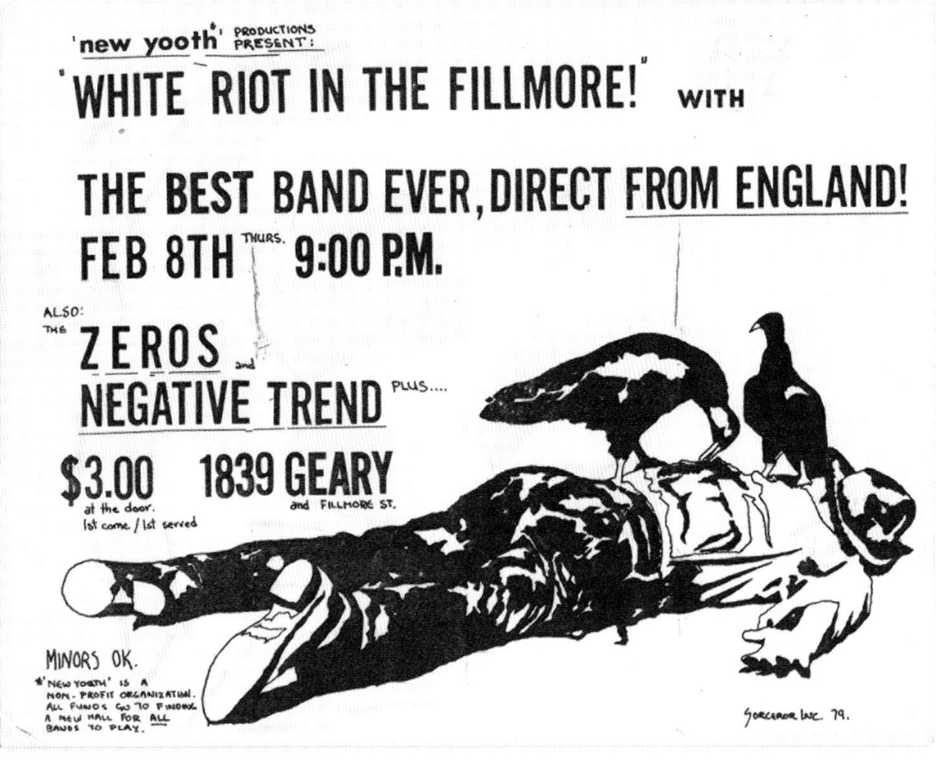

THE CLASH: (right) poster for concert at Ontario Theatre, Baltimore, MD (15 February 1979); (below) flyer promoting concert at the Masonic Auditorium, Detroit, MI (17 September 1979)

This flyer is from the band's second tour of the US. Three days later, during a concert at the Palladium in New York City, Pennie Smith took the famous photograph of Paul Simonon smashing his bass, which was used for the cover of the band's third album, *London Calling*, CBS (1979). This flyer was signed by the artist, Gary Grimshaw.

Andrew Krivine

THE CLASH: (above and below) posters for 'The Cost of Living' EP, CBS Records (May 1979), **Rocking Russian** design

THE CLASH: *London Calling* LP seriality poster, Epic Records (1979), **Ray Lowry** design, **Pennie Smith** photography

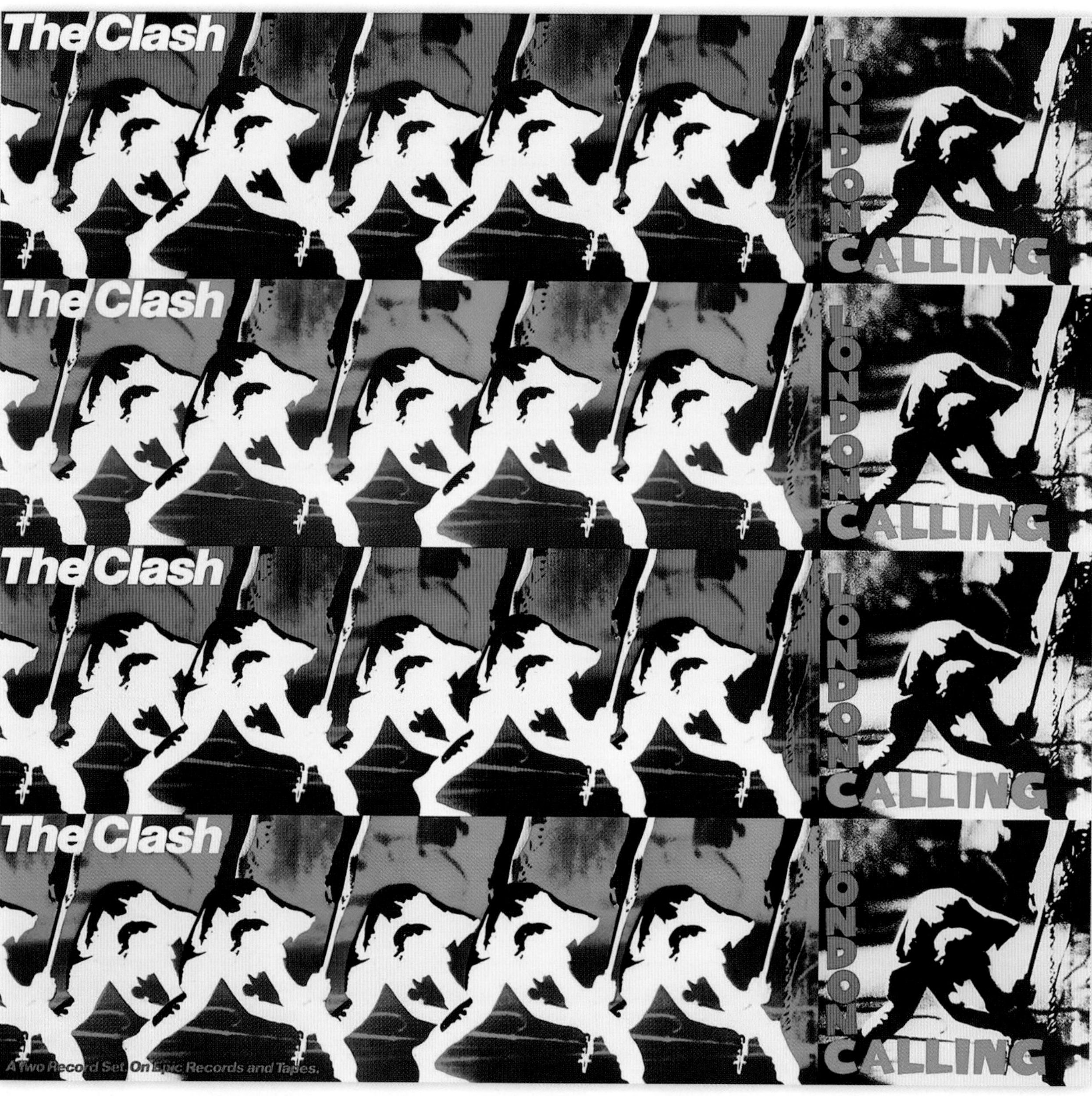

This serialization of the *London Calling* cover image is clearly influenced by Warhol's 'Triple Elvis' and 'Electric Chair' from the 1960s.

Andrew Krivine

THE CLASH: (above, left) *The Armagideon Times* #1 back cover; (above, right) *The Armagideon Times* #2 front cover: both published by The Clash, sold on their '16 Tons Tour' of the UK (1980), **Ray Lowry** design; (right) 'London Calling' 45 in-store poster (most likely a reproduction), CBS Records (1979)

This poster is for the release of the band's first compilation record, which was curiously issued in a 10-inch vinyl format. Of note: the man in the foreground is Don Letts, walking towards a phalanx of police at the Notting Hill Carnival, 1976. Don was one of the central figures on the punk scene; he worked at Acme Attractions and then BOY, directed the *Punk Rock Movie* while working as DJ at The Roxy club, directed the 'London Calling' video for The Clash and became a founder member of Big Audio Dynamite. The Clash frequently incorporated martial imagery in their promotional materials – in this case, Soviet bombers and tanks. A trace of the design influence of the Stenberg brothers is reflected in this poster.

Andrew Krivine

THE CLASH: *Black Market Clash* 10-inch compilation LP design CBS/Epic Records (1980), **Rocco Macaulay** photography

1

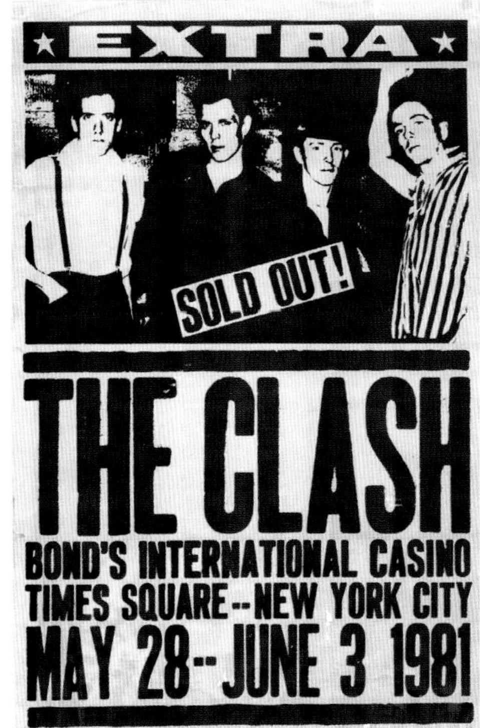

2

3

THE CLASH: 1 gig flyer for Victoria Hall, Hanley, Stoke-on-Trent, UK dates (Feb and June 1980); **2** concert poster for Bond's International Casino, NYC (May–June 1981); **3** concert poster with make-up dates for Bond's International Casino, NYC (extended residency, May–June 1981)

THE CLASH: poster for concert at Au Théâtre Mogador, Paris (September 1981), **Futura 2000** artwork (New York graffiti artist whose real name is **Leonard Hilton McGurr**)

THE CLASH: Impossible Mission tour poster, France, CBS Records (1981)

THE CLASH: (left) *Sandinista!* German LP poster, CBS Records (1981), **Julian Balme** design; (right) *Sandinista!* US poster, Epic Records (1980)

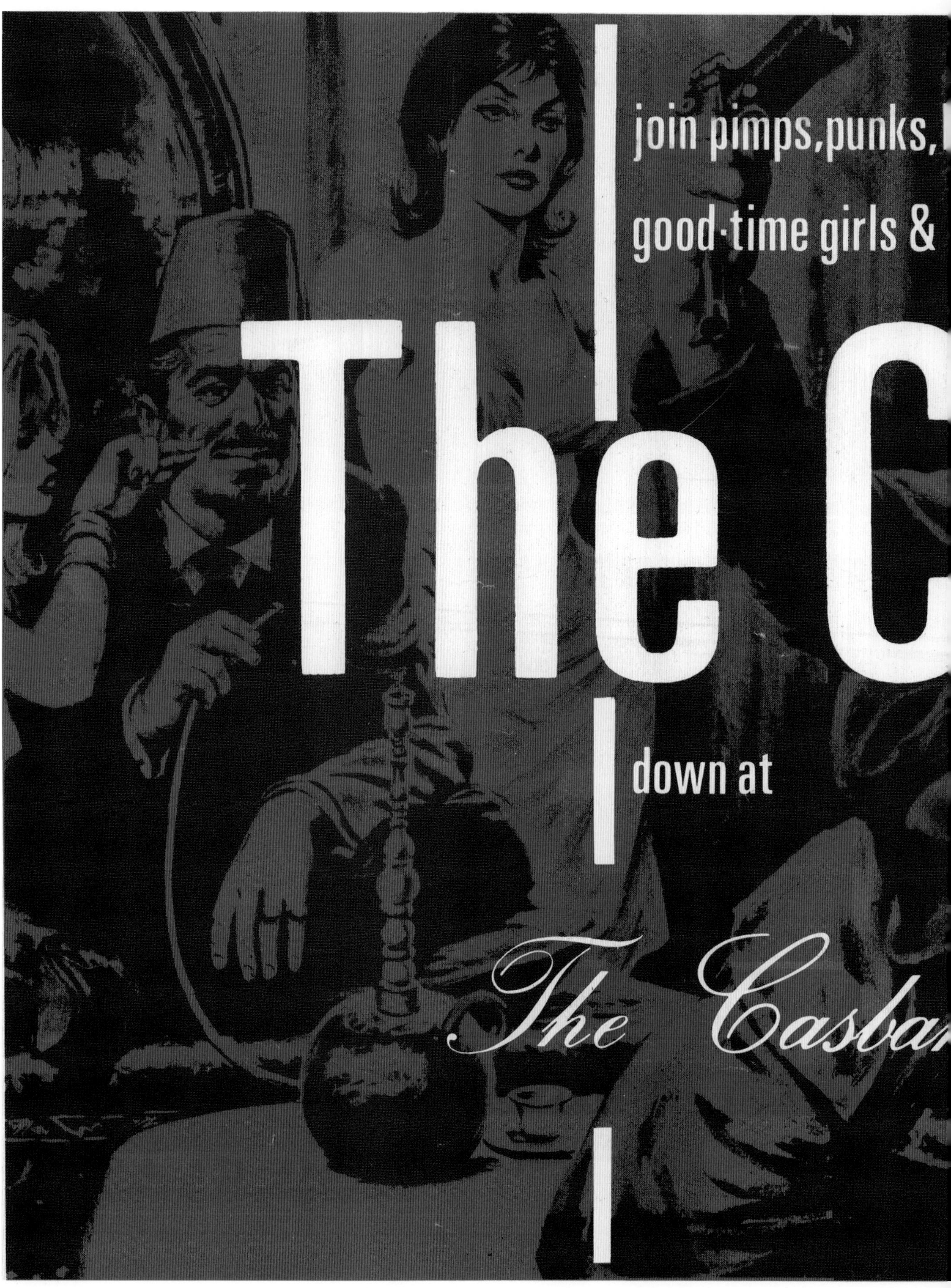
join pimps, punks,
good·time girls &
The
down at
The Casba

THE CLASH: The Casbah Club tour poster of the UK, US and Canada (May–August 1982)

1

2

THE CLASH: 1 *Combat Rock* set of four stickers, CBS Records (1982); **2** *Combat Rock* sticker, CBS Records (1982); **3** poster for concert at University of Houston, Nineden Ltd (June 1982), **Artists of Fortune** design; **4** Out Of Control tour poster, Rider College, New Jersey, NY (20 April 1984)

3

4

THE CLASH: Out of Control tour poster, Alumni Arena, Buffalo, NY (April 1984)

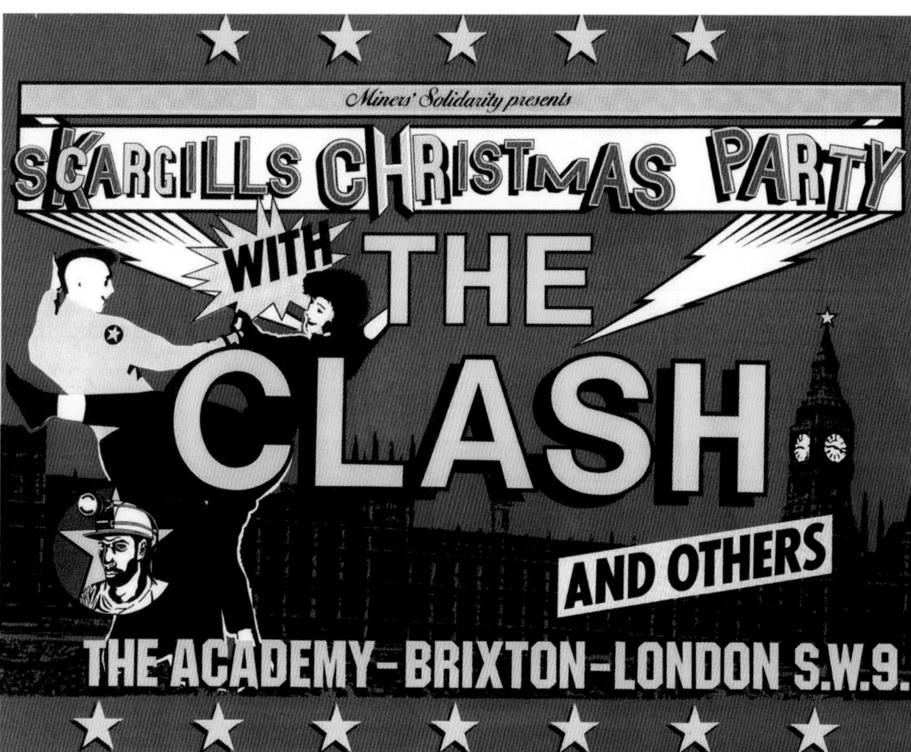

THE CLASH: (left) poster for miners' benefit gig titled Scargill's Christmas Party (7 December 1984); (below) *Cut the Crap* – two-sided LP flat, Epic Records (November 1985), **J.B.** design

Cut the Crap was The Clash's sixth and final studio album, released in November 1985. Both Mick Jones and Topper Headon had been fired prior to the recording, and as such it is widely perceived as not being a true Clash album. This poster by long-time design collaborator Julian Balme is clearly an homage to Martin Scorsese's cinematic 1976 masterwork, *Taxi Driver*.

Andrew Krivine

THE CORTINAS: (above) 'Fascist Dictator' 45 poster, Step Forward Records (1977), **Harry Murlowski** and **Peter Swan** photography; (right) 'Independence' 45 poster, Step Forward Records (1977), **X3 Studios**/**Bob Linney** and **Ken Maharg** design

THE
CORTINAS
X3 POSTERS 407-7811
new single on step forward records sf6
independence
+ DEFIANT POSE

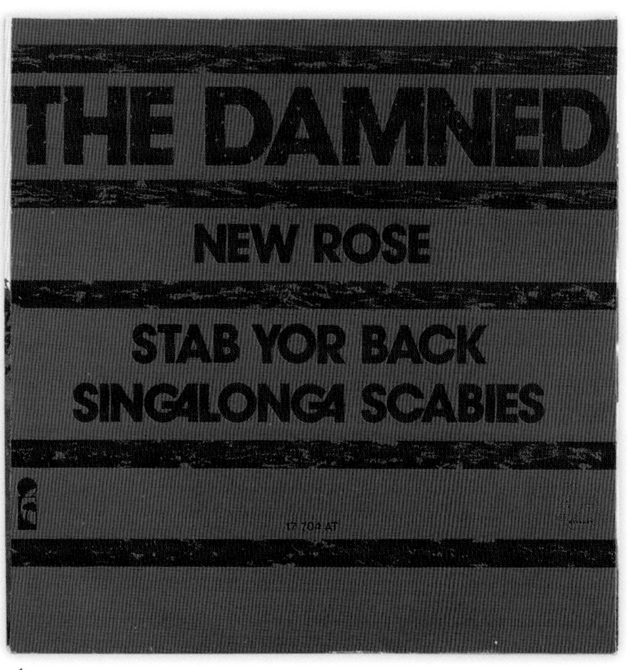

1

2

THE DAMNED: 1 'New Rose' 45 back cover, Island/Stiff Records Benelux (1976); **2** Stiff Records promotional clock (1977); **3** 'New Rose' unofficial 45 poster (*c.*1980) based on the sleeve for the French release of the single by Skydog Records (1977), **Bruno Caruso** design

3

THE DAMNED: (left and below) *Disciples Song Book* front and back cover, bio page, Stiff Records (1977), **Peter Kodick** photography, printed by *ZigZag* magazine

Dave Vanian; vocals

Nothing very much is known about Dave except that when Rat and Brian first saw him they reckoned he "looked like a singer" and took him on.

Brian James; guitar, vocals

Brian James does lots of the songwriting and all the guitar playing. He's 22 years old and has no comment to make on anything at all. He plays a red Gibson electric guitar which usually has six strings.

Captain Sensible; bass, vocals

"I played in Johnny Moped's brother's bedroom, and I think Johnny's a real cool meatball. I am 20 years old and my hobbies include big game ant eater hunting and drinking Fullers ESB. My brain is growing by the minute."

Rat Scabies; drums, vocals

"I am tall, good looking, arrogant and conceited. My hobbies include brick laying and eating manhole covers. I am 19 years old and play drums because I like hitting things. I got my first drum kit four years ago. My biggest influence is me, and I owe my success to me. I like scarring the Professor's brain with scalpels and bludgeons." (Rat Scabies is hung like a gnat. – Ed.)

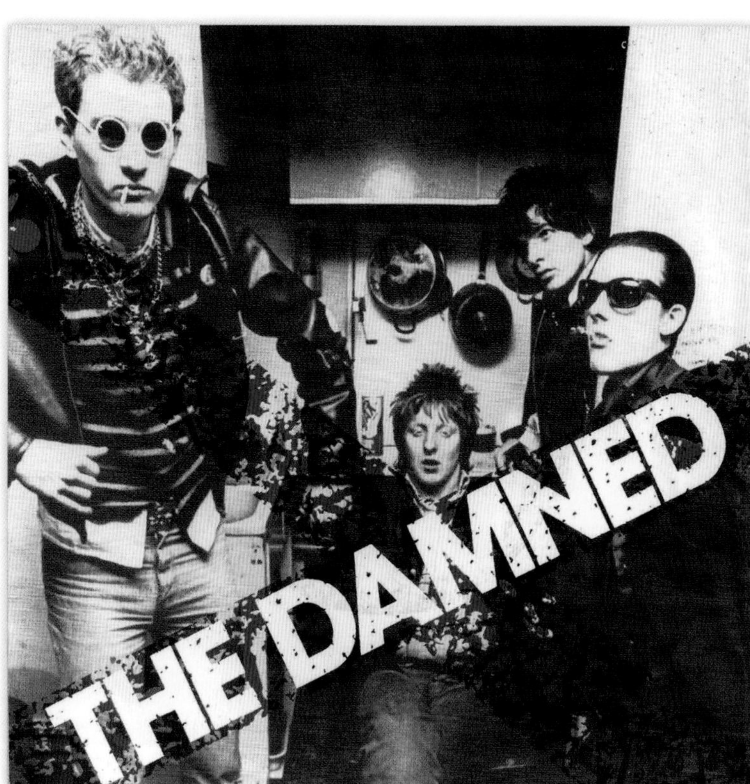

THE DAMNED: (left) 'New Rose' 45 front cover, Island/Stiff Records Benelux (1976); (below) UK tour poster for concert with The Dead Boys at the Elizabethan Rooms, Manchester (1977)

damnedeadboys
damnedeadboys
damnedeadboys
damnedeadboys
damnedeadboys
damnedeadboys
on tour
ELIZABETHAN ROOMS / SUN
MANCHESTER / 20th NOV

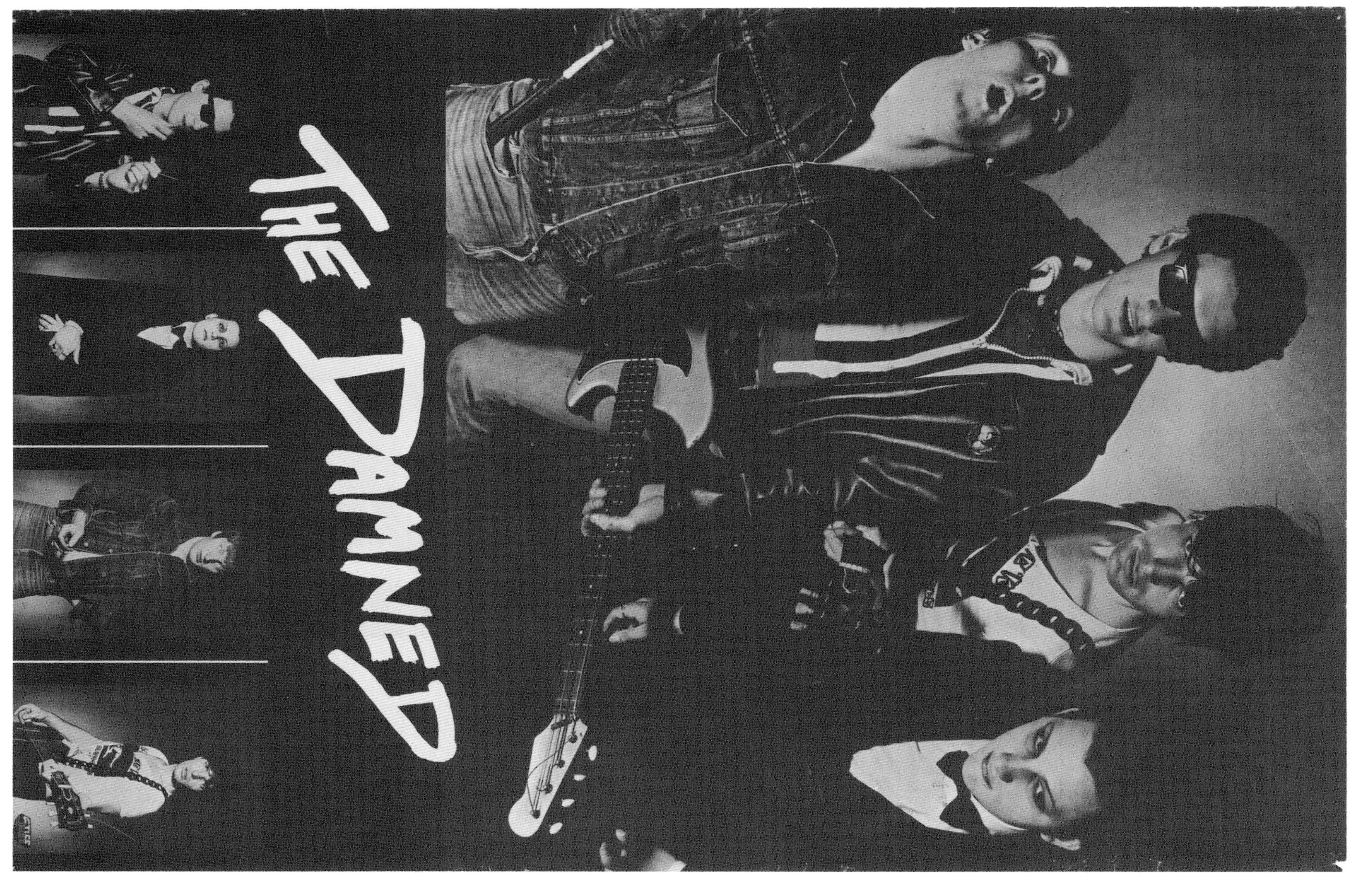

THE DAMNED: promotional poster, Stiff Records (1976), **Jake Riviera** design

THE DAMNED: 'Neat Neat Neat' unofficial 45 poster (*c.* early 1980s)

NED
NeAT
At
NEAt

THE DAMNED

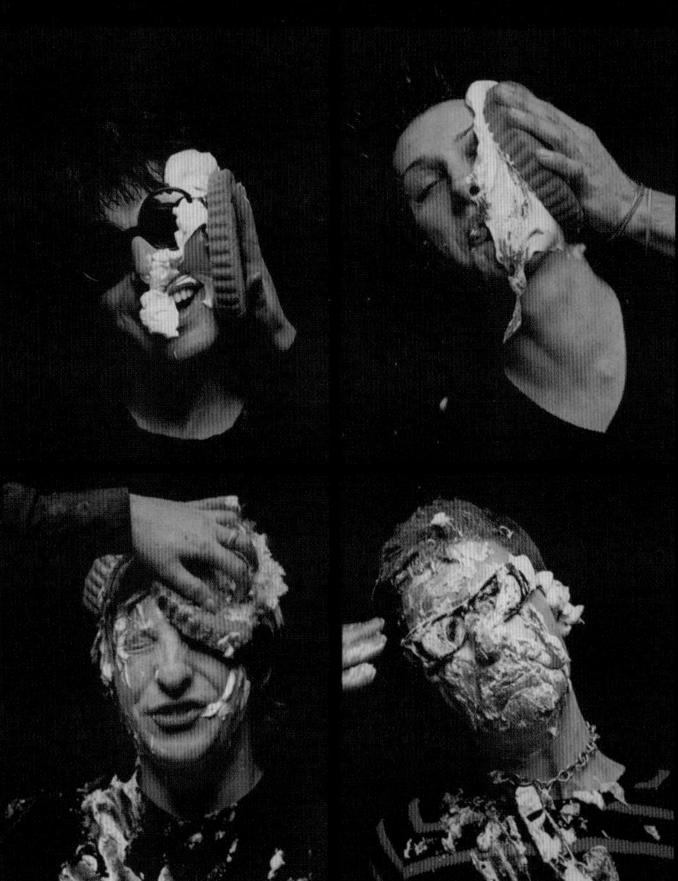

Album out now.
Play it at your sister.

32 Alexander Street London W2
"The sound is in the plastic"

THE DAMNED: *Damned Damned Damned* debut LP poster, Stiff Records (1977), **Barney Bubbles** design, **Pete Kodick** photography

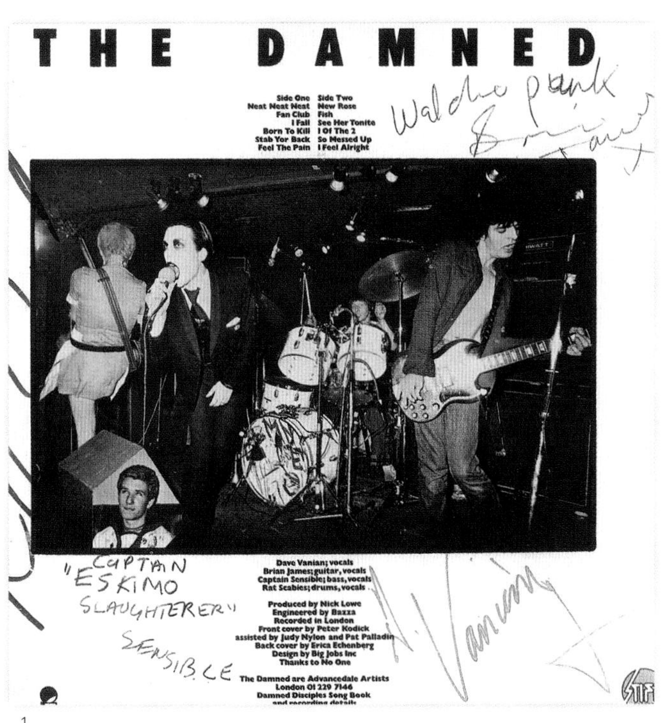

1

2

THE DAMNED: 1 *Damned Damned Damned* LP back cover (1977), **Big Jobs, Inc. (AKA Barney Bubbles)** design, **Erica Echenberg** photography, signed by the band; **2** tour poster with The Adverts (April 1977), vintage advertisement enlargement (*c.*1981)

1

2

3

THE DAMNED: 1 'Don't Cry Wolf' 45 poster advertising a purple vinyl version, Stiff Records (1977), **Chris Gabrin** photography; **2** 'Don't Cry Wolf' 45 in yellow vinyl Belgian pressing, Stiff Records (1977); **3** poster for 1st Anniversary concerts at Marquee, London, Stiff Records (July 1977); (opposite) *Music for Pleasure* British newsprint advertisement (*c.* October 1977), **Chris Gabrin** photography

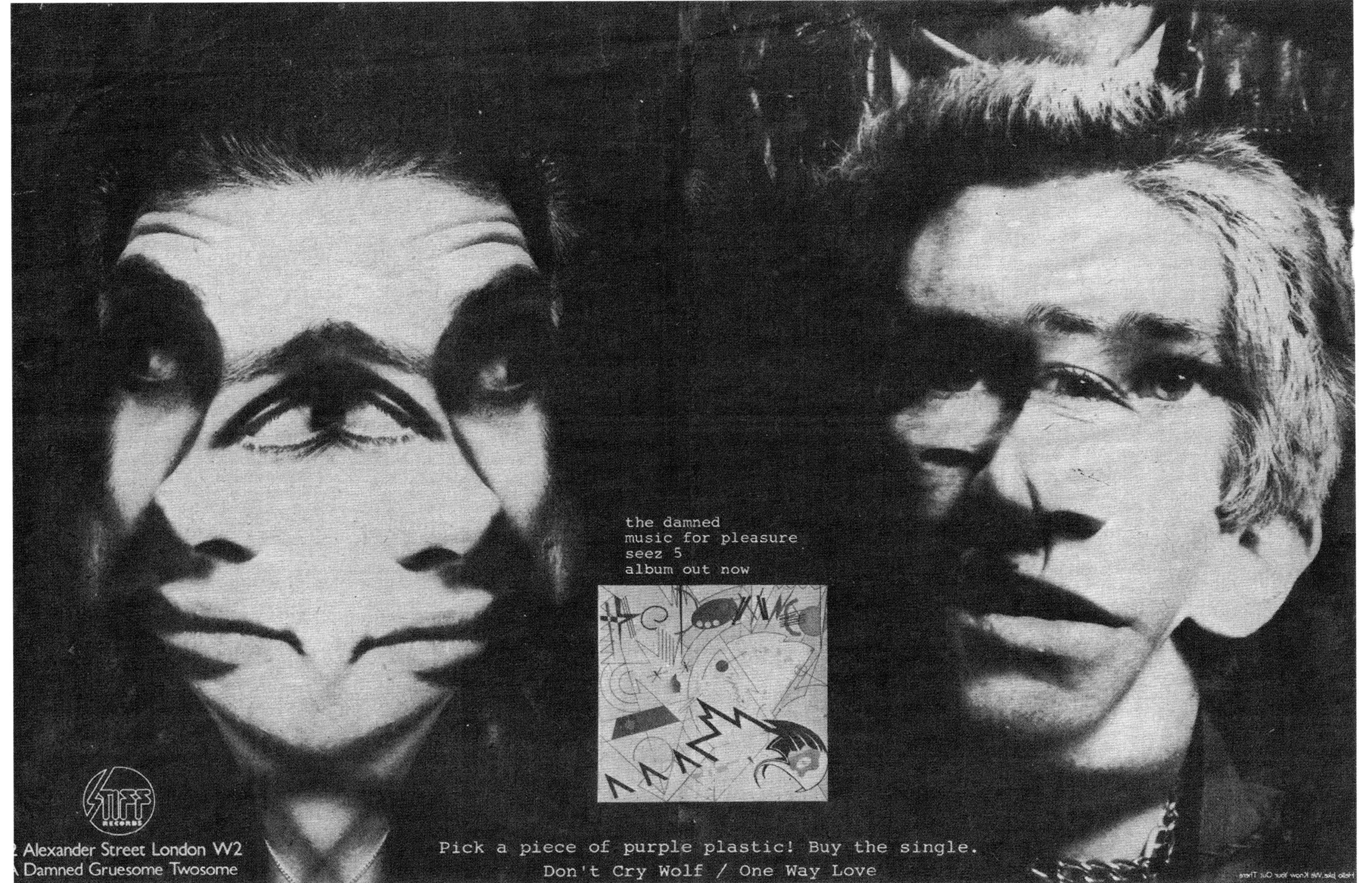
the damned
music for pleasure
seez 5
album out now
2 Alexander Street London W2
A Damned Gruesome Twosome
Pick a piece of purple plastic! Buy the single.
Don't Cry Wolf / One Way Love

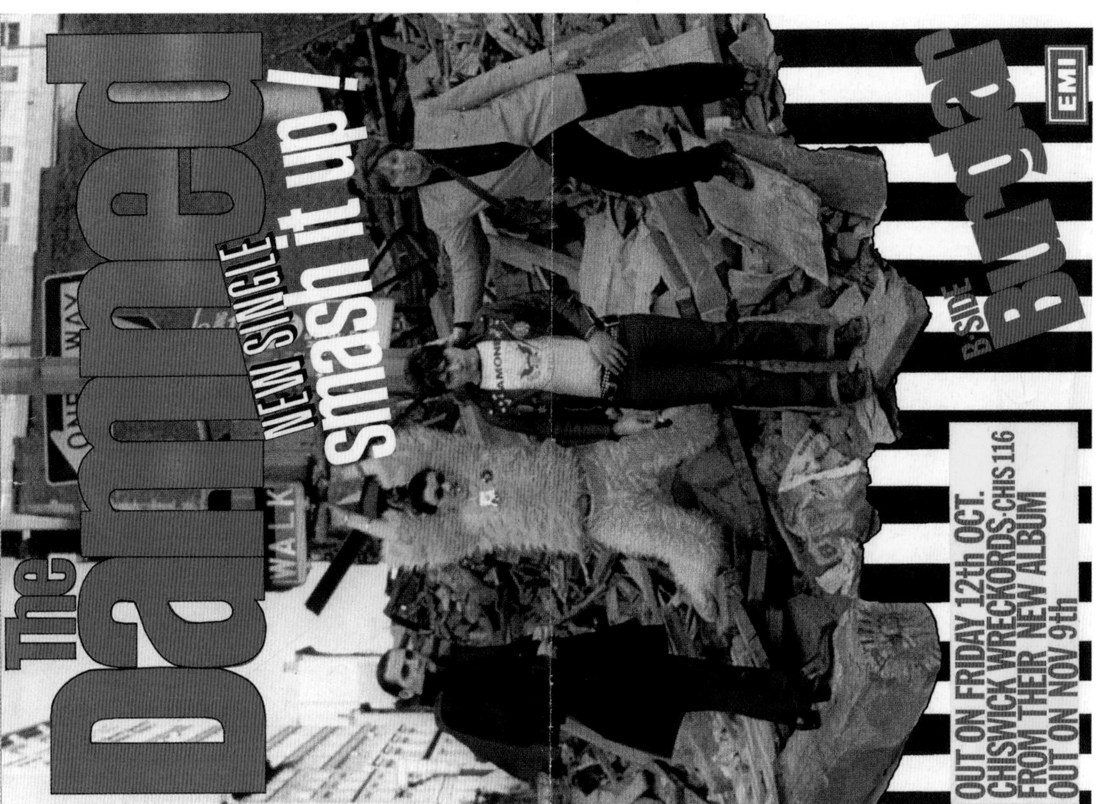

THE DAMNED: (above) 'Smash It Up' 45 flyer, EMI Records (October 1979)

THE DAMNED: 1 Just Can't Be Happy Today' 45 flyer, Chiswick Records (November 1979)

THE FACTORY AT THE RUSSELL CLUB

TICKETS FROM Discount Records

THE DAMNED

KiDS SHOW 5-30 till 8-00 75p

ROYCE ROAD

Mancunian Way

BUSES FROM:- PICC.- 263,257 ALBERT SQ. 81,84

the FACTORY

HULME

ROYCE ROAD

STRETFORD ROAD

OXFORD ROAD →

← OLD TRAFFORD

BiG KiDS 8-30 till 1-00

£1-30 advance £1-50 on door

7-4-79

THE DAMNED: (top) poster for kids show in Manchester (April 1979); (above) promotional badge for *Music for Pleasure* LP, Stiff Records (1977), **Barney Bubbles** design influenced by Wassily Kandinsky; **THE DRONES:** (right) 'Temptations of a White Collar Worker' EP front cover, O.H.M...S. Records (1977), **Roy Willan** design

NEW SINGLE AVA

EATE

Lock it up B/W Je

taken from their forthcoming album THE ALBUM released on NOV 11th

till available Outside View TLR001: T
Distributed by The Label

Along with Johnny Moped, Eater are one of the most beloved British punk bands from the earliest days, formed by a very young group of kids from North London (their drummer Dee Generate was just fourteen years old). Eater played often at such punk venues as the Roxy, Vortex and Barbarella's. Unfortunately they never achieved commercial success and disbanded in 1979. The band took their name from an early T. Rex song, and the single 'Lock It Up' is backed with their rendition of the classic Marc Bolan song 'Jeepster'.

Andrew Krivine

EATER: 'Lock It Up' 45 poster, The Label Records (1977)

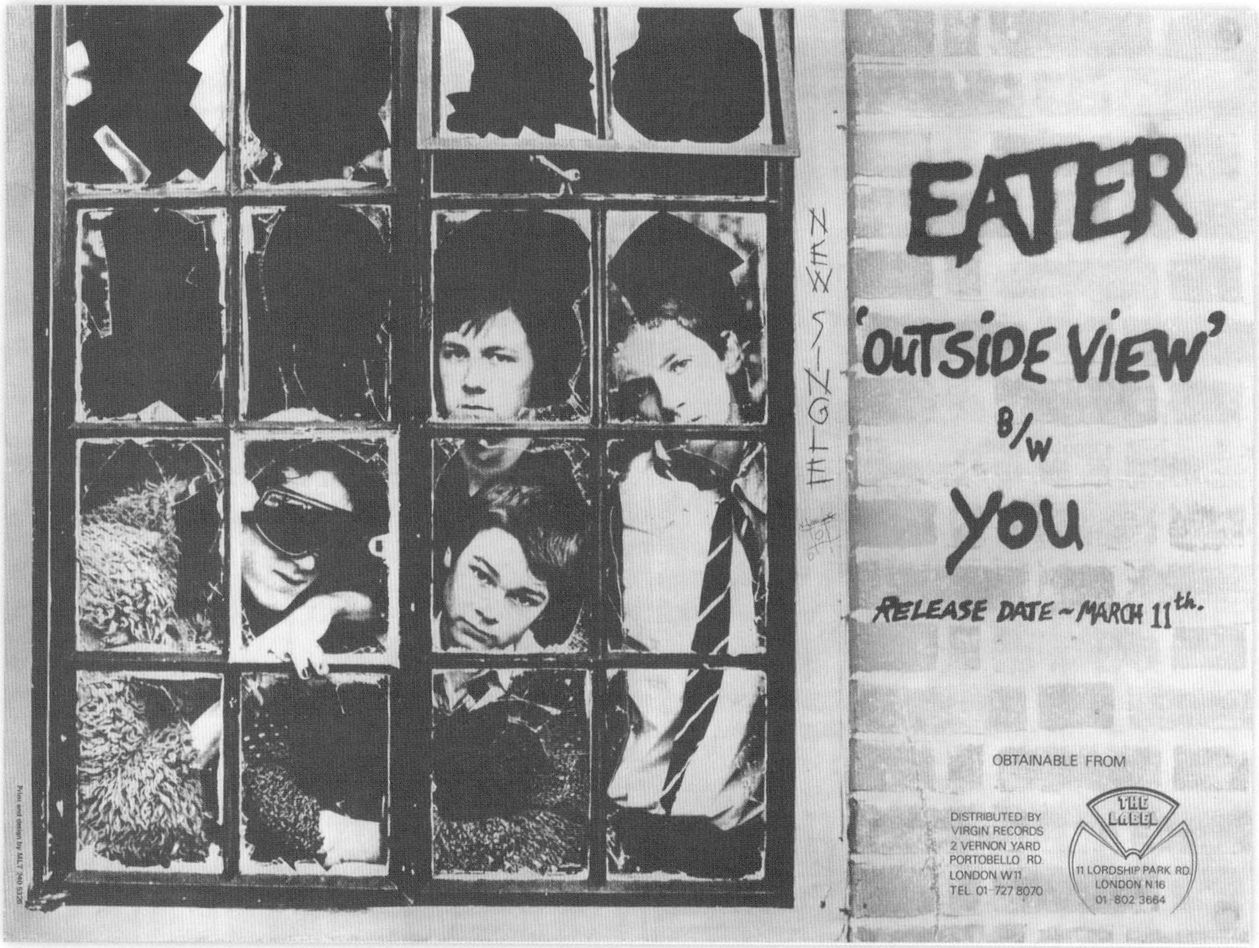

EATER

'OUTSIDE VIEW'

B/W

YOU

NEW SINGLE

RELEASE DATE ~ MARCH 11th.

OBTAINABLE FROM

DISTRIBUTED BY
VIRGIN RECORDS
2 VERNON YARD
PORTOBELLO RD.
LONDON W11
TEL. 01-727 8070

THE LABEL
11 LORDSHIP PARK RD.
LONDON N16
01-802 3664

EATER: (above) 'Outside View' debut 45 poster, The Label Records (March 1977); (below) 'Get Your Yo Yo's Out' EP front and back cover, The Label Records (1978), **Steve Joule** artwork

by ELIZAbeth

CREOLE CR 139

STOCK NOW TO MEET DEMAND

Available NOW from

EMI (SALES) OR CREOLE (SALES)

MANUFACTURED AND MARKETED
BY

Records 4 Bank Buildings, High Street, Harlesden, London, NW10
01-965 9223

ELIZABETH: poster for parody record by 'Elizabeth', a pseudonym of Jonathan King, British songwriter, performer, producer and record label owner, Creole Records (1977)

EDDIE AND THE HOT RODS: *Teenage Depression* LP poster, Island Records (1976), **Michael Beal** art direction and photography; (opposite) *Life on the Line* LP and US tour advertisement, Island Records (1977)

Teenage Depression is the first LP released by Eddie and The Hot Rods. Along with Dr Feelgood (also from Canvey Island, Essex) Eddie and The Hot Rods formed an essential 'genealogical bridge' between pub- and punk rock. Both bands were known for their propulsive, high-energy performances. This poster includes one of the most iconic images of the period. Several other bands would make extensive use of the typography found in this poster (Glaser Stencil Bold font by Letraset) in their materials.

Andrew Krivine

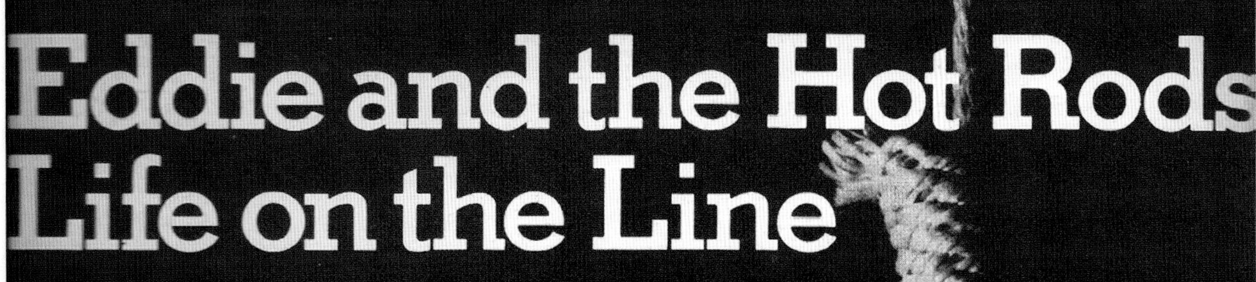

LOOK OUT AMERICA, IT'S THE VERY HOT RODS

Eddie and the Hot Rods', "Do Anything You Wanna Do" single was THE summer anthem of the year in Britain, a top ten smash loaded with high octane energy and excitement.

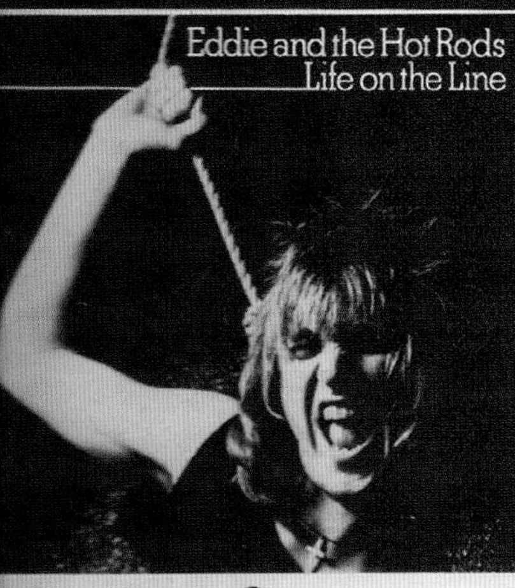

Their New Album Available NOW

EDDIE AND THE HOT RODS TOUR SCHEDULE

OCTOBER

30	Toronto, Masonic Aud.
31	Windsor, Embassy

NOVEMBER

3, 4, 5	London, Ontario
7	Ottawa
8	Montreal, Harlequin
10, 11, 12	New York, Max's
14	Philadelphia, Tower
15	Annapolis Pier 7
16	Washington, D.C., Bayou
17	Baltimore, Palace
18	Boston, Orpheum
19	New Jersey, Capitol Theatre
20	Pittsburgh
21	Cleveland, Agora
23	Detroit, The Masonic
25	Chicago, Aragon
26	Milwaukee
27	St. Louis

DECEMBER

2, 3	San Francisco, Mabuhay Gardens
8, 9, 10, 11	L.A., Whiskey

EDDIE AND THE HOT RODS: Life on the Line tour poster, Hamburg, Island Records (May 1978); (opposite, top) Summa Madness tour programme front (1977); (bottom) Summa Madness tour programme back with an advertisement for the 'Speed of Sound' live EP, Island Records (1977)

AT THE SOUND OF SPEED
EDDIE AND THE HOT RODS
TEENAGE DEPRESSION
ALBUM
Teenage Depression — ILPS 9457
SINGLES
Writing on the Wall/Crusin'(in the Lincoln)-WIP 6270
Wooly Bully/Horseplay — WIP 6306
Teenage Depression/Shake — WIP 6354
Might be Lying/Ignore them — WIP 6388
E.P.'s
Live at the Marquee — IEP 2
(Featuring: 96 Tears/Get out of Denver/Gloria/Satisfaction)
At the Sound of Speed (Live at the Rainbow) — IEP 5
(Featuring: Hard Drivin Man/Horseplay/Double Checkin Woman/All I need is Money)
SUMMA MADNESS TOUR U.K.'77
2nd June BIRMINGHAM TOWN HALL
3rd MANCHESTER APOLLO
4th GLASGOW APOLLO
5th June NEWCASTLE CITY HALL
8th BRISTOL COLSTOW HALL
9th LONDON RAINBOW
ISLAND
EDDIE AND THE HOT RODS

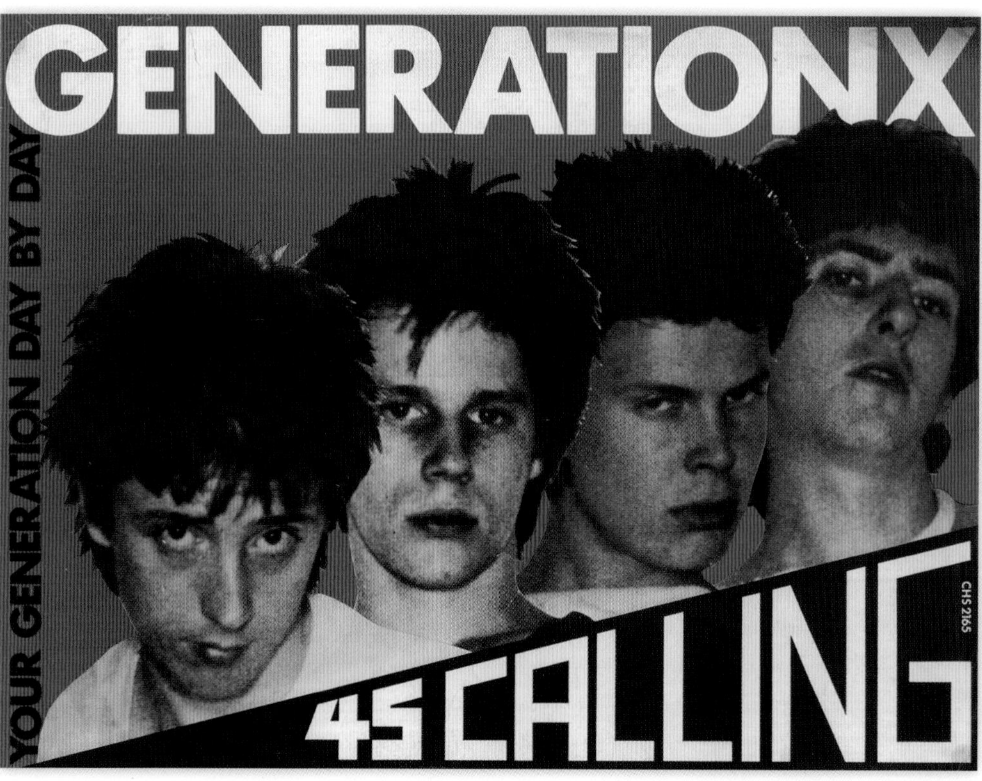

This poster promotes the band's first single, 'Your Generation'. Note the scowling image of a young Billy Idol (2nd right), before his spiked locks were dyed bleach blonde. Typography possibly drafted by Barney Bubbles, who designed the record sleeve.

Andrew Krivine

GENERATION X: 'Your Generation' 45 poster, Chrysalis Records (1977), **Barney Bubbles** design

This sleeve was designed by Barney Bubbles. Paul Gorman noted in his addictive 'Reasons to be Cheerful' blog that the Polish constructivist artist Henryk Berlewi's work (specifically, 'Mecano Facture, 1924–61') heavily informed this design.

Andrew Krivine

GENERATION X: 'Your Generation' – 45 front cover, Chrysalis Records (1977), **Barney Bubbles** design

1

2

3

Generation X new single
Your Generation Day by Day CHS 2165

generation generation
generation generation
generation generation
generation generation
generation generation
generationgeneration
generatigeneration
generagéneration
genegatioration
gegenerabion
generation
gegenerabion
genegatioration
generagéneration
generatigeneration
generationgeneration
generation generation
generation generation
generation generation
generation generation
generation generation

Chrysalis

Mail order copies from Rough Trade Records
202 Kensington Park Road. London W.11 (7274312)
70p + 10p P&P

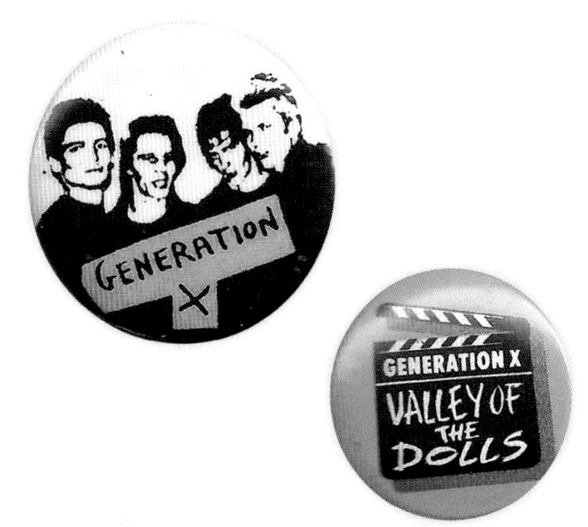

GENERATION X: 1 concert flyer for the Marquee Club, London (3 March 1977), **Jon Savage** design; **2** concert flyer for the Roxy Club, London (January 1977); **3** advertisement on the back cover of *Sniffin' Glue* #12 (September 1977)

GENERATION X: poster for residency concert at the Marquee Club, London, one of a set of four band member images: guitarist 'Derwood' (September 1977), **Barney Bubbles** design

Following the release of their debut single, 'Your Generation', Generation X lined up a series of four gigs at the Marquee, a high-profile rock venue on Wardour Street, London. Barney Bubbles had designed the single cover, drawing inspiration from constructivist artists such as El Lissitzky and Rodchenko to create a dramatic red-and-black typographic image based on the numeral 45. Bubbles was again commissioned to design the posters promoting the Marquee gigs, employing stills from a live performance clip of the band (one of each band member), along with his trademark geometric lines and dynamic composition.

Russ Bestley

GENERATION X: (left) 'Ready Steady Go' 45 poster, Chrysalis Records (1978), design influenced by Piet Mondrian

GENERATION X: (below) *Valley of the Dolls* LP poster, Chrysalis Records (1979); (above) promo badge for the LP, Chrysalis Records (1979)

1

2

3

THE JAM: 1 gig blank poster (1976); **2** *In the City* tour blank poster, Polydor Records (1977), **Bill Smith** art direction, **Wadewood Associates** artwork; **3** *This is the Modern World* LP poster, Polydor Records (November 1977), **Bill Smith** design, **Martyn Goddard** photography

THE JAM: 'The Modern World' 45 banner poster, Polydor Records (1977), **Martyn Goddard** photography

THE JAM: (above) 'News of the World' 45 advertisement from the *NME* (February 1978), **Bill Smith** design, **Martyn Goddard** photography; (right) 'A Bomb in Wardour Street' / 'David Watts' 45 poster, Polydor Records (1978)

THE JAM: (above) official fan club book (*c.*1978); (right) *Setting Sons* LP poster, Polydor Records (1979), **Bill Smith** design, **Andrew Douglas** photography

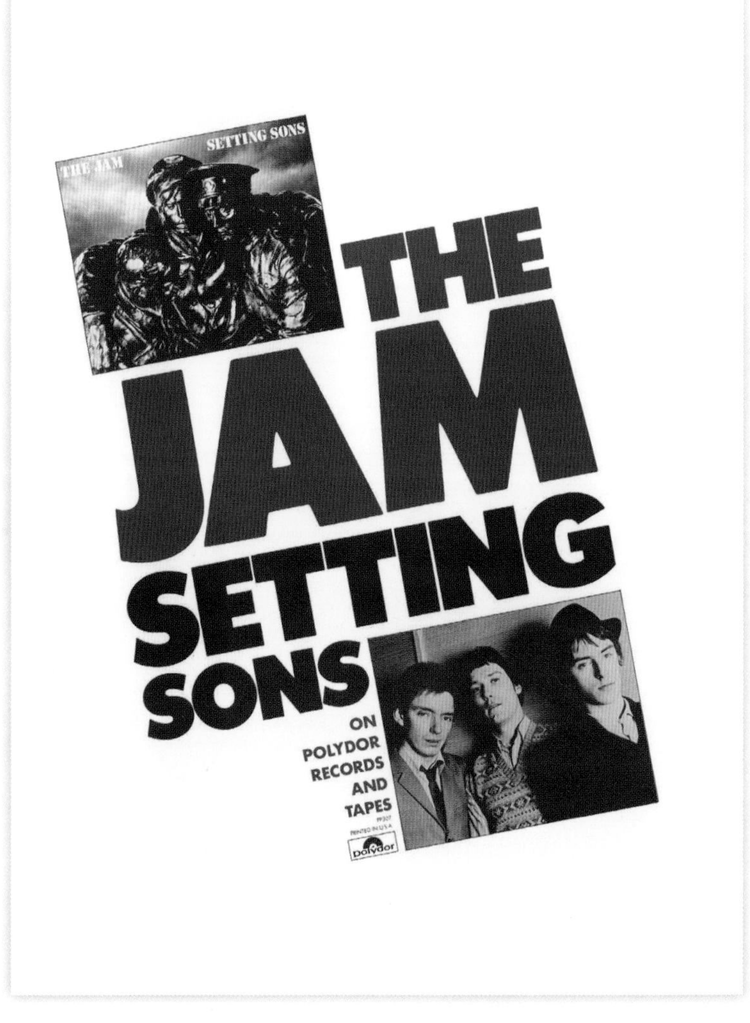

THE JAM: *Sound Affects* American LP posters, Polygram Records (1981), influenced by Roy Lichtenstein

MAGAZINE: (above) back of flyer for debut UK tour (1978), **Linder Sterling** design; (below) front of flyer for debut UK tour (1978)

MAGAZINE: *Real Life* LP dealer mail-out, Virgin Records (1978)

1

2

JOHNNY MOPED: 1 'No One' 45 poster, Chiswick Records (1977); **THE MOTORS: 2, 3, 4** posters for *Approved by the Motors* LP, Virgin Records (1978), clockwise from top right: featuring Adolf Hitler, Richard Nixon, Idi Amin; the set also included Jayne Mansfield

3

4

THE MOTORS: *Approved by the Motors* LP poster featuring Jayne Mansfield (1978); Mansfield died from severe head trauma suffered in a car crash in 1967

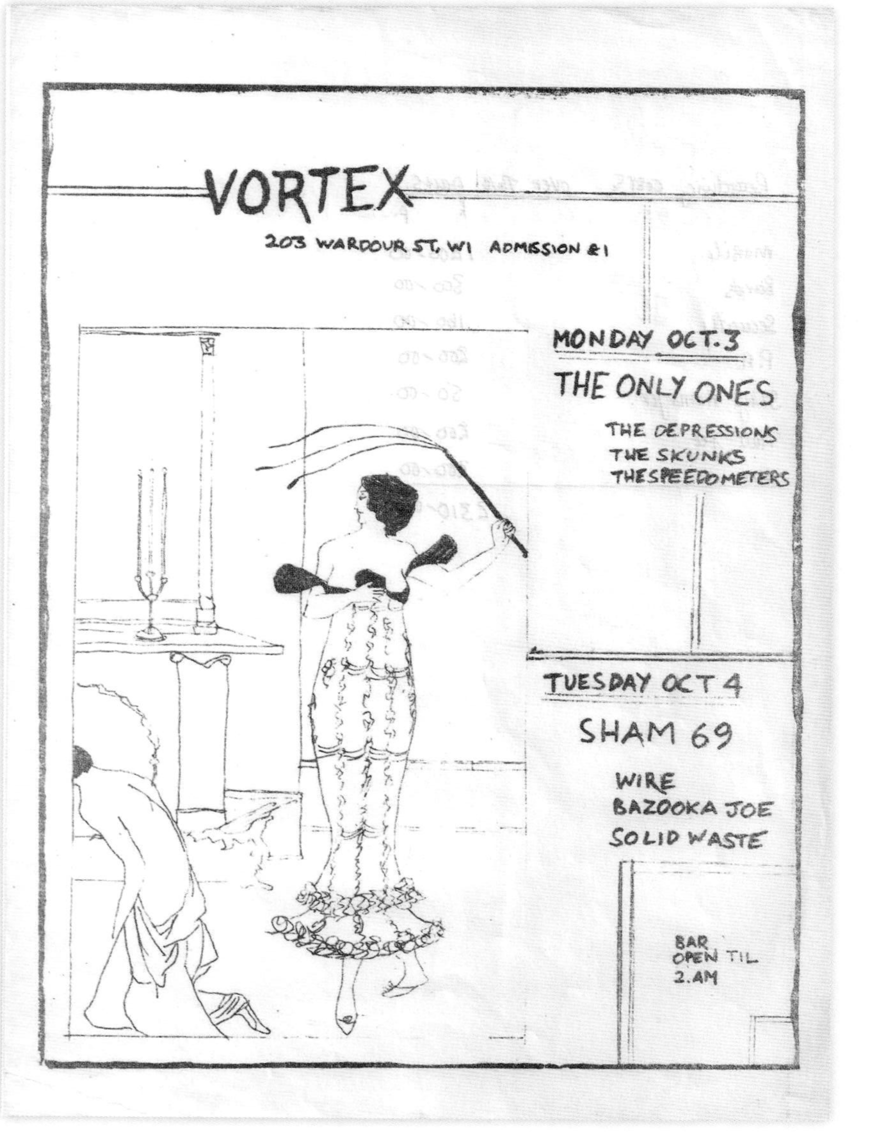

THE ONLY ONES: (left) flyer for Only Ones gig at The Vortex, London (3 October 1977); (top) 'Lovers of Today' 45 poster, Vengeance Records (1977), signed by the band

THE ONLY ONES: signed Planet Tour poster (1978), **Kavanagh** design

PENETRATION

MOVING TARGETS

Out now on Virgin Records. V2109

Virgin

PENETRATION: *Moving Targets* LP poster, Virgin Records (1978)

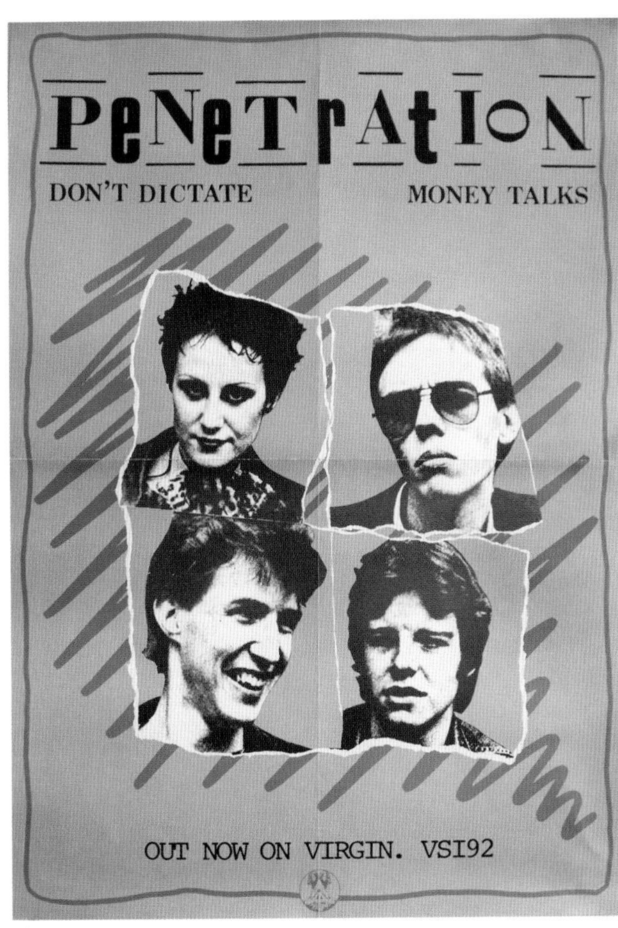

1

2

3

PENETRATION: 1 'Don't Dictate' 45 poster, Virgin Records (1977), **Russell Mills** design, **Peter Kodick** photography; **2** *Coming Up for Air* UK LP poster, Virgin Records (1979), **Keith Breeden** design; **3** montage poster, Virgin Records (1979), **Paul Slattery** photography

THE PUNK ROCK MOVIE: (left) flyer for NYC premier (May 1978); **PUNK:** book by Julie Davis, Davison Publishing (1977)

THE RINGS

I WANNA BE FREE

DEBUT SINGLE ON CHISWICK S14

ROXY CLUB: (left) flyer for the London club (March 1977), design by owner **Barry Jones**; **THE RINGS:** (right) 'I Wanna Be Free' 45 poster, Chiswick Records (May 1977)

SEX PISTOLS: (below) flyer (*c.*1975), **Jamie Reid** design, signed by Reid; (opposite) poster with Malcolm McLaren stamp on lower right corner, photos taken at the 100 Club Punk Festival (1976)

When the Sex Pistols first came together, they lacked a coherent graphic image. Helen Wellington-Lloyd, an early accomplice of manager Malcolm McLaren, produced some flyers for the band before Jamie Reid, a former colleague of McLaren at Croydon College of Art, was brought in to take charge of the band's graphic identity. Reid worked with various design ideas, some resurrected from his work at Suburban Press in the early 1970s. This is a very early flyer created in 1975, one of the first for the Pistols. Interestingly, it focuses on a cartoon image of guitarist Steve Jones – the group had at this point only recently abbreviated their name from QT Jones & His Sex Pistols, following the recruitment of vocalist Johnny Rotten.

Russ Bestley

SEX PISTOLS

SEX PISTOLS: poster for concert at the Top Rank, Cardiff (21 September 1976), reprint from 1980

This Sex Pistols poster advertises their gig at the Cardiff Top Rank on 21 September 1976, the day after the legendary 100 Club Punk Festival. The Pistols did perform in Cardiff this night, and scheduled a return to the venue as part of that December's Anarchy Tour, but that was cancelled and replaced by their now notorious appearance in nearby Caerphilly. The posters for the Top Rank 'Implosion' nights were never flyposted but displayed in illuminated boxes in the venue's doorway, and for this reason only one original poster is known to exist. The poster here was one of only a half dozen reprinted by BBC Wales in October 1980, for use as part of a backdrop to an interview segment on the Cardiff edition of the BBC 2 regional music and 'youth culture' show *Something Else* which featured live performances by The Damned and the Young Marble Giants, and was broadcast the following month. *Something Else* ran from 1978 through to 1982, with the format usually being two live performances interspersed with typical late-1970s-style 'kids on the street' interviews and monologues. The planned studio-based sequence, using the Sex Pistols posters with audience members talking about the punk scene in Cardiff, was abandoned so at the end of the day the original owner was allowed to take the posters home with him. When I bought it, the original owner told me, 'There's probably only a handful of local people who've seen this poster – those at the original gig and the production people at the BBC in 1980. If I hadn't been just a kid at the time of the filming, the TV people would have told me to **** off when I asked to take the posters home with me!'

Andrew Krivine

SEX PISTOLS: (left and above) pages from a promo folder created by the band's management company, Glitterbest (1977)

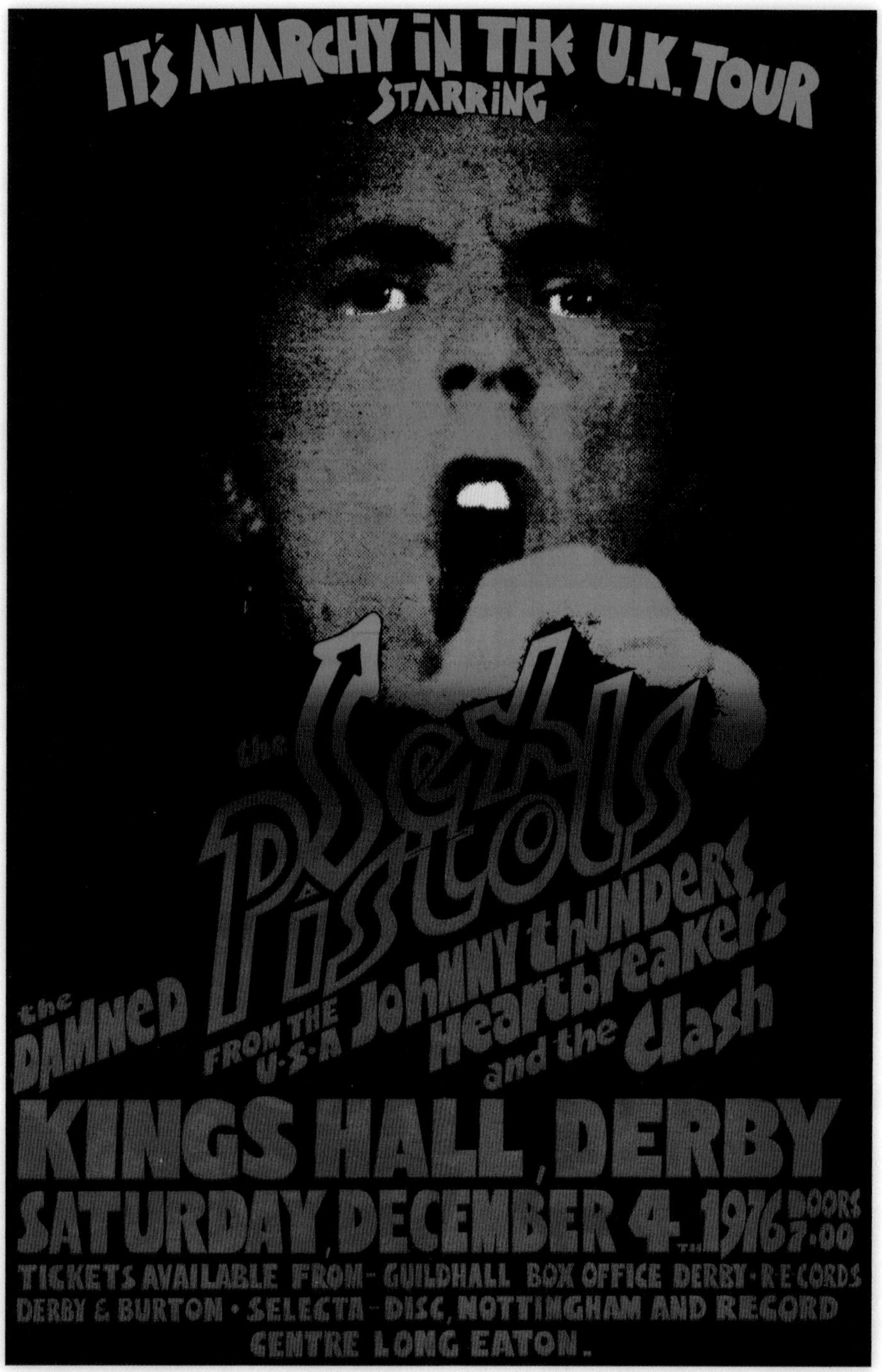

SEX PISTOLS: Anarchy in the UK tour poster for concert in Derby (4 December 1976), second printing, *c.*1978

This poster was for the Sex Pistols' ill-fated Anarchy tour and this concert never actually took place. It was cancelled by Derby City Council following the Pistols' refusal to audition in front of members of the local council, resulting in them banning that evening's show. The tour originally had over twenty dates scheduled across the UK, but due to the backlash following the Bill Grundy incident – where the band verbally abused their television host with a string of expletives, prompting one viewer to kick-in his brand new colour TV – only a handful of concerts actually occurred. The Anarchy tour had a higher attrition rate than Spinal Tap's Smell the Glove North American tour in 1982. Note: this specific copy of the poster is likely a second printing. Evidently, first printings have two spots where the red ink was not absorbed through the silkscreen in the 'P' and 'S' of the band's name.

Andrew Krivine

SEX PISTOLS: 'Anarchy in the UK' 45 poster, EMI Records (1976), **Jamie Reid** design, **Ray Stevenson** photography

Together with his design for 'God Save the Queen', this is the most iconic British punk design from the initial punk rock explosion. This copy was liberated from a wall in Acme Surplus, my cousin's warehouse/ office on the Portobello Road, London, in July 1977.

Andrew Krivine

SEX PISTOLS: *Anarchy in the UK* fanzine No.1 header, the 'zine was created for the tour by Glitterbest (December, 1976), **Jamie Reid, Sophie Richmond, Malcolm McLaren** and **Vivienne Westwood** design

SEX PISTOLS: 'God Save the Queen' 45 poster, A&M Records (1977)

This poster relates to one of the critical stories behind the legend of the Sex Pistols. They were signed to A&M Records for less than three weeks. Prompted by the band's outrageous public behaviour, Herb Alpert (co-founder and the 'A' in A&M) terminated the band's contract and ordered all copies of the pressing of this single destroyed. Only a handful of original copies of the A&M pressing of GSTQ exist. In a Sotheby's auction catalogue from June 2014 this poster was described as a 'black swan of sorts. Only one roll of circa twenty posters survived, as they were shipped from the London office to the Los Angeles office of A&M Records.'

Andrew Krivine

SEX PISTOLS: 'God Save the Queen' 45 poster, Virgin Records (1977), **Jamie Reid** design, photo appropriated from Cecil Beaton

Possibly the best-known image from the British punk scene, this Jamie Reid design is based on a portrait photograph of Queen Elizabeth taken by Cecil Beaton during the 1950s. The single release coincided with the Queen's Silver Jubilee and sold 150,000 copies within five days of release.

Andrew Krivine

1

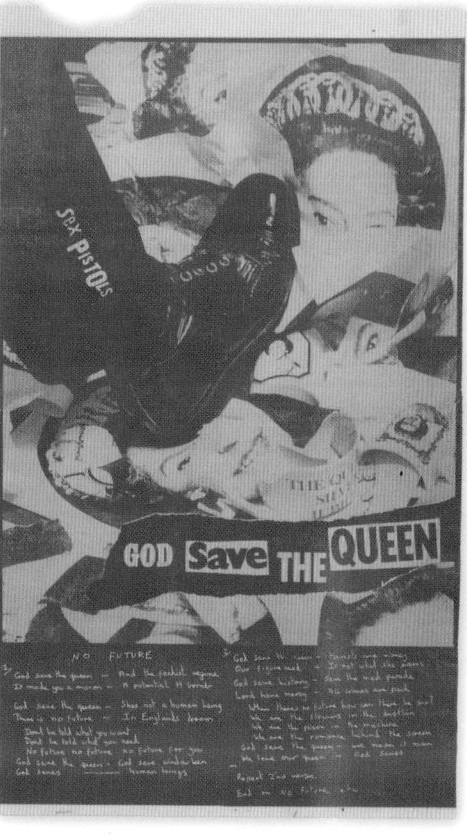

SEX PISTOLS: 1 'God Save the Queen' newsprint advertisement (June 1977), **Jamie Reid** design; **2** 'Pretty Vacant' 45 poster, Virgin Records (1977), **David Jacobs** concept. The 'Nowhere Buses' are from a pamphlet published by the American Situationist group Point-Blank!; **3** 'Pretty Vacant' cardstock flyer, Virgin Records (1977)

2

3

DANCE TO THE SEX PISTOLS

WE'RE SO PRETTY OH SO PRETTY

VACANT AND WE DON'T CARE

NEW SINGLE Sex Pistols pretty vacant

OUT NOW ON VIRGIN RECORDS VS 184

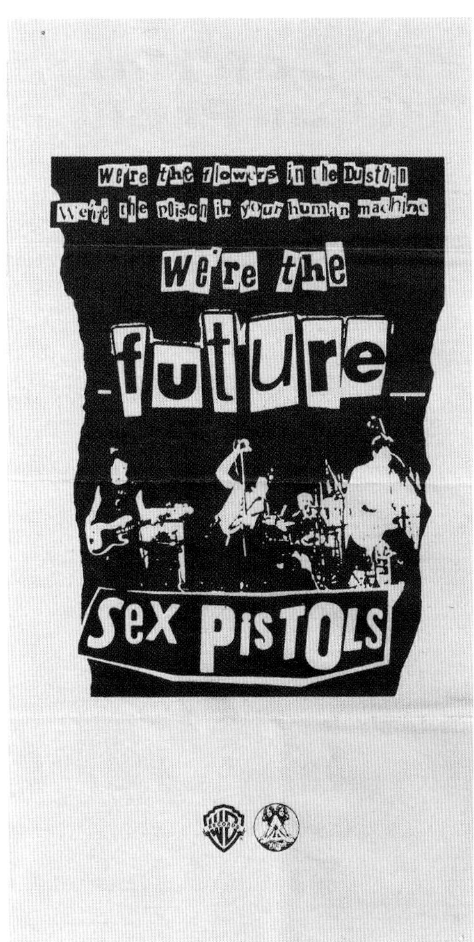

SEX PISTOLS: 1 *Never Mind the Bollocks* US advertisement, Warner Bros. Records (1977); **2** 'Holidays in the Sun' 45 poster, Virgin Records (October 1977), **Jamie Reid** design; **3** 'Holidays in the Sun' 45 poster, Virgin Records (October 1977), **Jamie Reid** design, based on Belgian Tourist Authority brochure

Warner Brothers secured the North American rights to the Pistols' recordings from Richard Branson's Virgin Records in 1977 and had great expectations for the group. The label spent lavishly on promotional materials for the Sex Pistols. In addition to printing copies of the 'collage' *Never Mind the Bollocks* poster design (which was included in initial American and British pressings of the album), Warners produced several of their own promotional pieces, including four poster designs, a cloth banner and a T-shirt which incorporated Jamie Reid's typography and was sent to journalists along with review copies of *NMTB*. In contrast to the canary yellow and red colours of the Virgin record sleeve, Warners opted for a neon pink and green combination as the central colour scheme. Warners took the Queen Elizabeth photograph from the 'God Save the Queen' 45 poster and serialized the image in this poster, a layout also seen in the American promotional poster for The Clash's *London Calling* (1980).

Andrew Krivine

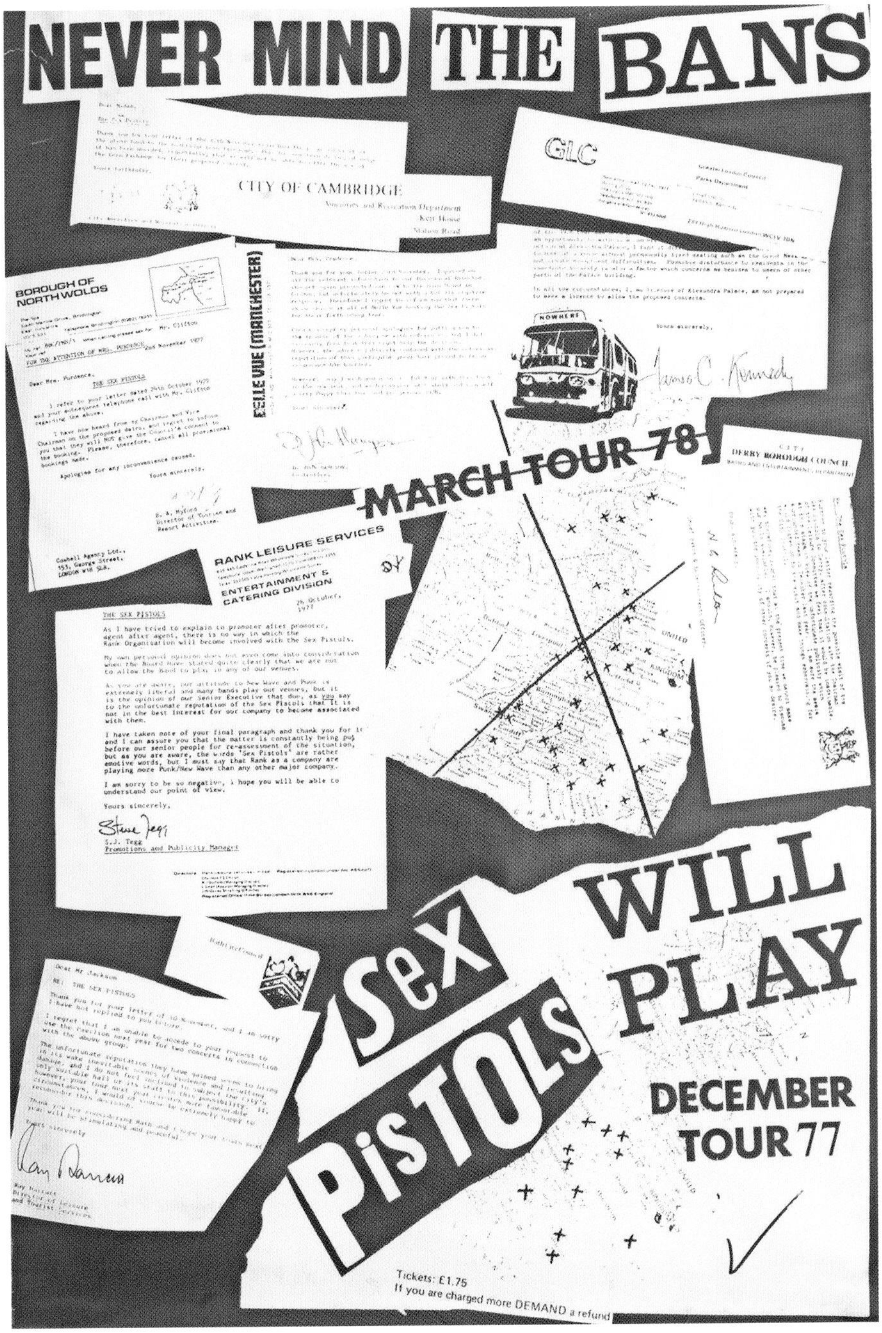

NEVER MIND THE BANS

MARCH TOUR 78

SEX PISTOLS WILL PLAY

DECEMBER TOUR 77

Tickets: £1.75
If you are charged more DEMAND a refund

SEX PISTOLS: (left) Never Mind the Bans tour poster (1977); (below and opposite) *Never Mind the Bollocks* US LP posters, Warner Bros. Records (1977), **Jamie Reid** design

1

2

3

SEX PISTOLS: 1 backstage pass to the Pistols' final performance, at Winterland, San Francisco, CA (14 January 1978); **2** poster for single recorded with Ronnie Biggs, 'No One Is Innocent', Virgin Records (1978), **Jamie Reid** design; **3** locally made poster for the Pistols' performance at the Longhorn Ballroom in Dallas, TX (10 January 1978)

SEX PISTOLS: *The Great Rock 'n' Roll Swindle* LP poster, Virgin Records (1979), **Jamie Reid** design; the poster was promptly withdrawn by Virgin Records in response to threats from The Walt Disney Company

Some Product
The lady loves...
Fatty Jones
Chocolate Box
Carri on Sex Pistols
Some Product. New album out now on Virgin. VR2.
Do not pay more than £3·20 for this valid piece of product

Some Product
Wouldn't you rather be Gobbin'?
GOB ALE
Carri on Sex Pistols
Some Product. New album out now on Virgin. VR2.
Do not pay more than £3·20 for this valid piece of product.

Some Product
I'd like to teach the world to Piss
PISS Lemonade
Carri on Sex Pistols
Some Product. New album out now on Virgin. VR2.

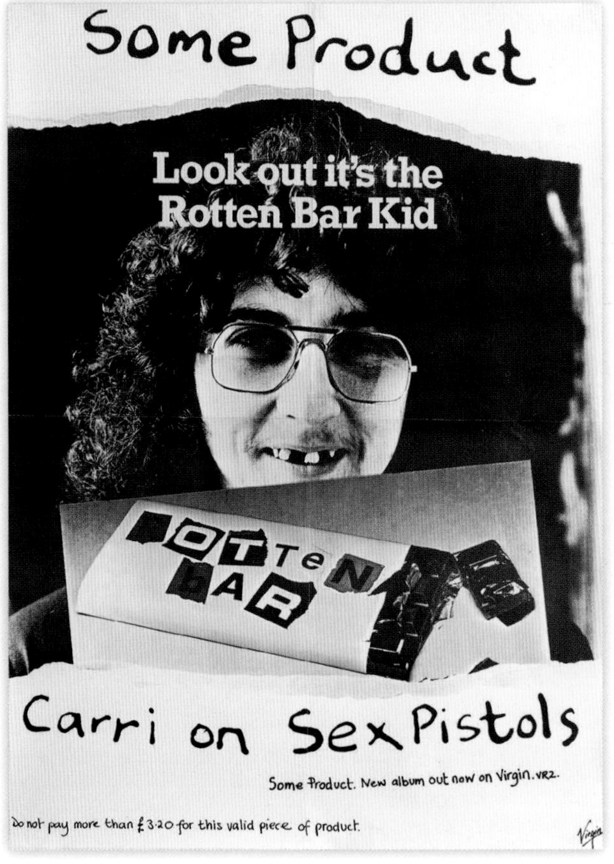
Some Product
Look out it's the Rotten Bar Kid
ROTTEN BAR
Carri on Sex Pistols
Some Product. New album out now on Virgin. VR2.
Do not pay more than £3·20 for this valid piece of product.

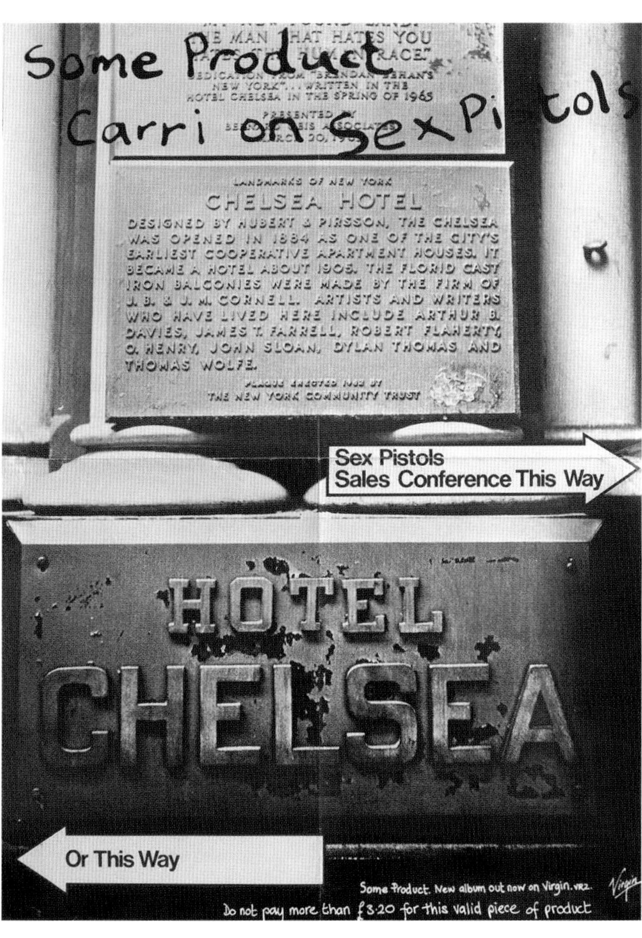

SEX PISTOLS: (above) stickers promoting *The Great Rock 'n' Roll Swindle* (1979); (below) 'Something Else' 45 poster, Virgin Records (1979), **Jamie Reid** design. The single was released in February, soon after Sid Vicious' death.

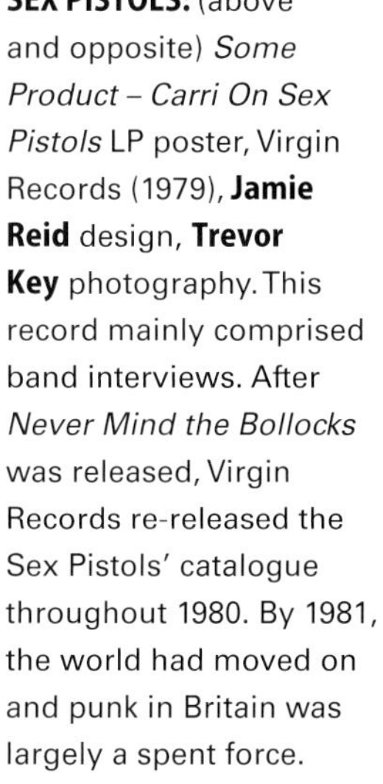

SEX PISTOLS: (above and opposite) *Some Product – Carri On Sex Pistols* LP poster, Virgin Records (1979), **Jamie Reid** design, **Trevor Key** photography. This record mainly comprised band interviews. After *Never Mind the Bollocks* was released, Virgin Records re-released the Sex Pistols' catalogue throughout 1980. By 1981, the world had moved on and punk in Britain was largely a spent force.

SEX PISTOLS: 'The Great Rock 'n' Roll Swindle' 45 poster, Virgin Records (1979), **Jamie Reid** design, **Trevor Key** artwork

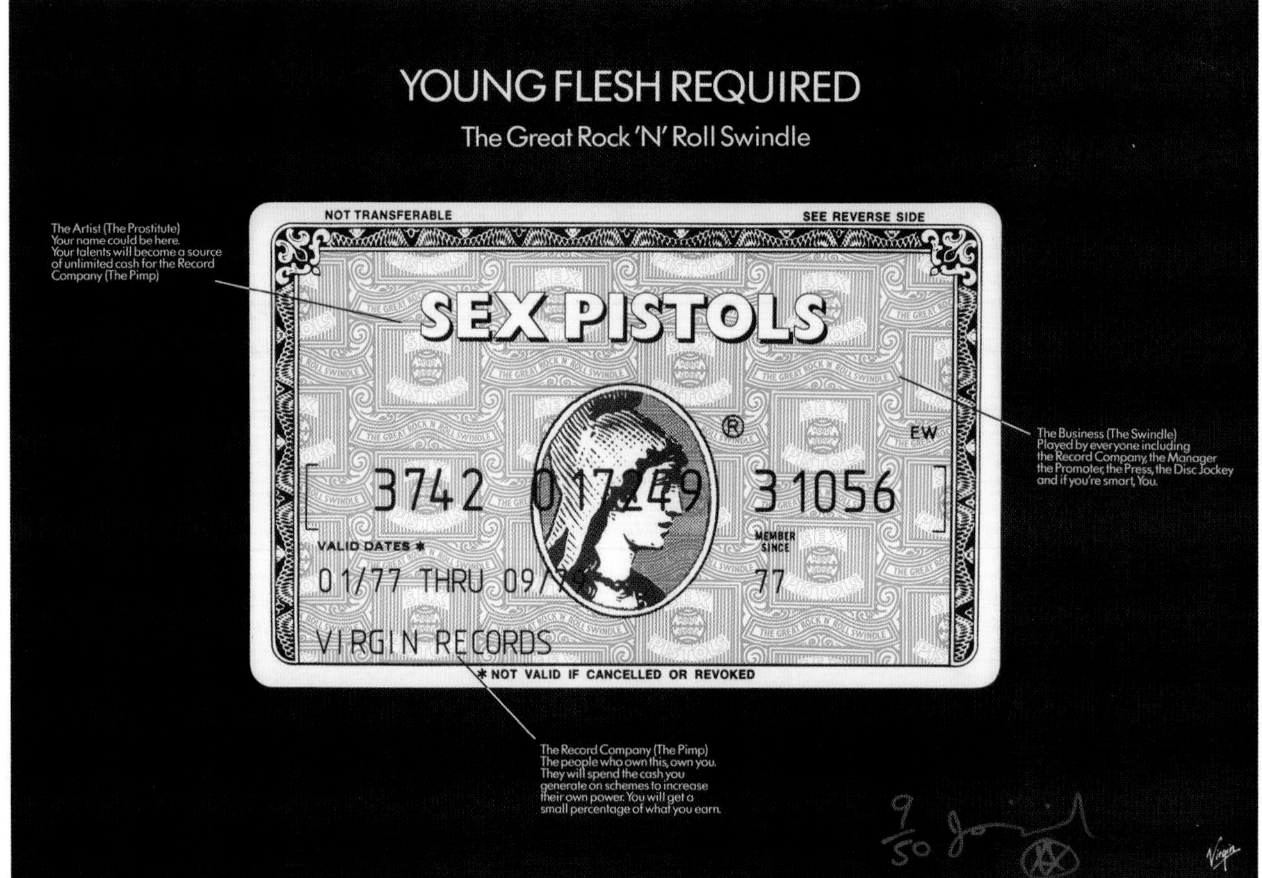

Undoubtedly one of Jamie Reid's most subversive designs, appropriating an iconic symbol of consumer capitalism. American Express was understandably outraged by the poster and threatened legal proceedings against Virgin, compelling the label to withdraw the poster almost immediately. In a dispiriting, self-consciously ironic twist, Virgin Money (started by record label founder, billionaire Richard Branson) announced in June 2015 that they were issuing two credit cards with the artwork from the 'Anarchy in the UK' and *Never Mind The Bollocks* records. Branson commented in a video promotion for the cards, 'I can't think of anything more appropriate than Virgin Money adopting the Sex Pistols on their credit card.' This poster was printed in both glossy and matte finishes, and this copy was signed and numbered by Jamie Reid.

Andrew Krivine

SEX PISTOLS: *Flogging a Dead Horse* LP poster, Virgin Records (1980), **Jamie Reid** design, **Trevor Key** artwork

1

2

3

SHAM 69: 1 What 'Ave We Got? tour blank poster, Step-Forward Records (October 1977). The photograph is of lead singer Jimmy Pursey in the process of being arrested in front of the Vortex Club on 23 September 1977, after playing an abbreviated set on the club's roof; **2** Rock Against Racism concert poster (1978), **Chris Reed** photography; **3** 'Angels With Dirty Faces' 45 flyer, Polydor Records (April 1978)

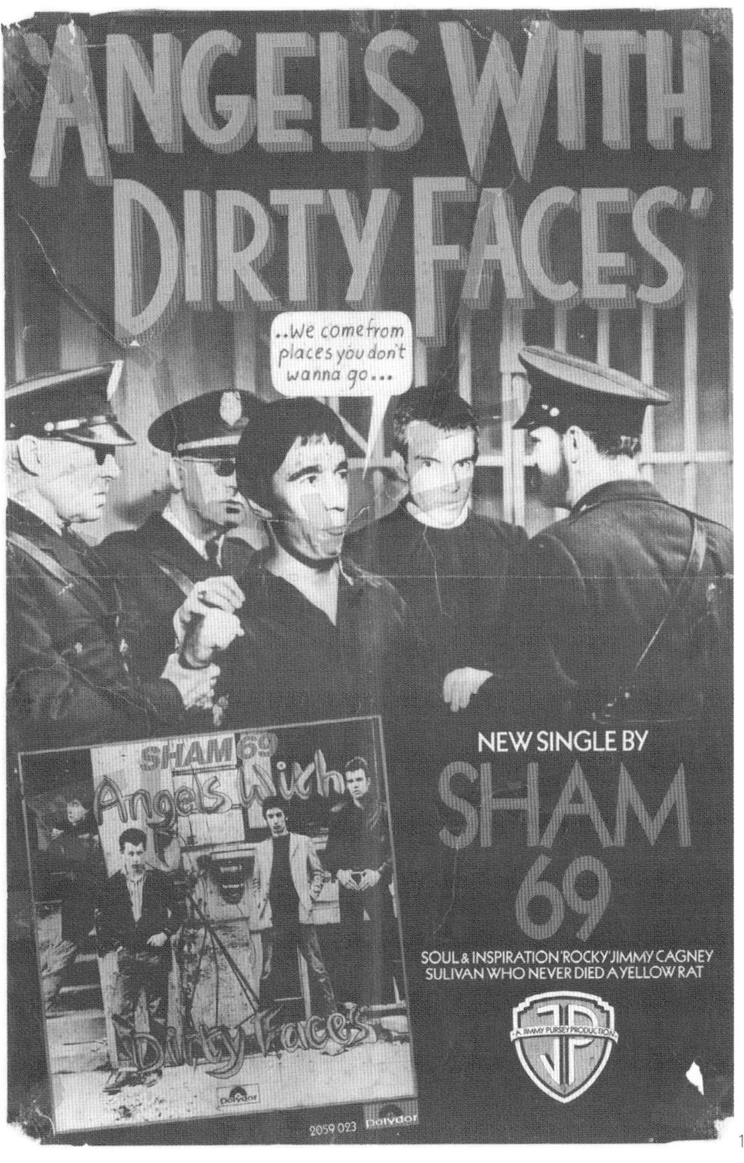

1

2

3

SHAM 69: 1 'Angels With Dirty Faces' 45 poster, Polydor Records, based on a movie still from the 1938 gangster film *Angels With Dirty Face*s (April 1978); **2** 'Hurry Up Harry!' 45 advertisement from *ZigZag* magazine (November 1978); **3** circular 'roundel' poster for a concert in Bradford promoting the single 'Tell the Children', Polydor Records (1980)

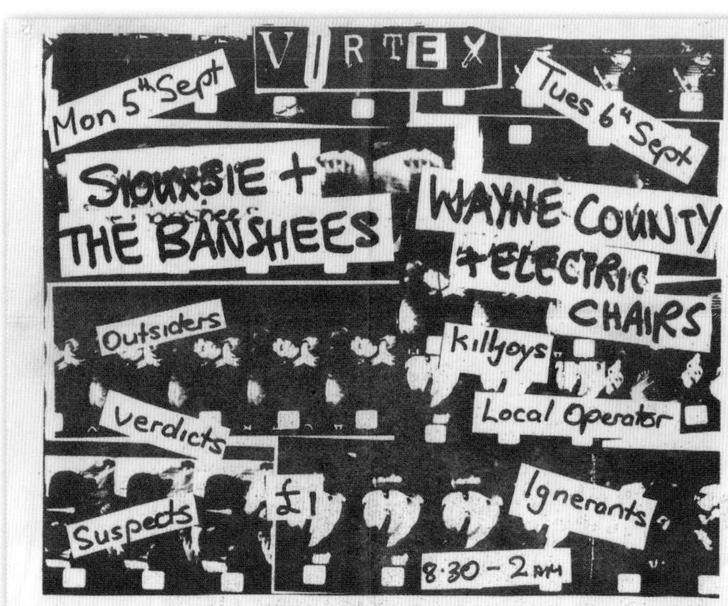

SIOUXSIE AND THE BANSHEES: flyer for concert at Vortex (5 September 1977)

SIOUXSIE AND THE BANSHEES: 'Hong Kong Garden' 45 poster, Polydor Records (1978), **Jill Mumford** design, **Sid Day** calligraphy

THE SLITS: (above) *ZigZag* No. 75 magazine cover, Kris Needs editor (August 1977) **Caroline Coon** photography; (left) flyer for performance with Sham 69 at The Other Cinema, London (21 August 1977), **Caroline Coon** photography

The rock magazine *ZigZag* had been around for years and, although I read the music press religiously, I can't say I paid it much attention. Then, in August 1977, a new editor, Kris Needs, took over and *ZigZag* began to concentrate on punk. His first cover featuring a picture of The Slits instantly signalled the new editorial direction. The Slits' first album, *Cut*, with its post-punk, reggae-influenced dub sound, was still a couple of years away, and when the cover story appeared, the four-woman band formed in 1976 was still playing raucous punk music. The cover caught my eye and I bought the issue. The image is a montage based on a black-and-white band photo in which the women stand side by side. The cover designer has cut out Viv Albertine and Palmolive, tilted their heads differently, and placed them in front of Ari Up and Tessa Pollitt, who now form the back row. Rough edges around their wild hair help to disguise the reassembly, as well as giving the picture great energy. The faces are treated graphically to make them look like cheap newsprint and this adds to the fanzine feel that also comes from the use of 'handwriting' for the cover lines. The clashing colours work brilliantly with the portrait. Revisited decades later, the cover's voltage has not lessened. Even though the image is an artful construction, the graphic adjustments are totally in keeping with the band's feminist self-image, and a world away from the sexualized packaging of female performers today.

Rick Poynor

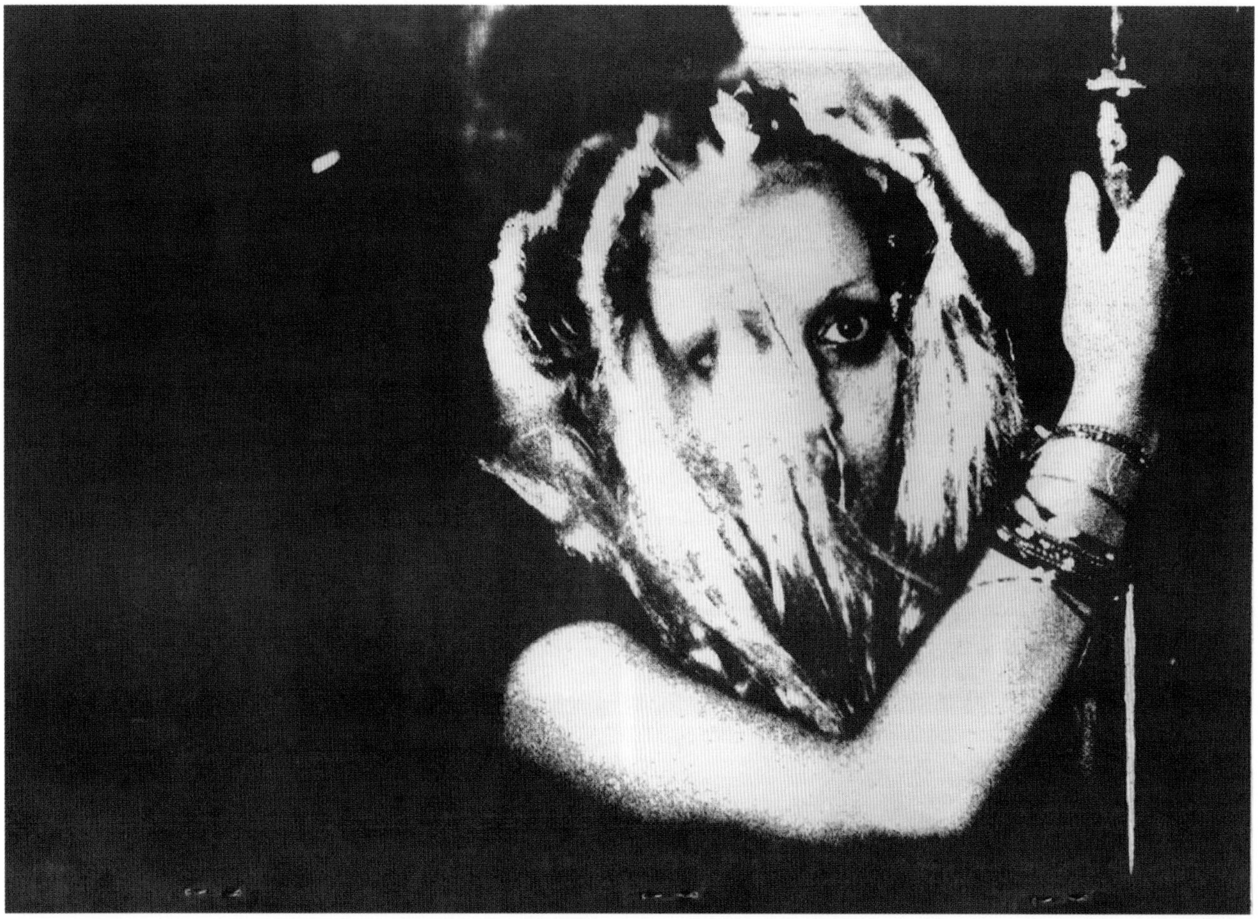

THE SLITS: Ari Up in *The Poser* photozine #5 (1979), editor Neil Anderson, London

SNIFFIN' GLUE: (left) issue #10, with editor Mark P's ATV on the cover (June 1977); (right) issue #7, Roxy DJ Don Letts on the cover (February 1977)

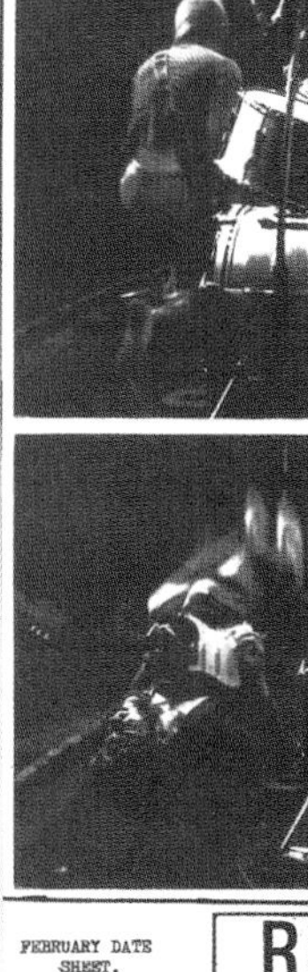

(Contd.from page 6).

After 'Wild Thing' comes Hendrix's 'Foxy Lady' and even that hippy Jesus is there with his poxy tambourine.

Some more chug-a-chug bass and guitar is stored up in the next song, 'Keep On To Me' which is loud, hard and full of energy. Then it's all over bar the shouting 'cept for some real fanatics who manage to rouse the band back for an encore.

The Gorillas are nothing to do with the new wave except that they're on the same level-you can talk to'em and they're not superstars. They're a peoples band as the variety in the audience proved. Nothing breathtaking or spectacular-just a rock band with guts.

Steve Mick.

JESSE HECTOR ROLLIN' ABOUT.

FEBRUARY DATE SHEET. ROXY CLUB FEBRUARY DATE SHEET.

41-43 Neal Street London W.C.2. Tel: 836 8811

Mon.14th: Damned & Adverts
Wed.16th: Vibrators & G.B.H.
Sat.19th: Cortinas & Bombers.
Sun.20th: Reggae night.
Mon.21st: Damned & Johnny Moped.
Tue.22nd: The Late Eddie Cochran.
Wed.23rd: Slaughter and the Dogs & G.B.H.
Thurs.24th: Jam & Rejects.
Fri.25th: } Possible biggie —
Sat.26th: } RING FOR DETAILS
Sun.27th: }
Mon.28th: Damned & Chelsea.
PHONE FOR DETAILS OF OTHER NIGHTS.

SNIFFIN' GLUE: issue #7, advertisement for the Roxy Club (February 1977)

ADVERTISEMENT FEATURE

SNIFFIN' GLUE: issue #7 Stiff Records advertisement (February 1977)

SNIFFIN' GLUE: The Clash in issue #8 (March 1977)

SNIFFIN' GLUE: *Sniffin' Glue – The Bible*, Michael Dempsey Press (1978)

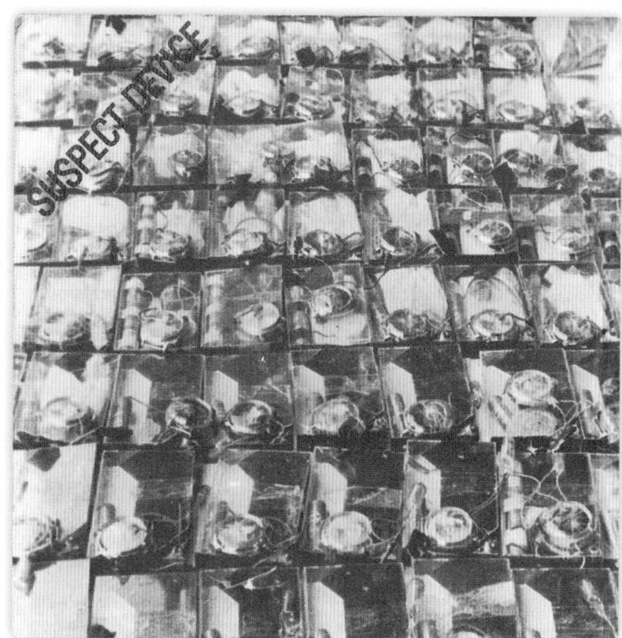

STIFF LITTLE FINGERS: (top left) 'Suspect Device' 45 front cover, Rough Trade Records (1978); (above) 'Gotta Get Away' 45 poster, Rough Trade Records (1979), **Janette Beckman** photography; **THE STRANGLERS:** (left) *Rattus Norvegicus* poster, United Artists (1977), **Paul Henry** design, **Trevor Rogers** photography; (below) 'No More Heroes' promotional sticker, A&M Records (October 1977)

SUBURBAN STUDS: tour blank poster advertising 'Questions' single, Pogo Records (1977)

THE VIBRATORS: (above) cover of six-page press kit, signed by the band, Epic Records (1977); (below) page from 'Baby Baby' press kit, Epic Records (1977)

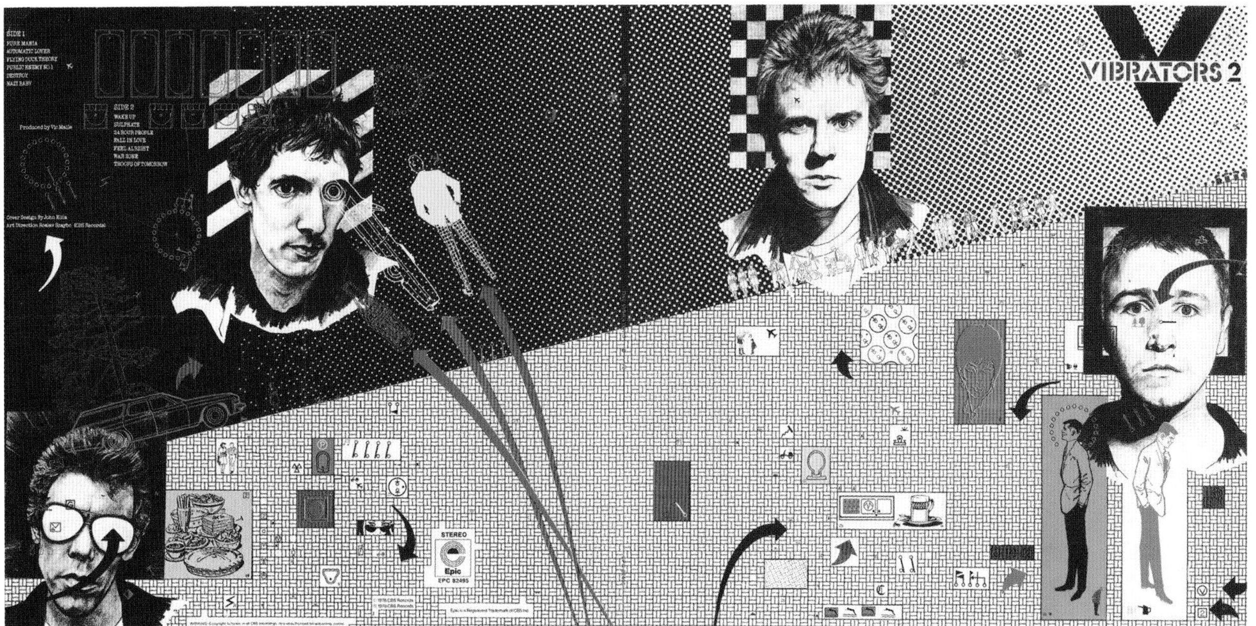

1

2

THE VIBRATORS: 1 *V2* LP poster, Epic Records (April 1978), **John Ellis** artwork; **2** 'Disco in Moscow' 45 poster, Rat Race Records (October 1980); **3** tour blank poster (*c.*1980), **John Callan** photography

3

X-RAY SPEX: (below) 'Oh Bondage Up Yours!' 45 cover, Virgin Records (1977), **Poly Styrene** (Marianne Joan Elliott-Said) design

This record sleeve was designed by the band's lead singer Poly Styrene, considered by many to be 'the Judy Garland' of punk for her powerful, quite unique voice. The lead track opens with the memorable spoken-word intro, '...some people think little girls should be seen and not heard, but I think... Oh Bondage, Up Yours!' Poly was also responsible for the record sleeve artwork on the band's second single, 'The Day the World Turned Day-Glo'.

Russ Bestley

X-RAY SPEX: (below) poster for concert at The Roundhouse, London (January 1978)

X-RAY SPEX: (above) *Germfree Adolescents* LP advertisement from *ZigZag* magazine (November 1978); (below) *Germfree Adolescents* LP poster, EMI Records (1978), **Cooke Key** design, **Falcon Stuart** artwork, **Trevor Key** photography

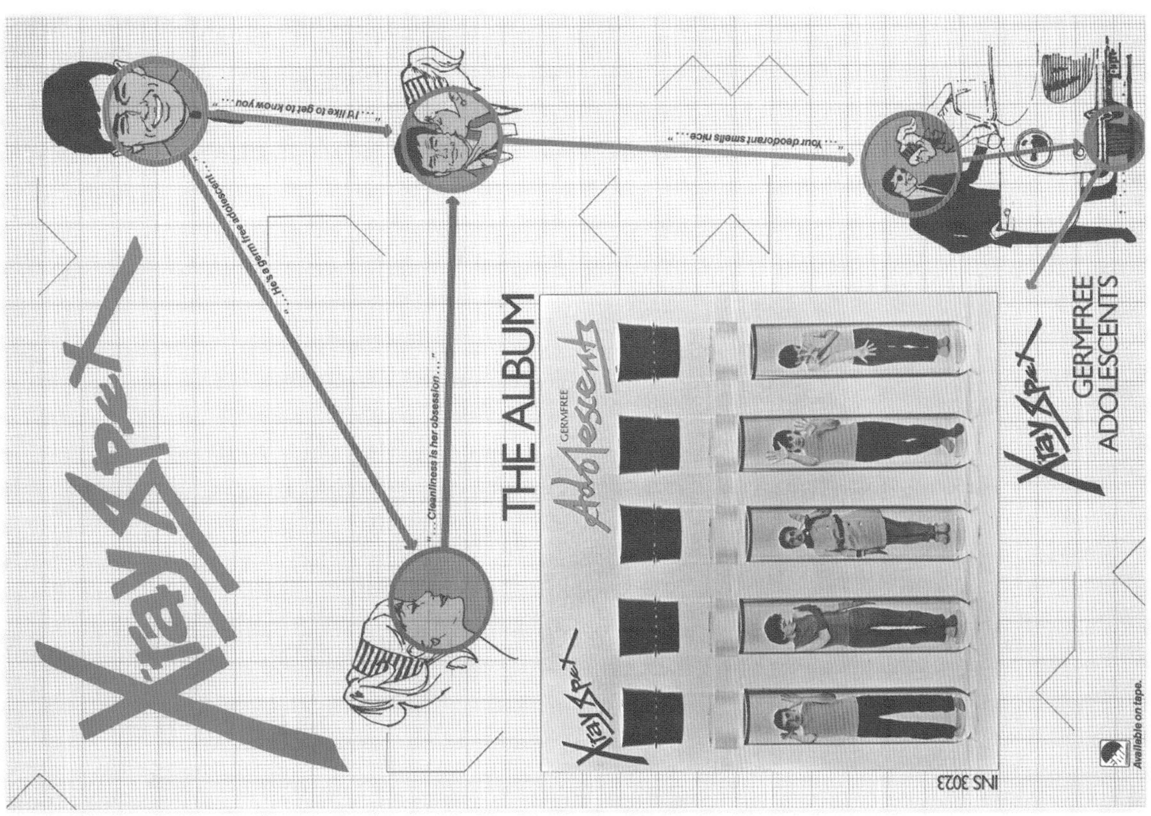

THE DAY THE WORLD TURNED DAY-GLO
IAMA POSEUR
THE NEW SINGLE

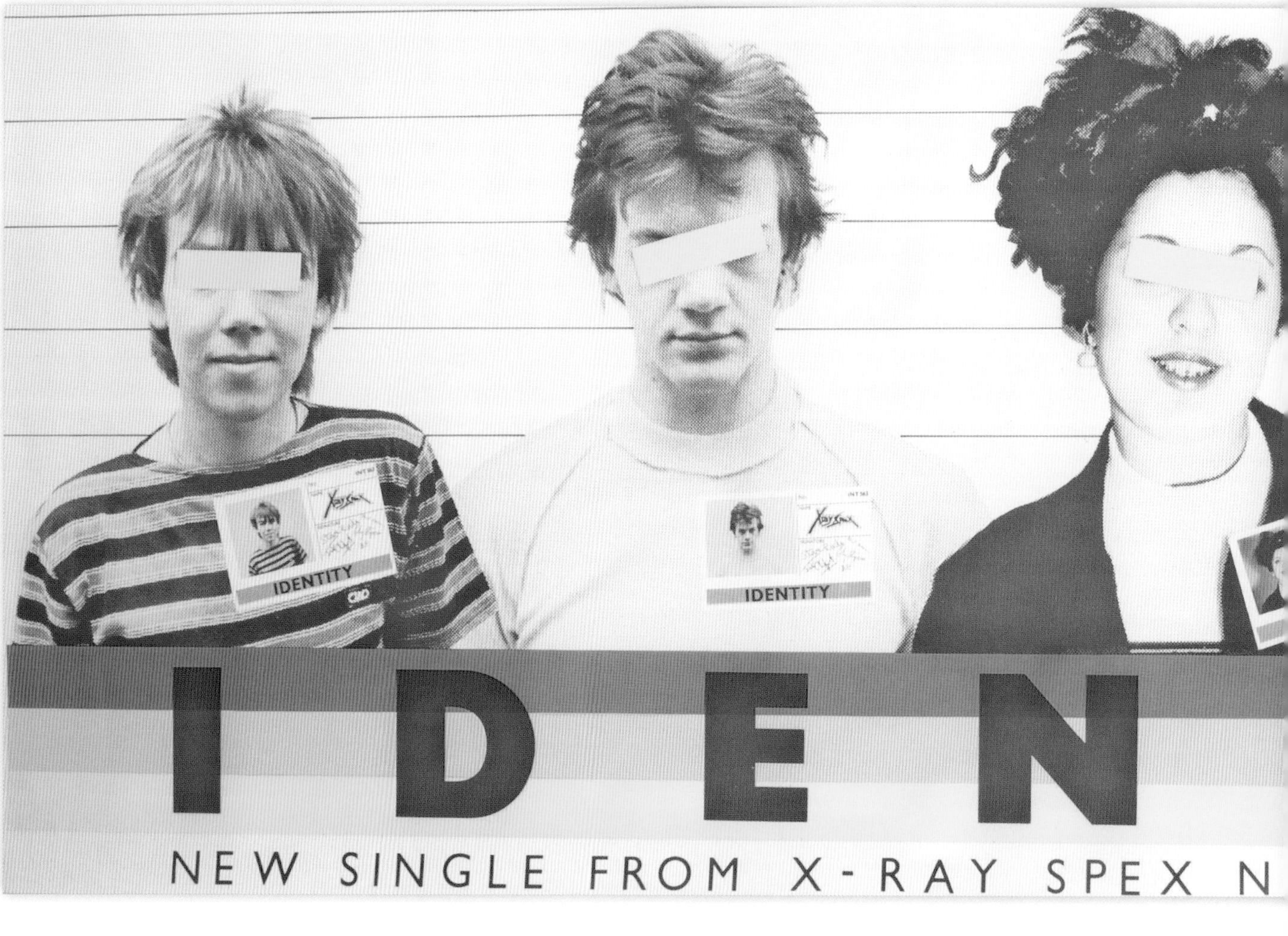

IDENTITY
IDENTITY
I D E N
NEW SINGLE FROM X-RAY SPEX N

X-RAY SPEX: (left) 'The Day the World Turned Day-Glo' 45 poster, EMI Records (1978), **Poly Styrene** artwork, **Cooke Key** design. The first 15,000 copies of the LP were pressed in orange vinyl; (below) 'Identity' 45 banner poster, EMI Records (1978)

SEVEN DEADLY QUESTIONS TO ART CHANTRY

1. Where were you in '76–'80?

When punk hit the Northwest (officially the very first punk club in Seattle opened in 1978; the first show billed as a punk rock show in Seattle was in 1976), I was still in college. The first 'official' punk poster I ever saw was hanging on a telephone pole in 1978. It stopped me dead in my tracks. I had no idea what I was looking at. Keep in mind that, in 1978, *Star Wars* and *Saturday Night Fever* were still playing in theatres. Disco chrome and neon lettering and (especially in Seattle) 'rainbows and earth tones' were all the rage. Seeing a black-and-white, scratchy, cruddy photocopy made out of garbage for a band called 'Negative Approach' completely dumbfounded me. I carefully peeled it off the telephone pole and carried home and hung it on the wall. I stared at it for weeks, trying to figure out what it was. It changed the entire direction of my life. I still have it, framed, on my wall.

The poster was made by a guy credited as 'FRANKO' (real name, Frank Edie, an artist). His cut-and paste, press-type ransom lettering, crude Xerox collage-look so profoundly impacted my aesthetic thinking that I still try to echo his work forty years later. But the classic cut-and-paste photocopied/quickprint/montage/collage punk poster had already existed in Seattle for nearly a decade prior to 1978. There was a theatrical/musical/drag troupe (several were former Cockettes) of performance artists in Seattle called Ze Whiz Kidz (their ranks boasted Tomata du Plenty and Gorilla Rose and Satz, among others – all later became punk stars). Ze Whiz Kidz had been doing posters for their performances since the late 1960s that were indistinguishable from what we later called 'punk' posters.

One person – Tomata du Plenty – was doing cut-and-paste cruddy scribbled punk posters

BLACK FLAG: flyer for performances at Hong Kong Café, Los Angeles, California (January 1979), **Raymond Pettibon** design

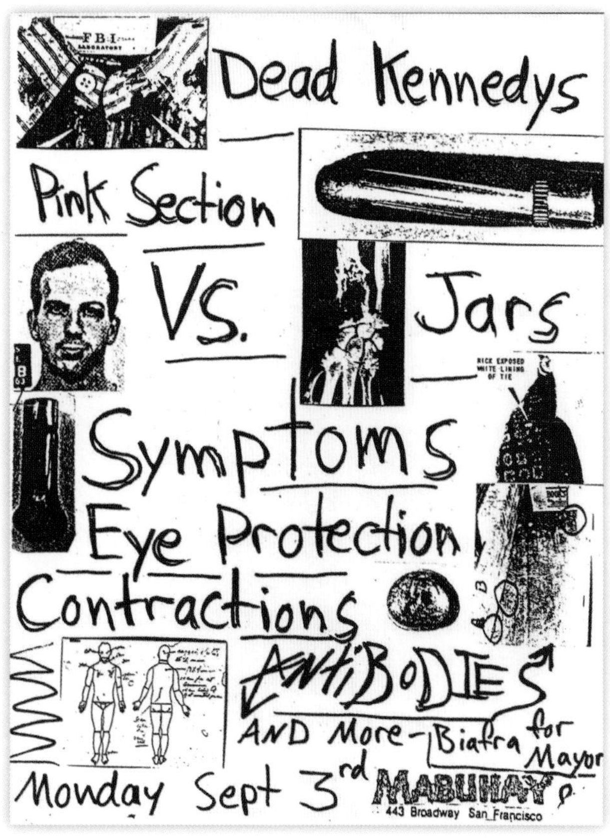

SCREAMERS: (left) flyer (1978), **Tomata du Plenty** design; **DEAD KENNEDYS:** (above) flyer (1979)

in 1970. By 1972, he and Gorilla Rose moved to New York City, where they became deeply involved in the underground arts music scene and worked with everybody from Bette Midler and The Harlettes to the New York Dolls to the gang at Max's Kansas City. Tomata was the one who started to launch performances at a little dive bar called CBGB's. He booked local bands like the Ramones and Blondie (née, The Stilettos). The first time either of those bands ever played CBGB's, they were opening for Tomata's drag theatre troupe (it was Blondie's first appearance). It was where the Ramones met Arturo Vega (who was in the performance troupe), and Arturo both costumed and did all the graphics for the Ramones (that logo!).

Tomata did posters for his shows that are the earliest real scratchy crude PUNK posters I've ever found anywhere. The posters in NYC were all so formal and 'showcard'-style simple (picture and type) but Tomata's work was already looking punk. One of the things that has always amazed me is how quickly punk culture spread across America. Compared to the hippie movement which took literally years to move across the continent (most of what we call the '60s' actually happened in the early 70s), punk seemed to conquer the entire planet in a few months.

Later, Tomata came back to Seattle, formed a band called The Tupperwares, and put on the first punk shows in Seattle. In fact, their first performances predate the first Sex Pistols gigs by half a year. The Tupperwares were forced to change their name (to the Screamers) and then moved to California (dragging along a young Penelope Houston of The Avengers). Il Duce of The Mentors also followed them, to work as a roadie for The Screamers. Later on, Satz left Ze Whiz Kidz, formed a band called The Lewd and moved to San Francisco.

ILLINOIS ENTERTAINER: Chicago free paper; the photograph is of Chicago mayor Jane Byrne (1980)

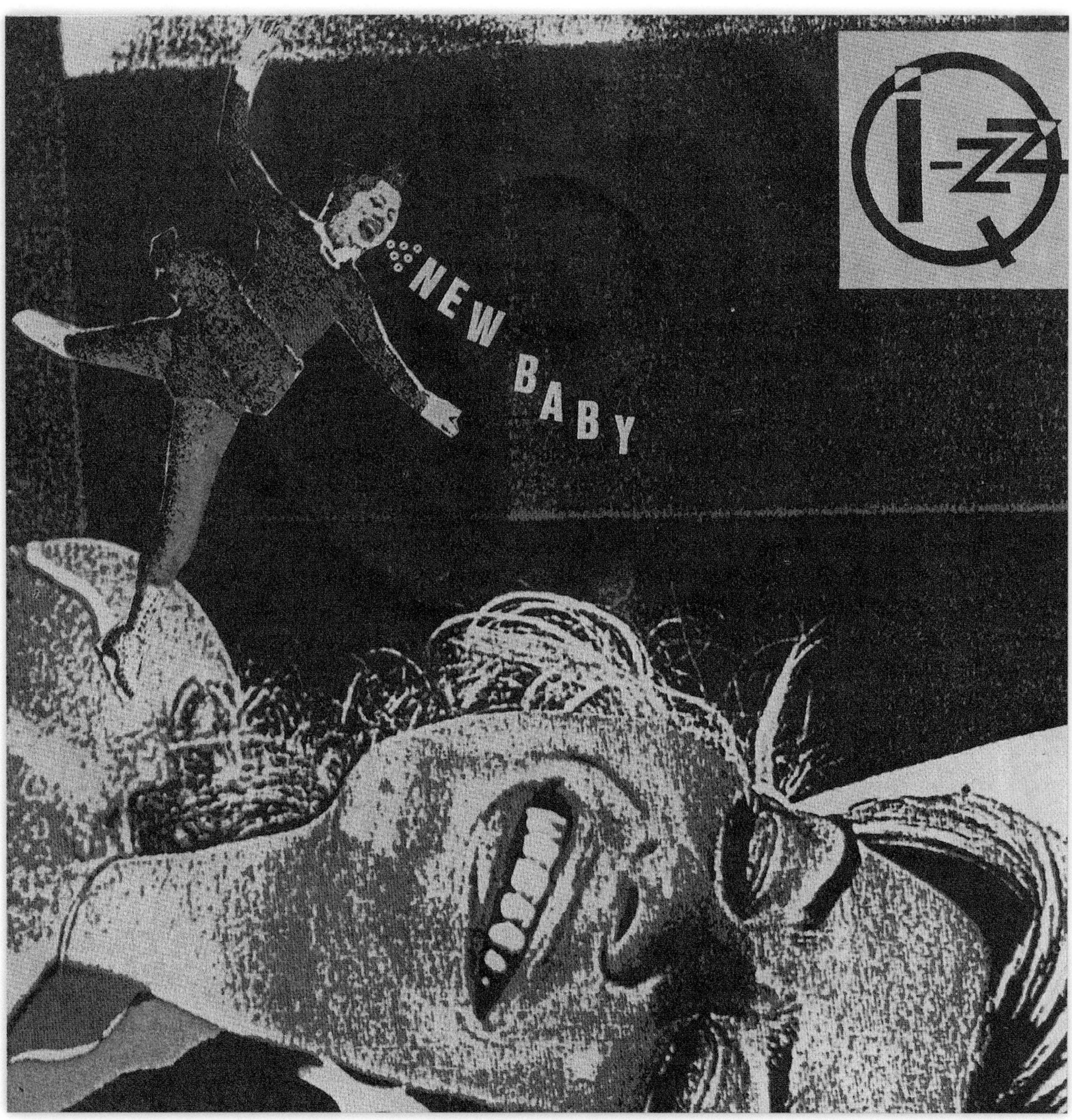

QI-ZZ: 'New Baby' 45 front cover, Hospital Records (1980)

Everywhere Tomata went, he made those scratchy, cheesy street posters for everybody. He was a sort of 'pied piper of punk', accidentally setting up scenes in every city he went to – Seattle, New York, San Francisco, Los Angeles. And everywhere he went, these crazy scratchy posters popped up with him. I'm not saying he invented the form. But he certainly was one of its earliest practitioners and influential poster artists. I doubt he even realized it.

2. Which punk piece would you most like to have/steal?

Once, when visiting NYC, just hanging around, I went to a gallery opening that had a number of my 'friends' showing (guys like Gary Panter and Joe Coleman and Robert Williams). Coincidentally, a gallery across the square was just taking down a Jamie Reid exhibit. When I realized, I immediately ran over to that location and saw that people were stacking frames and frames of stuff against the walls like cordwood. I ended up talking to the promoter of the show who let me wander around and look at stuff.

As I was flipping through all these infamous pieces of punk art, I tripped across the ORIGINAL PASTE-UP for the Sex Pistols' 'God Save the Queen' 45. I think my heart actually stopped beating for a moment. If there is another piece of physical artwork that is MORE iconic to late twentieth-century graphic design, I'd be hard pressed to think of what it might be. I was actually holding the HOLY GRAIL of punk graphics in my sweating, shaking hands.

The best part was that it was in a cheap thrift store frame (damaged, ebonized wood). The glass was completely gone (if there ever was any). So, the collaged pasted-up artwork was exposed to dirt and grime, which had become so thick it looked like it had been sitting in a garage for thirty years. It probably had. I blew on it to sweep off some dirt, but it was so stuck under the edges of the paper that it was literally outlined in filth. All the newsprint, ransom-style type had extremely yellowed over the years as well. Basically, it looked like hell; it was PERFECT!

I SO considered just taking off at a run with that thing. I was standing next to a doorway that was propped open. There was nobody anywhere near me. They just let me – a total stranger – fool around on my own. Nobody knew who I was. I was even leaving town the next day. I could have snagged it easily and NEVER, EVER been caught. I doubt they would have even noticed it was missing until the shipment got back to England. But I didn't steal it and have regretted it ever since...

3. Peter Saville or Barney Bubbles?

Definitely Barney Bubbles. Peter Saville has zero sense of humour. I really hate graphic design language that can't play. How do you engage another person's mind when your every word is didactic? I dunno. I met Peter Saville once. He was as serious as cancer and very beautiful. I've seen photos of Barney Bubbles. Now, there was a guy who only had his wit to survive. It was his incredible weapon of choice. And BB's wit was so DARK! In the world of punk, humour was the ONLY tool you had to make it through your daily life. You lived like a rat, but you actually thought it was funny, that in fact the whole stinking world was funny. You cursed it and then you laughed at it. What's more beautiful than that?

4. Who, in your view, most embodied the essence of the Sex Pistols: Jamie Reid or Johnny Rotten?

That's tough. Jamie Reid was the graphic design language, chosen by Malcolm and imposed on the band. Rotten was also chosen and imposed on the band. So, in a way they are the perfect echo for each other. They didn't CHOOSE to pair up on the project, but never before have two totally separate personal visions been as attuned to the basic primal scream as those two men were. Reid and Rotten created the visual dialogue of British punk; the gutter trash, the anti-design, the politics. Without either of these amazing men, I doubt much would have come of punk in England. They were (and still are) so PURE.

Do you know if they became friends? Did they talk? Did they compare notes? Even if they didn't, two more FEROCIOUS minds never worked together before or since. An amazing, and inadvertent, team from hell. Beautiful.

5. Which was a greater punk band: The Damned or Eater?

The recording of The Damned's 'New Rose' was one of those perfect moments caught in the studio. They even admitted they never sounded that good before or since. I see The Damned as a cartoon band playing dress-up and goofing. I never took them very seriously. That is except for 'New Rose', which is a perfect pop/punk tune unlike any other. Their later work left me cold. I ignored them.

Eater? They were SO YOUNG. Now we had super, super-young bands in America, too. The Zeros from LA were tiny children, for instance (they later spawned El Vez; Robert Lopez). The Zeros were classic Los Angeles punk aggro (a sort of proto-thrash). West Coast punks took themselves seriously. They really wanted to destroy the world. But British punk, it was always about fashion. Americans are shit at fashion.

I never listened to Eater, either. By the time their records were available (in the 'import' section in our record stores) there were more amazing punk bands who were LOCAL to listen to. Why would I listen to Eater, when I had The Telepaths or The Wipers to listen to in my hometown? The entire DIY ethic (so powerfully introduced into the punk dialogue by Jamie Reid) had completely captivated the West Coast punk scene. It somehow meshed well with the old 'back to nature' hippie era, when DIY was a religion. West Coast punks didn't give a fuck about anything except their immediate survival. They were like rats living in a post-apocalyptic world trying to eke out a living any way they could. 'England? What's that? Fashion? You crazy?'

6. Which one of your own works 'leans heavily' on which punk antecedent?

My entire graphic design output has always 'leaned heavily' on the carnal attitude of punk. It's one of the main reasons my career travelled the way it did. I scared away straight clients in huge numbers and attracted lunatics instead (mostly broke lunatics). So, all of my design language has been bridging the gap between the extreme underground and the mainstream. I've seen my career as a catalyst between both worlds; a bridge. I would learn some vicious stylistic 'word' from one side of the fence and then present it on the other side to an audience who could not understand it, but could react to it. Simultaneously, I brought the mainstream over that fence and threw them into the hungry mob to fend for themselves. Watching the normal people I knew trying to deal with the underground in a 'cool' way was always so ridiculous to me. It was wonderful comedy.

As a result, I was never fully trusted by either 'side'. I was too straight to be a punk (too old, too college, too normal). To the mainstream, I was a total freak and I scared the shit out of them. They hated me... so I straddled that fence and struggled to survive like everybody else. In the end, I never really succeeded in either world. But at the same time, I redirected those worlds as I saw fit. It was one hell of a perch to be sitting on when the 'grunge' scene broke open in a media feeding frenzy. I actually got to witness a cultural explosion up close and personal. It was like watching the Haight-Ashbury scene, or Swinging London, or NY punk go nova right in front of you. Even I could toss pebbles in that crazy pond and watch the ripples they made turn into cultural tidal waves. It actually got real frightening and people began to die. It's something I'm very glad I got to see, but I don't ever want to see it again. Once is plenty.

7. Which side of the pond (US or Britain) do you feel produced artists that have had the greatest influence on late 20th-/early 21st-century poster design?

We Americans are SO enamoured of all European design that to say we were able to produce work over the last half-century that was in any way pure and separate from work in, say, England, would be silly. It's just not how language works. At the same time, we do have an extremely different voice over here that remains distinct even now. We Americans and the British may speak roughly the same language, but we are so VERY different.

An example; back in the mid-80s the British arts magazine *Creative Review* wrote an article about my work. Now this was before the whole music scene erupted in Seattle, and the work they knew me for was a lot more associated with other aspects of the arts – theatre, dance, festivals and magazines. Things of that sort. I barely had any record covers in my portfolio back then. When they saw my work (sent at their request), they interviewed me, and the woman I talked to seemed sort of distant and cold. I just assumed it the proverbial British 'stiff upper lip' routine, though.

When the article came out, the title was something like 'the VULGAR art of Art Chantry'. The writer's distance and coldness was actually DISLIKE! She did not understand me or my work at all. She just thought I was a crude vulgarian white trash American. It was actually sort of perfect. It helped me to realize how completely AMERICAN my design dialogue actually is. People in

DEAD KENNEDYS: *Fresh Fruit for Rotting Vegetables* double-sided poster LP insert, Alternative Tentacles Records (1980), **Winston Smith** design

other countries (England, Germany, Japan, etc.) just DON'T get my work. That's because my work is all SPOKEN in a common popular AMERICAN language form – a slang (if you will) spoken in a guttural accent that defies other cultures to totally understand it. This is an attribute I learned from working in punk.

The first time I saw that beautiful crude punk poster by FRANKO, I was enthralled. It explained so much about this design language I practice as my art. I immediately did my own very first punk rocket soon thereafter (for Penelope Houston's band The Avengers). I worked up this little flyer, attempting to erase EVERYTHING I had learned about graphic design. Instead, I tried to put it together as if I had never tried to do anything like this before in my life. I didn't really succeed in my goal, but I produced a cool little crude poster. It was posted up all over the small town I was living in at the time.

The next morning after it was hung around town, I saw that every single poster had been torn from the wall and shredded. The entire city had been CLEANSED of my poster art overnight! Try to imagine making any sort of poster at all that would result in every single copy being attacked and destroyed? We can't do it today. We're too worldly and cynical, now. Back then, it was easy, the graphic language of punk was so off-putting and UGLY that people would attack the posters PHYSICALLY.

At first this hurt my feelings. But as I thought about it, I realized that, even though they attacked my posters, they certainly SAW my posters. In fact, the concert sold out. This is seemingly contrary to every notion of marketing and aesthetics. But, if you think about it, the punks had no way to communicate with each other back in those days. Nobody could afford telephones. They couldn't advertise in newspapers (couldn't afford to buy them either). So, the ONLY way punks back then had to speak to each other (there were so few around) was by postering. When you saw a punk poster and you were also a punk, you'd think, 'my people are having a meeting'. It was exclusive. Punks didn't want 'normal people' to attend. So, the style of language literally scared straight people away from their shows. The punks didn't want them around, so they used a marketing technique of the narrow demographic – only other punks understood what was being said.

This technique is not new or even rare. The hippies did the same thing with their psychedelic posters. You couldn't read them!! You had to be 'high' to understand, right? 'Normal' people saw them and turned away in FEAR. Back in the 1960s, straight people ALSO attacked psych posters and shredded them off walls. But the hippie freaks still saw them and knew there was a meeting of the tribe to attend. Simple, direct and beautiful.

So, when a punk puts a dead baby on a poster, they aren't trying to promote the killing of babies. They are trying to speak to their cohort exclusively and letting them know when to get together for a powwow. If the straights freak out and attack, all the better: *'We don't want them around anyhow.'*

DEAD KENNEDYS: *Fresh Fruit for Rotting Vegetables* double-sided poster LP insert, Alternative Tentacles Records (1980), **Winston Smith** design

LOS ANGELES (AP) — Five Nobel laureates have given sperm to an exclusive sperm bank to be matched with the "right" women in hopes of producing exceptional children, the businessman behind the scheme says.
IF YOU LOVE YOUR CAR DIE FOR IT.
PUT ON YOUR THINKING CAP
Tina has never had a Teddy Bear.
SPECIAL WEAPONS AND TACTICS S.W.A.T.
Cambodia's Pol Pot
MASTERSCAM VICIOUS CIRCLE CREDIT CARD
People used to play with toys; now the toys play with them
AT LONG LAST, UNCLE JOHN'S FORTUNE IS MINE!
He who loves me follows me
Chi mi ama mi segua.
jesus jeans
Die,
Suckers
IN GOD
WE TRUST
SATURDAY NIGHT
A CHURCH IN DECAY
A POPSTAR FOR THE 80's
Hitler dedicating first VW plant in 1938
The Claws of The Lobster
Seduction
Roll-a-Role
LIE CHEAT & STEAL
Xaviera's Happy Hooker Game
TASTES RICH SMELLS RICH LOOKS RICH TASTED RICH SMELLS
WORLD'S HIGHEST STANDARD OF LIVING
There's no way like the American Way
CHARLES MANSON'S EYES
JIMMY CARTER'S EYES
Food Club
PINK SALMON
NET WT 15½ OZ · 439 GRAMS
SALMON AND NOODLE CASSEROLE
THE BLACK TUNA GANG
DON'T LIVE IN FEAR!
Protect Family, Home, Business
K-9 COMMAND DOGS
Trained Dogs For Sale
Student With Library Card Designs Bomb
Losing makes him mad
BILLY
INTERNMENT
TOP CAT
Ah Men
ALBUQUERQUE, N.M. (UPI) — The Postal Service has suspended a mailman for allegedly spraying Mace at a 3-year-old boy
Berkeley in 1964: Now they scramble for grades
IT'S MADE IN DUPLICATE
DIAL-A-KISS
HEAR A SPECIAL MESSAGE FROM GENE, PAUL, ACE OR PETER
Call 999-2222
Washington — The Army ordered $10.2 million worth of new machine guns even though the same weapons were available from surplus stocks in the Air Force and Navy, congressional auditors said yesterday.
WARGASM!
THAT'S ENTERTAINMENT
TIME Cult of Death
BRING US TOGETHER AGAIN
As real-estate salesman Geoffrey Keys, 26, explains the procedure: "Male goes to Harvest House for female in Danskin top, short shorts, and impenetrable sun glasses. Goes home and shoves 2.5 grams of coke up her nose and pops as many Flight 714 Quaaludes as necessary for an evening of sexual bliss."
Rotting vegetables
(Eres Putrescentia)

THE DELINQUENTS: tour flyer (1981)

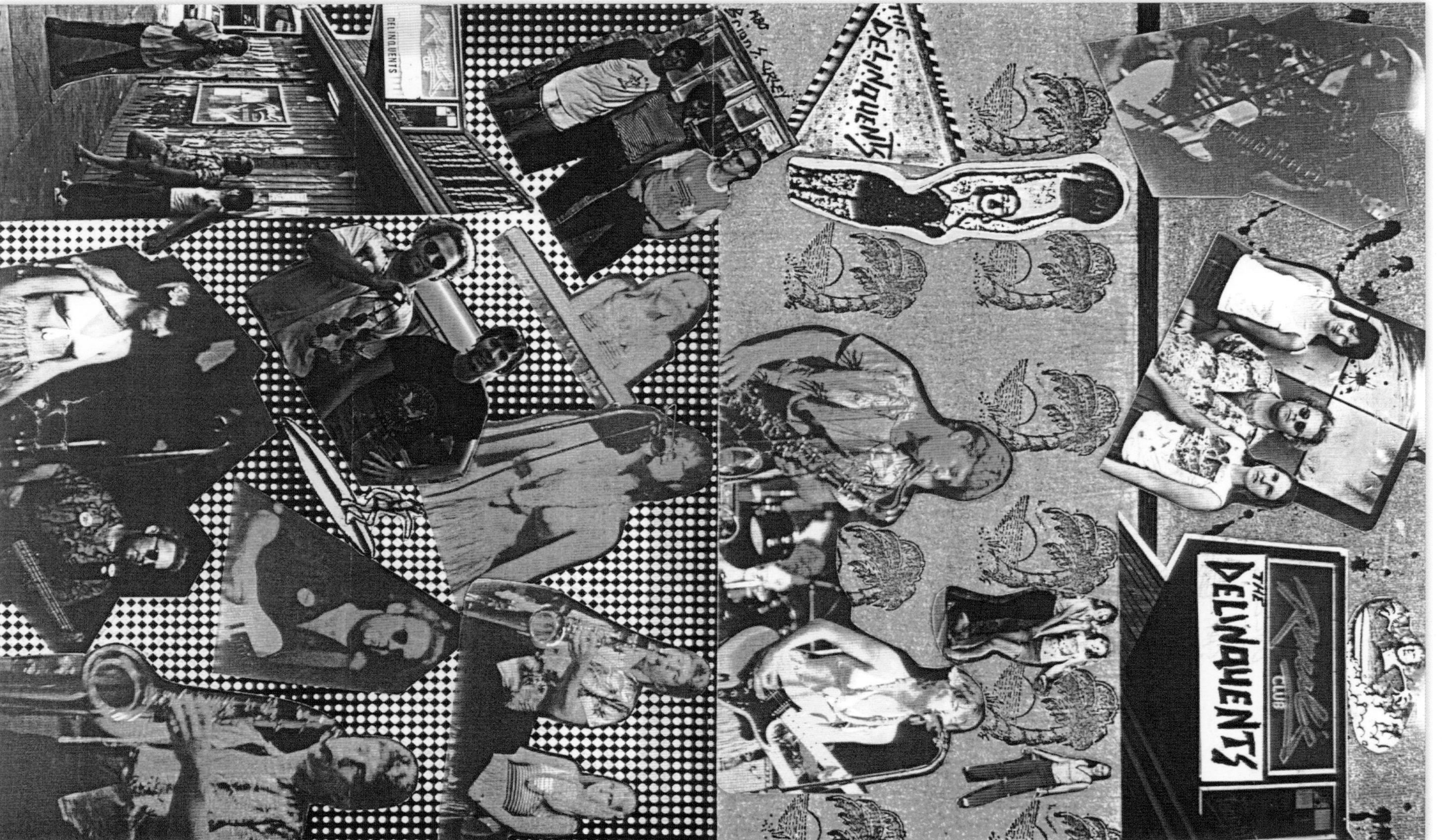

MORNING AGAIN IN AMERICA

One widely received historical narrative contends that the roots of punk were laid down in mid-1970s New York City then migrated to London in 1976–7 and became a spent force in Britain by the end of 1978. Worse even, some of the more doctrinaire punk chroniclers go further, asserting that punk was dead by April 1977, following the ousting of Roxy club founders Andrew Czezowski, Susan Carrington and Barry Jones (the so-called 100 days). This view, to my mind, is insupportable; rather, I believe punk to have been resurrected in the New World after 1978.

In my *weltanschauung*, American punk had two distinct phases: initially, from 1974 to 1977 and centered in New York, but with vibrant outposts in LA and San Francisco; in the second phase North America became punk's standard bearer in the late 1970s continuing well into the 1980s. (North America here includes many excellent punk bands from Canada.) Animated by a loathing of the neon-saturated and often soft-focus video artifice of MTV, hardcore punks launched a direct aural assault on the smug, hollow optimism of that time, epitomized by Reagan's 1984 reelection mantra, 'It's morning again in America'. The brilliant corrective to this neo-conservative, partisan mood is, without question, Dead Kennedy's single 'Kill the Poor'.

While a few punk bands doggedly carried on during the Thatcher years in Britain (mostly 'Oi' bands, including Anti-Pasti, Angelic Upstarts, Cockney Rejects, and The Exploited), punk's creative centre had shifted decisively over to the Western Hemisphere. American groups like Angry Samoans, Bad Brains, Black Flag, Circle Jerks, Dead Kennedys, Fear, Suicidal Tendencies, and TSOL (together with their Canadian peers) are potent representatives of the second era of punk in North America.

Andrew Krivine

1 ANGRY SAMOANS: *Back From Samoa* LP poster, Triple X Records (1982); **2 THE AVENGERS:** lyric book cover (1978), **Penelope Houston** design; **3 BAD BRAINS:** 'Destroy Babylon' 45 poster/tour blank, Bad Brain Records (1982)

1

2

3

BLACK FLAG: Creepy Crawl '80 tour flyer for gig at The Island, Houston, TX, Blue Light Productions (1980), **Mark Greene** artwork

1

2

3

BLACK FLAG: 1 'Police Story' promotional sticker (1981), **Raymond Pettibon** (credited as Chuck Higby) artwork; **2** flyer for benefit concert at La Casa de la Raza, Santa Barbara, CA (1983), **Raymond Pettibon** design; **3** flyer for performances at S.I.R, Los Angeles, CA (November 1982), **Raymond Pettibon** design

BLACK FLAG

Tues WITH THE MiDdle Class AND SOCIAL DISTORTION

TASTE THE MOMENT!

Weds WITH THE Adolescents

Jan 6 & 7 AND CHINA WHITE

Pettibone

Art is Religion

A kiss and a fix aren't enough anymore

STARWOOD

8151 santa Monica Blvd

BLACK FLAG: flyer for concert at The Starwood, Hollywood, CA (January 1981), **Raymond Pettibon** design

1

2

3

BLACK FLAG: 1 *My War* LP poster, SST Records (March 1984), **Raymond Pettibon** design (under the alias Napoleon Bolero); **2** flyer for gig (8 November 1984), **Raymond Pettibon** design; **3** 'The Process of Weeding Out' EP poster, SST Records (1985), **Raymond Pettibon** design

1

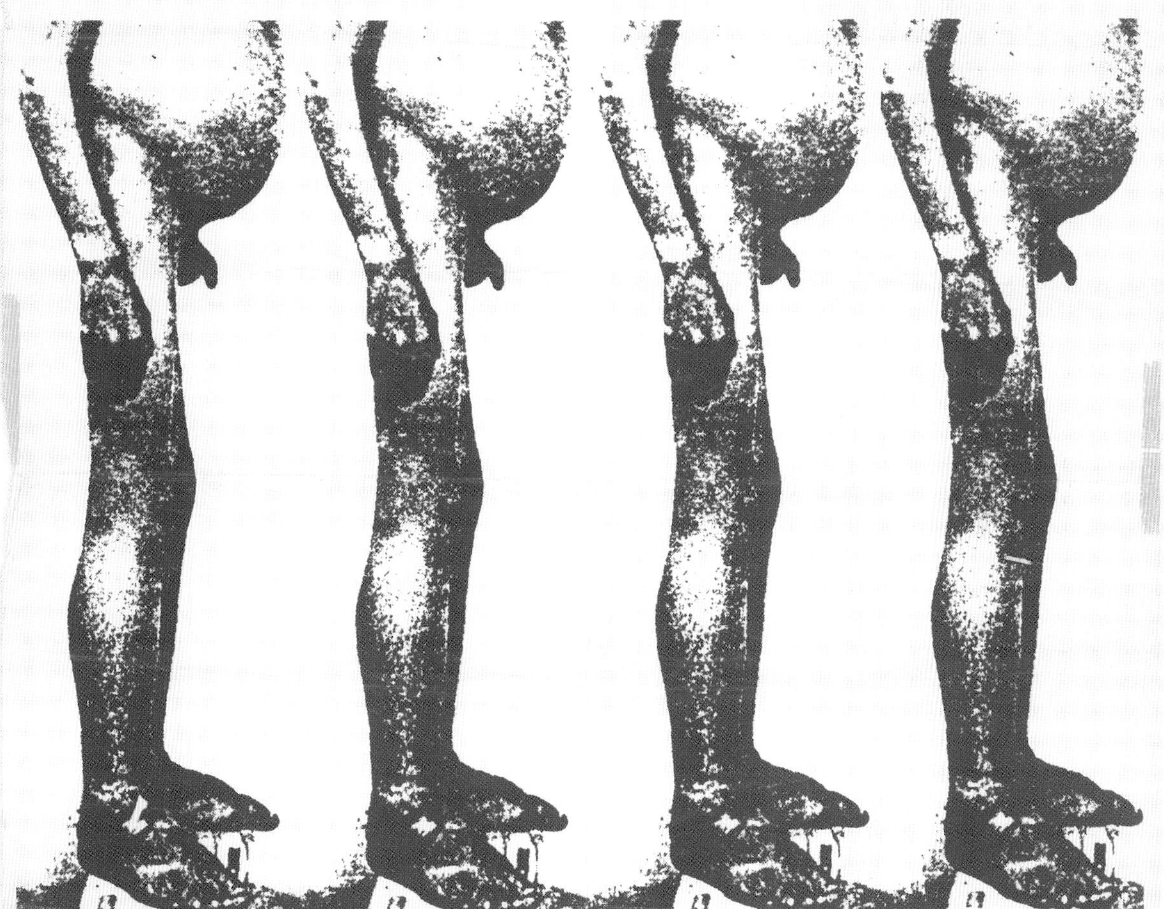

BUTTHOLE SURFERS: *Pee Pee the Sailor* EP poster, Alternative Tentacles Records (1983), **Winston Smith** design

1

2

3

CIRCLE JERKS: 1 flyer for concert at Florentine Gardens, Los Angeles, CA (25 November 1981); **2** *Wild in the Streets* LP poster, Faulty Products Records (1982), **Glen E. Friedman** photography; **3** sticker, Faulty Products Records (1982); **4** *Golden Shower of Hits* LP poster, LAX Records (1983)

4

1

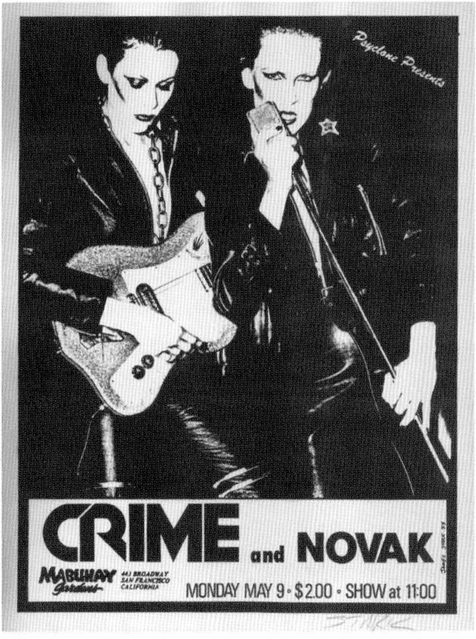

2

CRIME: 1 poster for gig (4–5 August 1977); **2** poster for gig (9 May 1977), **James Stark** design; **3** flyer for gig (2 February 1979)

3

CRIME
with VKTMS and SITUATIONS
THIS FRIDAY 2/2/79 MABUHAY 443 Broadway 11PM

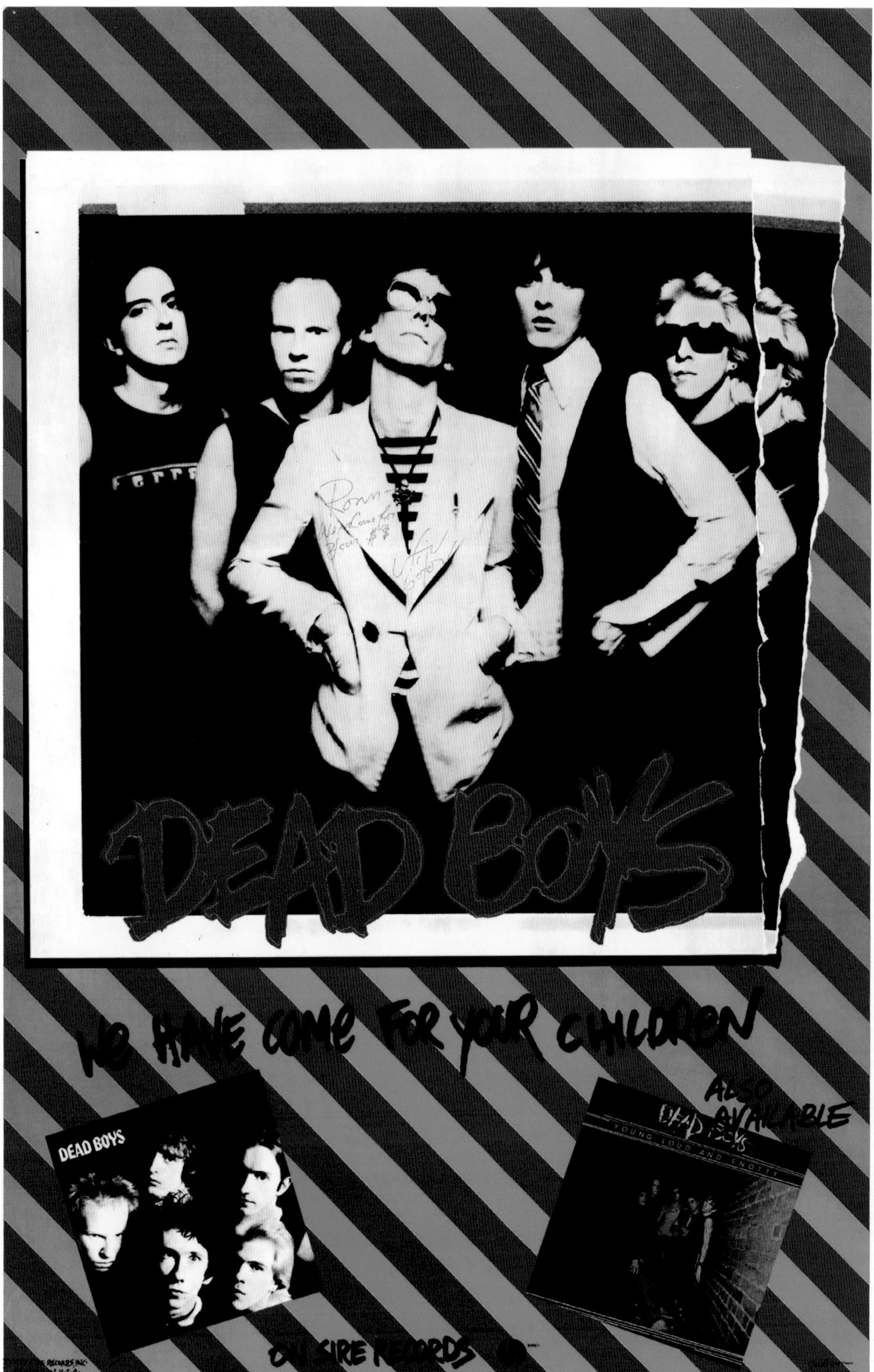

DEAD BOYS: *We Have Come For Your Children* LP poster, Sire Records (1978), **Ronn Spencer** design; **Mick Rock** photography

DEAD KENNEDYS: (left) newsprint advertisement for concert at Washington Hall, Seattle (July 1979); (below) 'California Uber Alles' 45 cover inner spread, Optional Music (1980)

1

2

3

DEAD KENNEDYS: 1 'Kill the Poor' 45 front cover, Cherry Red Records (1980), **Greg Wright** artwork; **2** 'Too Drunk to Fuck' 45 poster, Alternative Tentacles Records (1981), **Fallout Productions** & **Biafra** design; **3** flyer for concert at Mabuhay Gardens, San Francisco, CA (1981)

2

1

DEAD KENNEDYS: (bottom) *Fresh Fruit for Rotting Vegetables* LP poster, IRS Records (1980), **Fallout Productions** design; (top) poster for 'In God We Trust' EP poster, Alternative Tentacles Records (1981), **Jello Biafra**, **Winston Smith** artwork

1

2

3

FEAR: 1 placard for concert at Hong Kong Café, Los Angeles, CA (November 1979); **2** poster for concert at On Broadway in San Francisco, CA (June 1983); **3** band photo poster, Slash Records (*c.*1981)

1

2

3

4

FLIPPER
POSTER
GENERIC FLIPPER
SUBTERRANEAN RECORDS

FLIPPER: 1 flyer for concert at The Farm, San Francisco, CA (*c.* July 1982); **2** tour blank poster, Subterranean Records (1982); **3** 'Get Away' 45 poster, Subterranean Records (1982); **4** *Generic Flipper* LP poster, Subterranean Records (1982), **Saneway Stores, Inc.** design

FLIPPER: *Gone Fishing* LP flyer, Subterranean Records (1984)

FRIED ABORTIONS: (above) flyer for concert at Sound of Music, San Francisco, CA (4 February 1981), **Winston Smith** design; (right) flyer for concert at The Bandshell, Golden Gate Park, San Francisco, CA (17 July 1981); Michael Earl Saunders (lead singer of the Angry Samoans) played drums for Fried Abortions from 1980–2

GERMS: (above) poster of cover for LA fanzine *Slash* #9 (1978); (left) 'Germs Return!' sticker for final performance, at the Starwood in Los Angeles, CA (3 December 1980)

1

2

3

GUN CLUB: 1 poster for debut album *Fire of Love*, Ruby Records (1981); **2** *The Birth, The Death, The Ghost* LP poster, ABC Records (1984)

HÜSKER DÜ: 3 'In the East' tour blank poster (1983); Hüsker Dü took their name from the Danish memory game, 'Do You Remember?', which was introduced in the US during the 1950s

HÜSKER DÜ: 'Eight Miles High' 45 poster, SST Records (1984), image based on photograph by **Naomi Petersen**

HÜSKER
ZEN ARCA

HÜSKER DÜ: *Zen Arcade* LP poster, SST Records (1984), **Fake Name Graphx** design

MEAT PUPPETS: poster for concert at The Stage, New York City (October 1984)

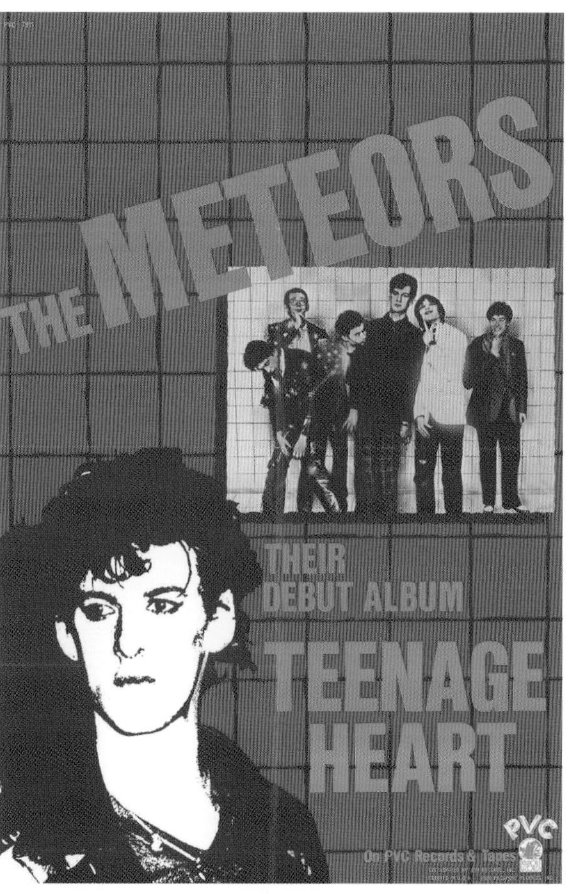

THE METEORS: *Teenage Heart* LP poster, PVC Records (1980)

MINUTEMEN: flyer for concert at Godzilla's, San Francisco, CA (19 March 1982), **Orlando X** artwork

THE MUMPS: (left) fan club flyer (*c.*1979), photograph from the 1960 film *Village of the Damned*; (below) 'Rock & Roll This, Rock & Roll That' EP poster, Perfect Records (1978)

THE MUTANTS: poster for gig at Savoy Tivoli, San Francisco, CA (6 April 1980)

THE NUNS: 1 poster for concert at Mabuhay Gardens, San Francisco, CA (24 November 1977); **2** flyer for Mabuhay gigs (8–9 September 1978); **3** poster for gig at The Stone, San Francisco, CA (June 1981)

1

2

3

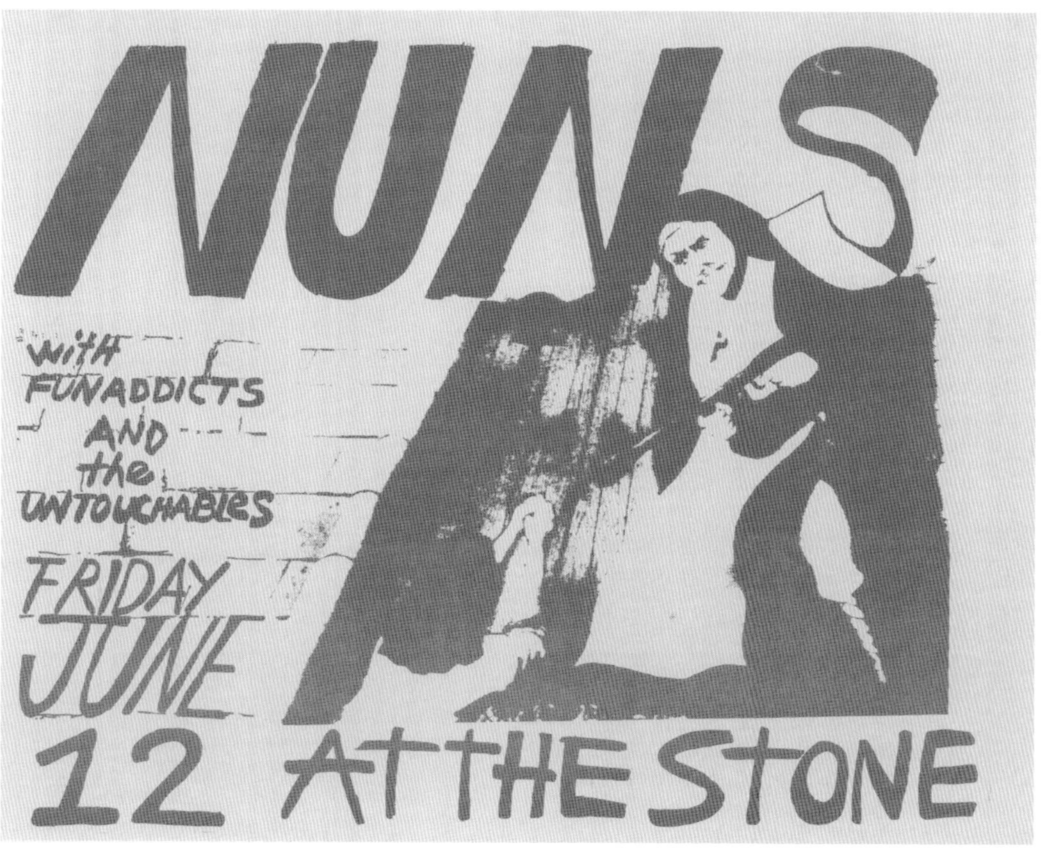

SCREAMERS
SCREAMERS
SCREAMERS
SCREAMERS
SCREAMERS

SCREAMERS

JULY 5•6•7•8

WITH LOUNGE LIZARDS THURS. & SUN.

HURRAH

36 WEST 62ND ST., N.Y.C.

SCREAMERS: residency flyer at Hurrah, NY (July 1979), **Gary Panter** artwork/design

SIC F*CKS: flyer for concert at Trax, New York City (April 1982)

SOCIAL DISTORTION: (below) flyer promoting unreleased LP, 13th Floor Records (1984)

1

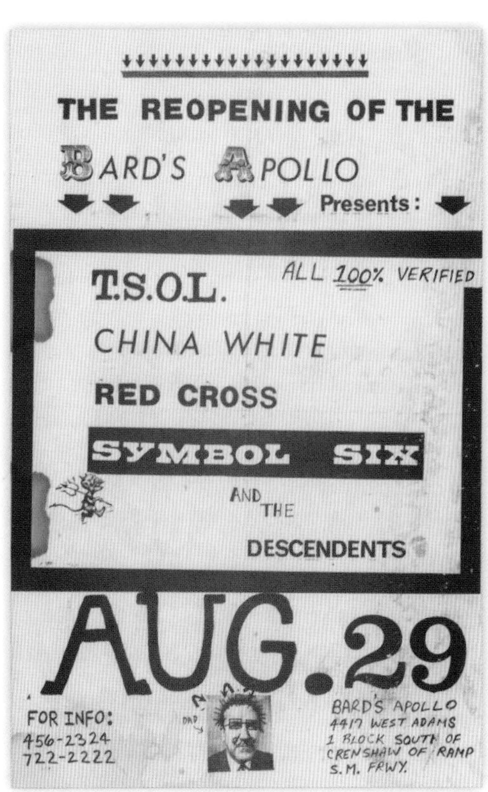

2

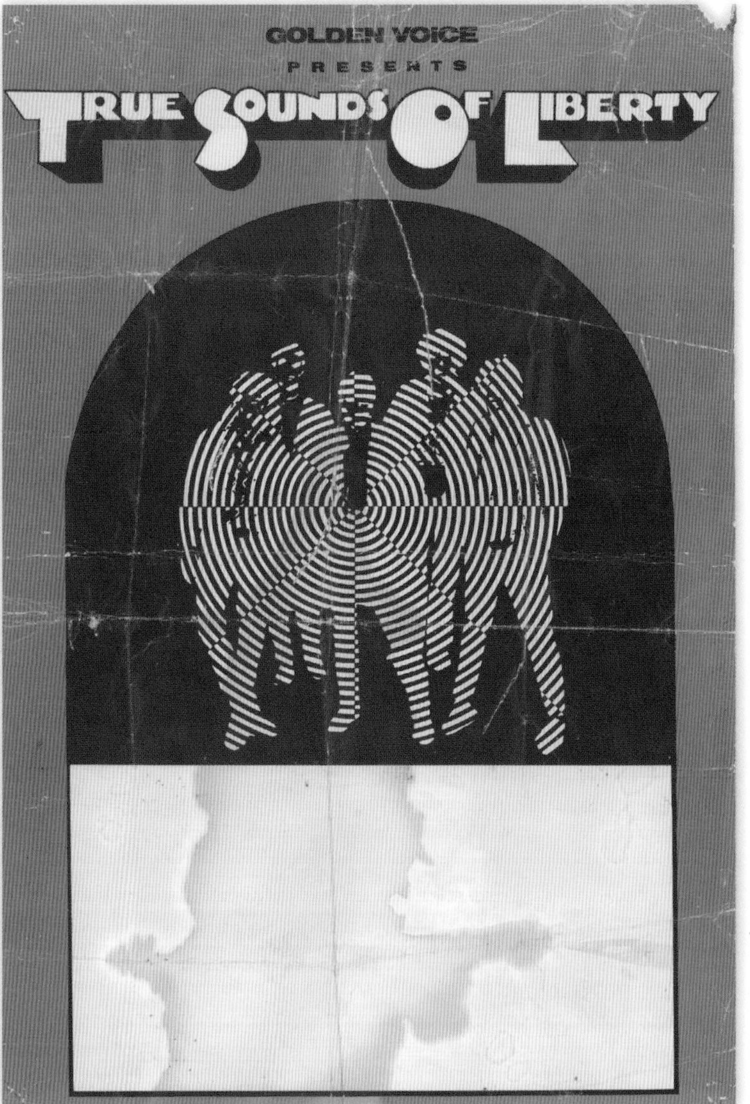

3

TRUE SOUNDS OF LIBERTY:
1 flyer for concert at Bard's Apollo, Los Angeles, CA (29 August 1981); **2** 'Weathered Statues' EP sticker, Alternative Tentacles Records (1982); **3** tour blank poster (*c.*1984), drawing on colours and typography of a Bill Gold and Philip Castle-designed poster for the Stanley Kubrick movie, *A Clockwork Orange* (1971)

1

2

3

4

X: 1 poster for concert at Russian Center, San Francisco, CA (24 October 1981); **2** flyer for concert at Starship, Milwaukee, WI (1981); **3** *Los Angeles* LP poster, Slash Records (1980), **Frank Gargani** photography; **4** poster for concert at University of Kentucky, (*c.* 31 October 1982)

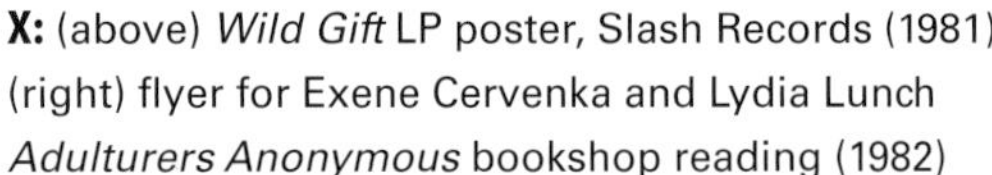
X: (above) *Wild Gift* LP poster, Slash Records (1981); (right) flyer for Exene Cervenka and Lydia Lunch *Adulturers Anonymous* bookshop reading (1982)

X: *More Fun in the New World* tour poster, Elektra Records (1983)

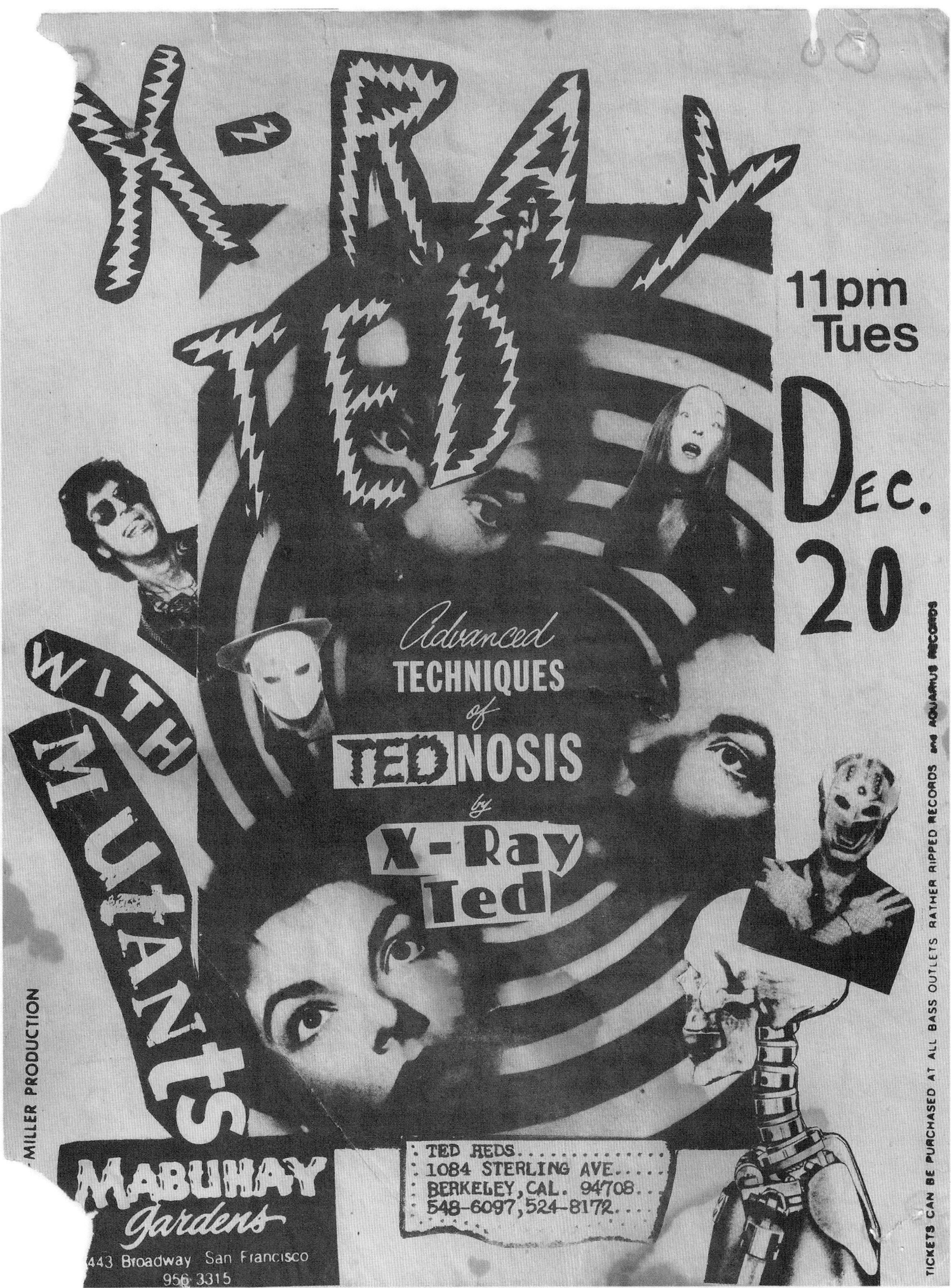

X-RAY TED: flyer for gig at Mabuhay Gardens, San Francisco, CA (20 December 1977)

I'M DEAD I'M DEAD I'M DEAD

By Mal Peachey

The influence on British punk of late-night cinema double-bills showing cheaply made sci-fi and horror movies is not often discussed among academics or broadsheet critics. Yet it was hugely influential in a way that most socio-economic theories on punk's development fail to recognize. It is, of course, a cliché that any popular 'history' of punk will mention the 'Winter of discontent', high unemployment, city streets filled with uncollected trash and prog-rock as major factors in punk's emergence. All tales of England in 1976 will mention how industrial strikes by coal and steel workers had led to power cuts and a three-day working week, and with it a sense that the very fabric of British society was ripping apart. Hence why the disaffected, alienated and disenfranchised youth of inner-city London (and surrounding suburbs, especially Bromley) took to tearing their clothes, making their hair stick up in spikes, piercing themselves with safety pins and smearing heavy black eyeliner on their white-pancaked faces – all designed to increase the shock effect intended to outrage the older generation.

While some of that is true (the three-day week was only in operation for the first three months of 1974 though; the trash collectors' strike and 'Winter of discontent' were actually in 1979), look again at the make-up of the first British punks. That hair and eyeliner, those fishnets, ties and self-piercing wasn't inspired by Harold Wilson, Arthur Scargill or Margaret Thatcher. The Roxy and its clientele looked far more like Frank N'Furter's Time Warpers from Richard

THE BATCAVE: front of flyer for London's premier goth club (1982)

O'Brien's *The Rocky Horror Show* or Alice Cooper, than anyone else around at the time. Then there's the naming of the only true punk club in London: is it a coincidence that Lou Adler, the co-owner of the LA Roxy (which opened in 1973) first took *The Rocky Horror Show* to the USA, and subsequently produced the movie in 1975?

In the 1970s when British pubs closed and gigs ended strictly at 11pm every night (apart from Sunday, when it was 10.30pm), discos and clubs (which closed at 1, or 2am) charged an entry fee, sold alcohol at inflated prices and played only disco and funk records. After-hours clubs were either members-only or illegal, and usually only to be found in major cities. Which meant that for late-night entertainment under-18s had to meet at their homes and risk annoying parents and neighbours, or hang around in the cold, dark streets and parks once the local youth club had closed. The only places in the UK which offered at least a modest level of warmth, comfort and entertainment after the pubs shut and gigs ended were the ageing, semi-decrepit and struggling cinema chains which were increasingly being forced into running bingo sessions from lunchtime to 10pm before reverting to their original use after pub closing time. That was when double-bills of cheap-to-hire horror and sexploitation b-movies from the 1930s to 50s flashed across the screen, playing to audiences of young people in various states of boredom, inebriation, amphetamine-fuelled excitement or stoned amazement.

Richard O'Brien's *Rocky Horror Show* stage musical, first staged in 1973, was a brilliant satire on the late-night double-feature culture which had developed at the end of the 1960s, playing what are now considered to be classic black-and-white sci-fi and horror movies like *Flash Gordon* (1936), *King Kong* (1933) and *Frankenstein* (1931). O'Brien created a fabulous transgender, trans-sexual camp musical with a glam-rock soundtrack and proto-punk fashions (it's not a coincidence that the 'creature' Rocky in *The Rocky Horror Picture Show* of 1975 looks a lot like Iggy Pop in his gold lamé pants and blond hair phase). When the stage show toured the UK between 1973 and 1976, increasing numbers of people in the audience dressed like members of the cast and joined in with the singing, shouting lines at the stage. On the movie's release people went to the cinema wearing torn fishnet stockings, shabby black tails and dark glasses, carrying buckets of rice to throw at the screen during the wedding scene, and glasses of water to throw over one another during the rainstorm. They behaved just like... well, punks, actually.

By the end of 1977, The Damned's singer Dave Vanian had adopted something of a camp vampire look with his jet-black widow's peak, Edwardian undertaker coat and blood-red lips. While he was doubtless paying homage to Bela Lugosi and/or Christopher Lee's portrayals of Dracula on screen (just as O'Brien's character Riff Raff does), he must have witnessed – or heard about – the incredible power, thrill and fright of The Cramps in action. Read Michael Wilde's essay on the impact that Lux Interior, Poison Ivy Rorschach, Bryan Gregory and Nick Knox had on him and others (p.244), and you can see the bare roots of the goth scene which grew up in the UK.

The Damned were never considered to be a 'goth band' until the mid-1980s, possibly because they were too self-consciously ironic. Fellow Brit punk founder Siousxie Sioux helped to forge the subculture from her first recordings – not only via her Teutonic voice and the band's sombre sound, but as much for her strictly black-and-white fashion sense.

Toward the end of 1979, a would-be art-rock band from Northampton named Bauhaus released a single titled 'Bela Lugosi's Dead' and truly launched goth, the song becoming the movement's anthem. That same year The Cure released an album of decidedly un-goth rock songs titled *Three Imaginary Boys,* wrapped in a distinctly non-goth sleeve, and in truth they were never a goth band, but they're often mentioned among goth pioneers, possibly due to the fact that founder and head man Robert Smith has worn the eternal goth look of panda eyes and dyed-black birds-nest hair, shapeless black sweaters and skull jewellery for over forty years.

At the end of the 1970s, several British bands emerged from the post-punk scene intent on creating a definite goth movement, and for a while it centered around The Batcave in London's Soho. The scene developed around Alien Sex Fiend, Sex Gang Children and Specimen, all of whom adopted a predominantly black-and-white graphic style. Their flyers and single sleeves used spidery type, pseudo-horror movie graphics, film noir-style photography, or featured crypt-like statuary or band photos with members sporting exaggerated, overgrown and over-dyed towering quiff-with-mullet haircuts.

In goth promotional materials, nineteenth-century gothic and BDSM imagery as well as pentagrams and runic symbols are often displayed. The occult and paganism came to permeate the goth aesthetic, which lost its reverence for the schlock horror movies that had so inspired the movement's progenitors; just as cinema chains closed down many theatres, and late-night double features became as much a part of the past as the movies which they'd been so dependent upon.

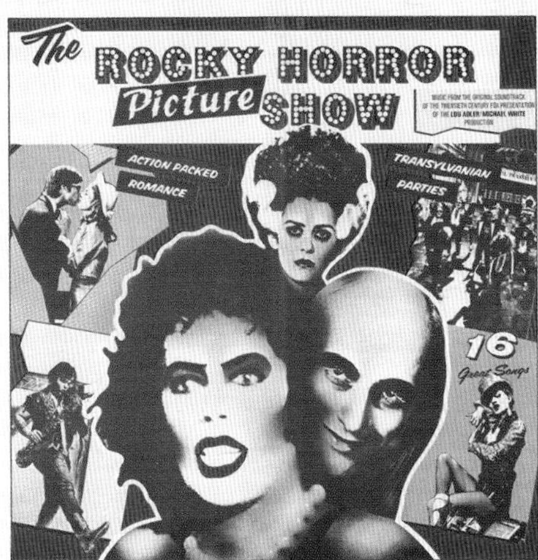

THE ROCKY HORROR PICTURE SHOW: soundtrack LP poster, Jem Records (1980), **John Pasche** and **Gull Graphics** design

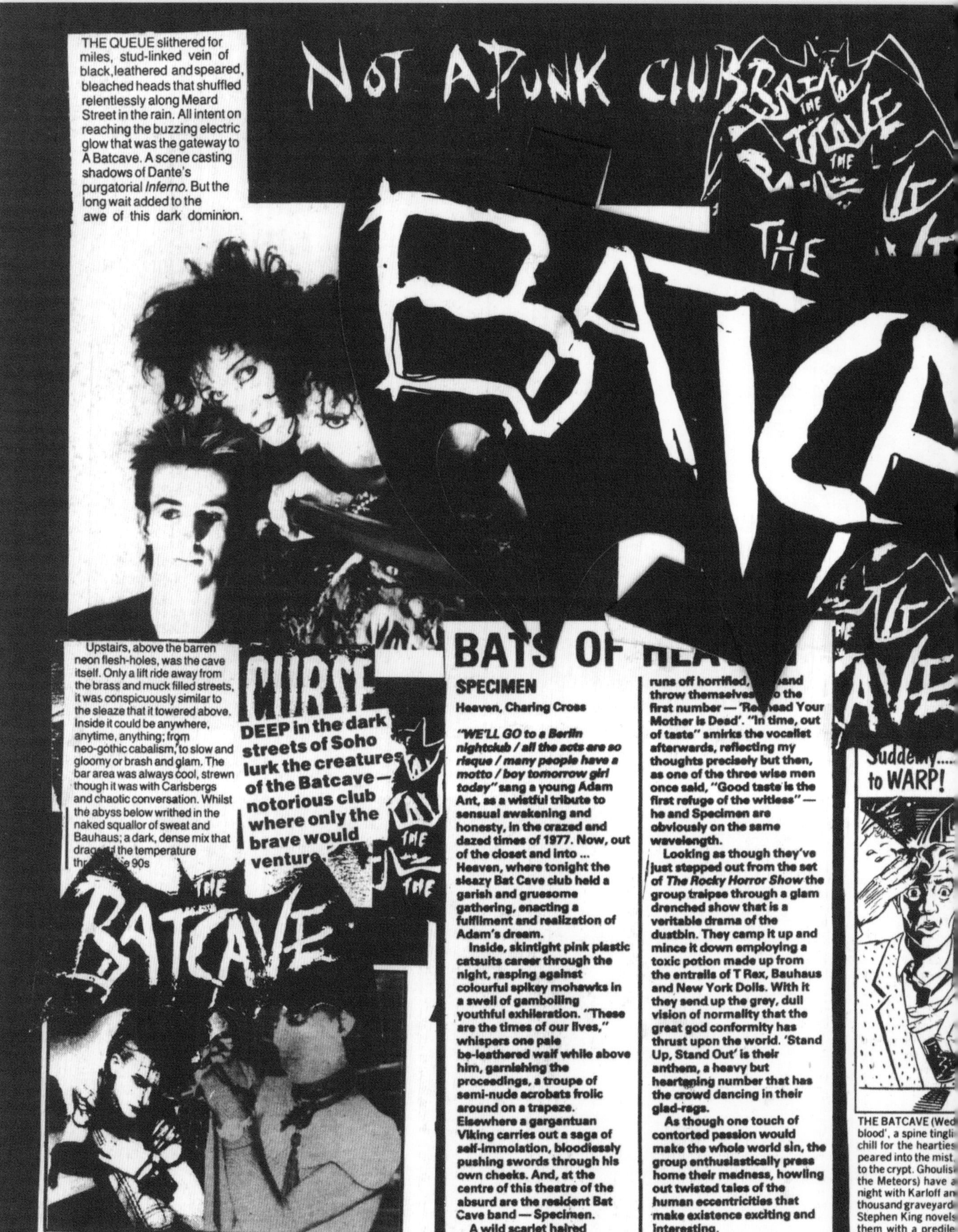

NOT A PUNK CLUB

THE BATCAVE

THE QUEUE slithered for miles, stud-linked vein of black, leathered and speared, bleached heads that shuffled relentlessly along Meard Street in the rain. All intent on reaching the buzzing electric glow that was the gateway to A Batcave. A scene casting shadows of Dante's purgatorial *Inferno*. But the long wait added to the awe of this dark dominion.

Upstairs, above the barren neon flesh-holes, was the cave itself. Only a lift ride away from the brass and muck filled streets, it was conspicuously similar to the sleaze that it towered above. Inside it could be anywhere, anytime, anything; from neo-gothic cabalism, to slow and gloomy or brash and glam. The bar area was always cool, strewn though it was with Carlsbergs and chaotic conversation. Whilst the abyss below writhed in the naked squallor of sweat and Bauhaus; a dark, dense mix that drag... the temperature thr... e 90s

CURSE

DEEP in the dark streets of Soho lurk the creatures of the Batcave — notorious club where only the brave would venture

THE BATCAVE

SPECIMEN (above) invite all those "with a taste for leather and lace" to attend their first performance at the Embassy Club on March 9 at midnight. **Paint** will also be attending and by requesting invitation tickets on the door leather-and-lace lovers will get in for £2 rather than the usual £6!

BATS OF HEA...

SPECIMEN

Heaven, Charing Cross

"WE'LL GO to a Berlin nightclub / all the acts are so risque / many people have a motto / boy tomorrow girl today" **sang a young Adam Ant, as a wistful tribute to sensual awakening and honesty, in the crazed and dazed times of 1977. Now, out of the closet and into ... Heaven, where tonight the sleazy Bat Cave club held a garish and gruesome gathering, enacting a fulfilment and realization of Adam's dream.**

Inside, skintight pink plastic catsuits career through the night, rasping against colourful spikey mohawks in a swell of gambolling youthful exhilaration. "These are the times of our lives," whispers one pale be-leathered waif while above him, garnishing the proceedings, a troupe of semi-nude acrobats frolic around on a trapeze. Elsewhere a gargantuan Viking carries out a saga of self-immolation, bloodlessly pushing swords through his own cheeks. And, at the centre of this theatre of the absurd are the resident Bat Cave band — Specimen.

A wild scarlet haired damsel wanders on stage and is passed a strange missive by the guitarist; she reads it and runs off horrified, ... and throw themselves ... o the first number — 'Re...ead Your Mother is Dead'. "In time, out of taste" smirks the vocalist afterwards, reflecting my thoughts precisely but then, as one of the three wise men once said, "Good taste is the first refuge of the witless" — he and Specimen are obviously on the same wavelength.

Looking as though they've just stepped out from the set of *The Rocky Horror Show* the group traipse through a glam drenched show that is a veritable drama of the dustbin. They camp it up and mince it down employing a toxic potion made up from the entrails of T Rex, Bauhaus and New York Dolls. With it they send up the grey, dull vision of normality that the great god conformity has thrust upon the world. 'Stand Up, Stand Out' is their anthem, a heavy but heartening number that has the crowd dancing in their glad-rags.

As though one touch of contorted passion would make the whole world sin, the group enthusiastically press home their madness, howling out twisted tales of the human eccentricities that make existence exciting and interesting.

In Heaven, as they say, everything is fine.

Richard North

THE BATCAVE

Suddenly..... to WARP!

THE BATCAVE (Wed... blood', a spine tingli... chill for the hearties... peared into the mist, ... to the crypt. Ghoulis... the Meteors) have a... night with Karloff an... thousand graveyard... Stephen King novels... them with a predile... guaranteed 'no funk... horridly 'normal' fas... Crowley). If you don'... one Hell of a night o...

THE BATCAVE: back of flyer for London's premier goth club (1982)

ALIEN SEX FIEND: (above, left) flyer (*c.*1983); (above, right) *Maximum Security* LP flyer, Anagram Records (1985)

BAUHAUS: (right) 'The Passion of Lovers' 45 poster, Beggars Banquet Records (June 1981)

BAUHAUS: (right) *Mask* LP/ UK tour poster, Beggars Banquet Records (October 1981), **Daniel Ash** artwork; (below) French Beggars Banquet poster (*c.*1982)

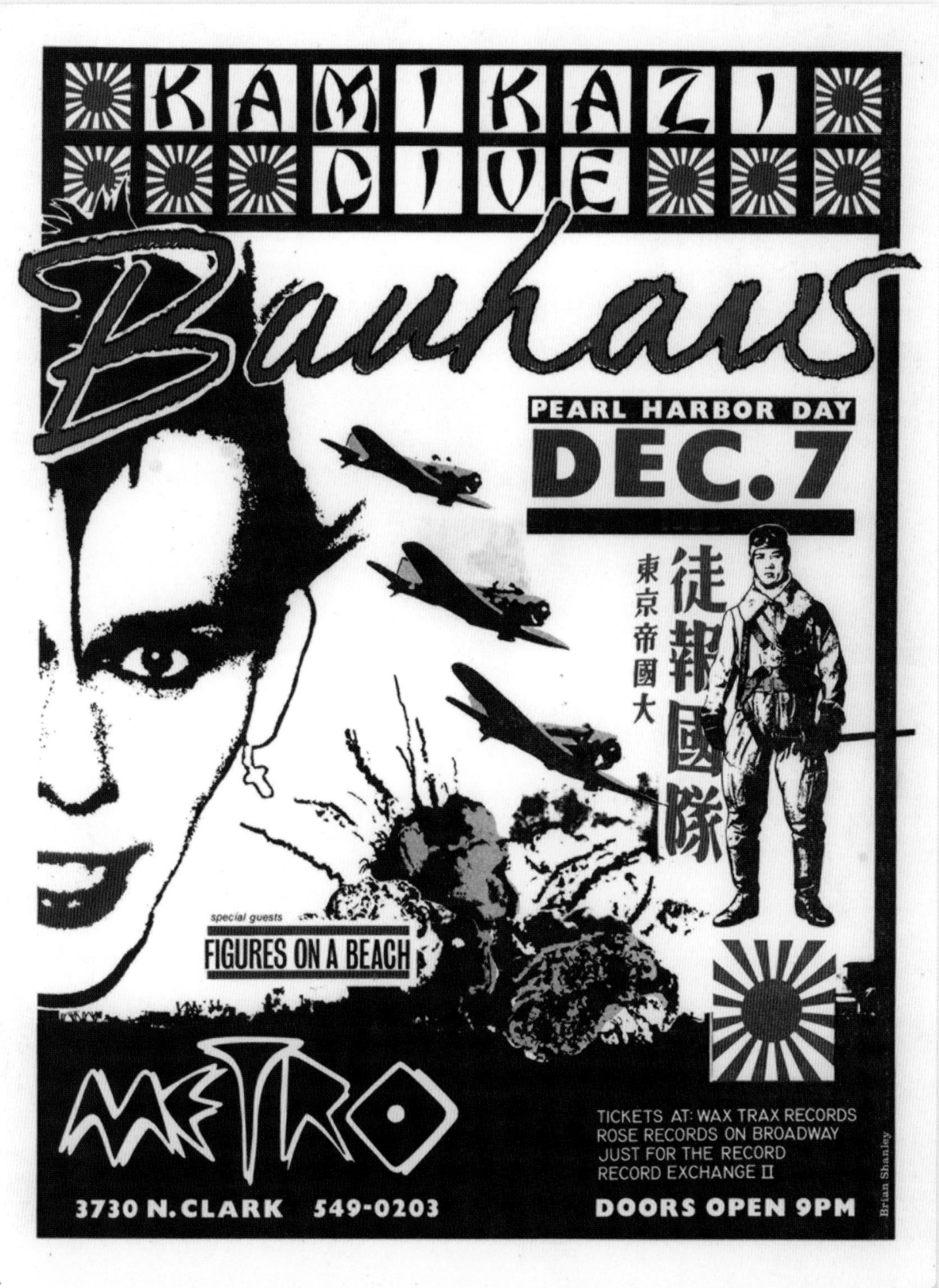

BAUHAUS: original flyer mock-up for concert at the Metro, Chicago, IL (7 December 1982)

An unusual flyer design promoting British post-punk/early gothic band Bauhaus at the height of their popularity on their US and Canada winter tour. The typography for the band's name here is taken directly from the sleeve of their single 'Ziggy Stardust', a cover of David Bowie's 1972 classic and a major chart hit for the band in the spring of 1982, but most other visual components are rather incongruous with any of the band's other graphics. Singer Pete Murphy's face is prominent, but the Kamikazi Dive theme and Japanese elements are slightly at odds with the typical graphic styles associated with the band – even their classic logotype fails to make an appearance.

Russ Bestley

BAUHAUS: *Sky's Gone Out* LP/concert poster for performance at Gaumont, Ipswich, Beggars Banquet Records (July 1983), **Daniel Ash** artwork

THE BIRTHDAY PARTY: flyer for concert with Mass and In Camera at the Clarendon Hotel, Hammersmith, London (30 October 1980), **Gary Asquith** design

THE BIRTHDAY PARTY: *Prayers on Fire* LP poster/ US tour blank, Thermidor Records (1981)

BLACK FLAG: flyer for concert at City Club, Detroit, MI (3 September 1982)

CRAMPED

By Michael Wilde

I feel like I knew The Cramps before I ever heard them play. In one sense it's true; I remember one steamy night downtown, on a 2am orange juice run with a friend who had moved to the city earlier that year (1976), when his name was called out from the shadows. 'Lux!' he replied congenially (they had known each other from earlier Vip Vop days). For the next twenty minutes four of us were hanging out on a stoop in the dark. Nobody made any introductions. Lux was squatting, smoking a cigarette, and somebody else was leaning against the iron railing: a fawn in clear, silvery high heels – or more properly, the satyr from the Martell cognac ad *c.*1905, with pale deeply pockmarked skin, a shock of blond hair and a grim Rapidograph-drawn line of a mouth, giving me what can only be described as the Evil Eye. This was the first trans I'd ever seen – but trans what? (I couldn't say.) He seemed part hell spawn, part sparrow, and as far as 'the eye', I know it when I'm given it: it's only happened two times in my life and this was one of them. He stared at me fixedly the entire twenty minutes, without uttering a vowel. I later found out this was Bryan Gregory, whom I came to recognize from their first single, 'The Way I Walk', featuring a green and grainy image of The Cramps backlit against some trees, or maybe from the bottom of a fishbowl (your choice). So I 'met' them first (at least Lux and Bryan), although to say 'meet' might be

THE CRAMPS: (above) flyer (1976), **The Cramps** design; (opposite, top) flyer for gig at CBGB's, New York City (24 May 1977), **The Cramps** design; (opposite, bottom) flyer for gig at CBGB's (January 1979)

stretching it. We were together on a tiny stoop in the middle of the night. Lux was amiably chatting away. They may have been taking a break from Max's that night (the neighbourhood was right) because somebody (a groupie?) showed up with a joint and started jabbering about the club. Lux was polite. We took our cue and booked. I remember his voice as being a little bit goofy and very soft-spoken.

My next run-in was when I actually saw them play. I was attracted immediately by the whole gestalt, I recognized all the images on their flyers, created by Lux and Ivy together, they used collage, favouring the heads and faces of well- and little-known horror movie images pasted onto the bodies of beach blanket bingos, including one for the CBGB theatre show that uses Barbara Shelley's vampire head from *Dracula, Prince of Darkness* (1966) on the body of a bobbysoxer; Lon Chaney's Erik as Poe's Masque of the Red Death from the 1925 *Phantom of the Opera* relaxing in an Eames chair; the human alligator from *The Alligator People* (1959) sipping a Coke; the original King Kong (1933) about to play a record on a portable turntable; and the ape from *Bela Lugosi Meets a Brooklyn Gorilla* (1952) doing the Twist with a chain in his nose, as well as the *Famous Monsters of Filmland* font incorporated into their moniker. That drew me like a fly to a Venus flytrap; The Cramps were my people, from the beginning. None of the other bands and nothing in the

rest of punk and everything that followed came close. The only other performer I've seen emit that much unhinged insane energy on a stage is Iggy, but even he was never quite as demented. It's as though Lux was channelling every single grade-Z movie and lunatic record out there, fine-tuning and refocusing them into white-hot light. You didn't so much as leave a Cramps concert as tremble out of one. The songs themselves don't do it justice. When I listen to 'Surfin' Bird', for example, I'm forever aware that vinyl, as lucky as we are to have it, can only capture 30 or 35 per-cent of what actually took place. My friend Paul Rodriguez – he's the tall kid in white shirt, over-alls and glasses sitting front-row centre looking off to the right on the back cover of *Gravest Hits* (1979), the photo taken at their Saturday, 1 April 1977, concert at CBGB's 2nd Ave. theatre, a dere-lict building on 4th Street and 2nd Avenue whose life as a venue for bands was short – recalls The Cramps' beginning to play 'Big Bird' that night, 'but Lux couldn't be seen at first. Then he strutted onto stage with a gallon jug of red wine hooked through his finger, took a long draught until wine ran down his front, raised the bottle over his head and brought it down onto the stage with all of his might. The bottle bounced across the stage and rested, unbroken, next to the drum set. Everyone booed. Lux repeated this twice with the same result then walked offstage. He returned with a hammer. He entered the audience with the mic in his mouth, somehow screaming and moaning despite it. He crawled on the floor, walked across people's heads, shook, rattled, shivered and convulsed. Bryan was rolling around onstage. His black-and-white polka dot-ted-guitar screaming to Lux's hiccups. He rolled through the shards of the wine bottle and began bleeding from several places. Ivy stared off into space, expressionless, like she and her rhythm guitar were playing from a remote island. Nick was inscrutable behind his shades, as always. By the time they finished, the stage and Bryan were covered in blood and wine. The drum set was destroyed, The Cramps logo on the bass drum fluttering where it had been kicked in. The lights came up and we all looked at each other as if to say, "...Oh...My...God...What Just Happened?"'

Another friend recalls attending the Alex Chilton-produced recording sessions for The Cramps' *Songs the Lord Taught Us* at the fabled Ardent Studios, of how Bryan had a 357-looking Magnum strapped to his leg which he placed religiously atop his amp, bookended with lighted candles (he doesn't know whether it was loaded or not). Later that night they played at a local bar and Lux began tearing up the joint: literally ripping up the baseboards from the apron of the stage until the owner ran out with a baseball bat and started swinging it at Lux's head. My friend recalls them fondly as 'really nice people'.

Much has been written about The Cramps, and from all who ever met or knew Lux (or 'Rick' in the early days when he was a painter of strange and psychedelic canvas), the word most often used for him is always 'sweet' or as Lux himself would say, 'the nicest guy you'll ever meet'; I can't help but wonder, though, at the genie on-stage – the one who in some fairytale came out of the bottle in a great hazardous cloud of spar-kling green gas, the terrifying troll with crazy hair who held our howling beating hearts in his hand, madly refusing to ever let go.

THE CRAMPS: *A Date With Elvis* LP poster, Big Beat Records (1986), **Stephen Bickerstaff** design

THE CRAMPS: flyer for concert at CBGB's, New York City, NY (24 May 1977), **The Cramps** design

THE CRAMPS: flyer for performance at CBGB's, New York City, NY (February 1978)

THE CRAMPS: (above) 'Rock Rock Rock It' flyer yellow version (1977), **The Cramps** design; (below) 'Human Fly' / 'Domino' 45 poster, Vengeance Records (1978), **The Cramps** design, **Steven Blauner** photography, courtesy of **Michael Wilde**

THE CRAMPS: 'Human Fly' colour 45 poster, Vengeance Records (1978), **X3 Studio/Bob Linney** and **Ken Maharg** design

'Human Fly' was the band's second single, on Vengeance Records. The label was founded by The Cramps, exclusively to issue their records, and continues to release their catalogue into the twenty-first century.

Andrew Krivine

THE CRAMPS: concert poster for the Hurrah club (Halloween 1978), **The Cramps** design, courtesy of Michael Wilde

THE CRAMPS: reproduction gig poster for Max's Kansas City, New York City, NY (November 1978), **The Cramps** design

THE CRAMPS: (below) flyer for concert at Max's Kansas City, New York City, NY (December 1978), **The Cramps** design

- 13 June 1978 photo taken at Napa State mental institution
- 3–4 September 1978 poster for NYC venue Hurrah
- key framing information via banal support structure of photo credit 'Photo taken by an inmate at Napa State Mental Hospital'
- gig as method of producing image / association with the downtrodden; Napa State is to The Cramps as Folsom Prison was to Johnny Cash
- means of representation is shaky / queasy / unfocused, signifying the view of the insane
- also signifiers of avant-garde developments in photography
- tag line adapts 'They're Coming to Take Me Away, Ha-Haaa!', a 1966 novelty single by Napoleon XIV, linking mental institution happening to gig at NYC's Hurrah's – implying that it's going to get crazy for the audience
- deliberate composition
- comic book horror logo is crisp and well-executed
- Apollinairian typography is crude, yet deliberately set, expressing overall concept of disorientation
- not a flyer, but a promo image
- a composite incorporating a photographic print, 2 sizes of press type and a cutout band logo on top * a promo image used behind glass in 'coming soon' displays at the entries of clubs
- actual marketing efforts
- halftone image indicated offset printing, meaning at least 500 copies produced to promote the show
- LUXurious!
- 'Somebody told me you people are crazy! But I'm not so sure about that; you seem all right to me.'

Glen Cummings / Adam Michaels

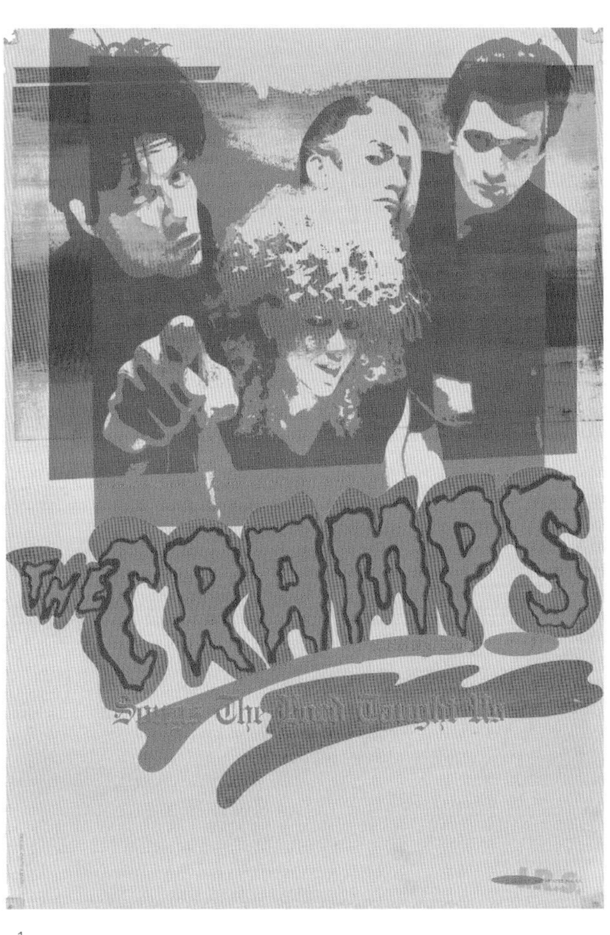

1

2

3

THE CRAMPS: 1 *Songs the Lord Taught Us* LP poster, IRS Records (1980), **X3 Studio/Bob Linney** and **Ken Maharg** design; **2** *Songs the Lord Taught Us* LP poster, Illegal Records (1980); **3** *Smell of Female* French LP poster, New Rose Records (1983), **Nancy Ribiere** photography

THE CRAMPS: *Off the Bone* compilation LP poster, Illegal Records (1983), **Dead Jaw** design

THE CRAMPS: (left) poster for concert with Specimen at the Hammersmith Palais, London (29 May 1984)

THE CRAMPS: (above, left) *Bad Music for Bad People* LP poster, EMI Records (1984), **Stephen Blickenstaff** artwork; (above, right) *A Date With Elvis* LP poster, Big Beat Records (1986), **The Cramps** design and photo, **Phil Smee** title lettering

1

2

3

EFFIGIES: 1 flyer for concert at Clutch Cargo's, Detroit, MI (17 July 1982), image of Peter Boyle as the monster in Mel Brooks' *Young Frankenstein* (1974); **2** 'We're Da Machine' EP poster, Ruthless Records (1983), **R. Broecker** design

FLESH EATERS: 3 flyer for concert in Los Angeles, CA (*c.* February 1982)

holy city
ZOO
WORD OF MOUTH
Mon 10th May
MODERN ENGLISH
Tues 11th May
APOLLO
Wed 12th May
THE LAUNCHING OF EGO
Mon 17th May
CHINA CRISIS
Tues 18th May
LOST CAUSE
Wed 19th May
THE NIGHT SHOW
Mon 24th May
THE OUTRAGOUS
TRUE LIFE CONFESSIONS
Tues 25th May
PYRAMID
Mon 31st
TEARS FOR FEARS.
Tues 1st June
BABYLON REBELS
THE NERVOUS KIND
HOLY CITY ZOO·MEMBERS CLUB · BIRMINGHAM · 021-233-1266 *

HOLY CITY ZOO: Birmingham club calendar poster (May 1982), featuring Peter Murphy of Bauhaus

THE MISFITS: (left) 'Bullet' 45 tour poster, Plan 9 Records (1978), **Glen Danzig** design; (below) flyer for concert at Max's Kansas City, New York City, NY (August 1978)

1

2

3

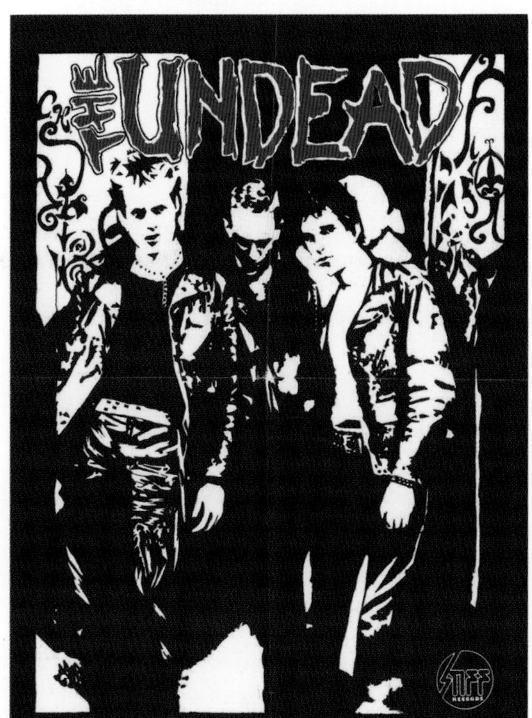

4

MISFITS: 1 poster for concert at Mabuhay Gardens, San Francisco, CA (24 June 1983);

THE SISTERS OF MERCY: 2 'Alice' 45 front cover, Merciful Release (1982), the gold latticework appropriates Henri Matisse's 1952 cutout work 'Blue Nude II';

SPECIMEN: 3 'Returning (From A Journey)' 45 flyer, London Records (1983);

THE UNDEAD: 4 'Nine Toes Later' EP poster, Stiff Records (1982)

THE UNDEAD: 'Never Say Die!' 45 poster, Post Morten Records (1985)

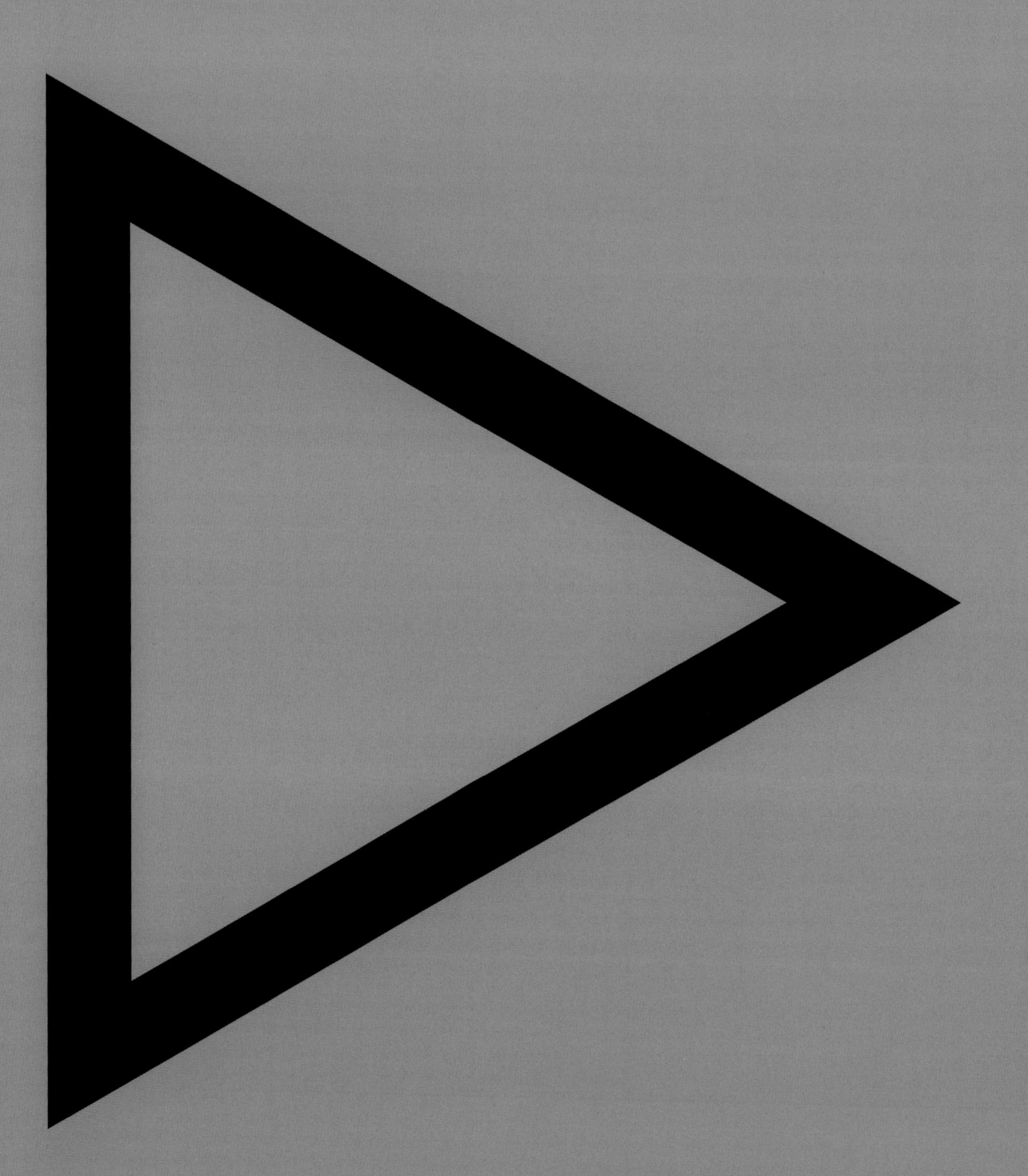

WARDANCE: POST-PUNK APOCALYPSE IN FULL COLOUR

By Andrew Krivine

For the sake of simplicity, the definition of 'post-punk' used here encompasses those acts who came out of, and after, the initial punk explosion but who took something from it. Some may seem incongruous in this context, but not to my mind. Nineteen seventy-nine was a messy transitional year: amidst the dying embers of punk's first wave and the stillborn mod revival (which, in retrospect, barely lasted beyond the summer), the first green shoots of post-punk appeatred. (As an aside, to their credit, The Jam, one of my favourite bands, who were at their creative zenith in 1979, wisely avoided being too closely associated with the mod revival despite efforts by the music press to tag them as its founding fathers.)

Post-punk was coming together in 1979 but emerged in full flower in 1980, heralding a second burst of music and design creativity. The works set forth in this chapter are as sophisticated, intriguing and eclectic as those produced during the punk era. Within this chapter is included a small sample of the British anarcho-punk movement which, led by the Crass collective, really began in earnest following the election of Margaret Thatcher as prime minister. There are also works advertising gigs and releases by politically aware bands such as Gang of Four from Leeds and Pop Group from Bristol, who mixed funk and free-form jazz with a punk aesthetic. From Manchester, A Certain Ratio and Joy Division (closely followed by New Order, of course) created hard-edged, semi-industrial rhythms to create a sound of their city, and Peter Saville turned that sound into a visual aesthetic unique to its time and place, while drawing on past art movements and styles. In 1978 the band Killing Joke formed in West London and a year later started their own record company and named it Malicious Damage. The band and label's visual identity was designed and refined by Mike Coles, whose work is as provocative and

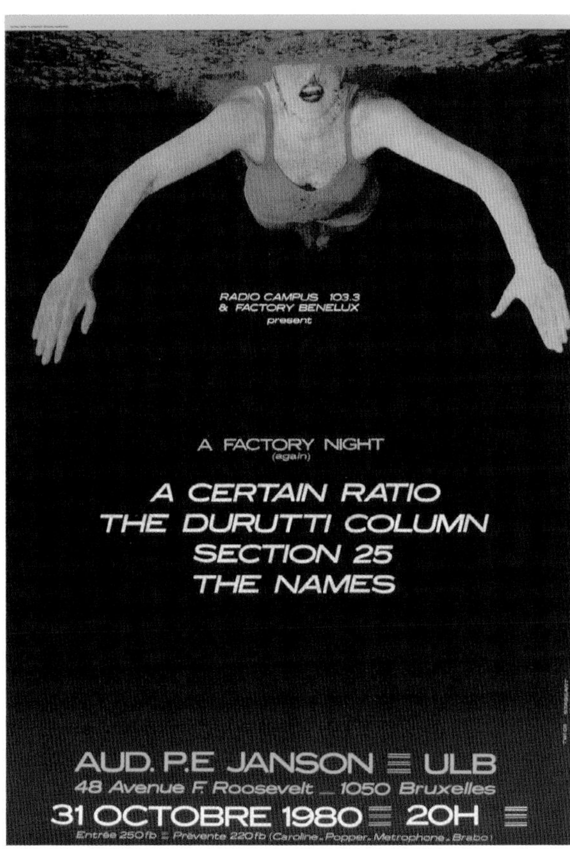

A CERTAIN RATIO: poster for concert in Brussels (31 October 1980)

thoughtful as any to be found in this book. As the 1970s ended it seemed revolutionary that graphic designers such as Cole, Peter Saville and Malcolm Garrett were as well-known by the record-buying public as the members of bands whose music their work adorned.

It's no accident that matters of graphic design became part of the music press discourse at a time when changes in printing technology were allowing the inclusion of colour pages in what had previously been a strictly black-and-white 'inky' affair. The design of sleeves and advertisements were discussed by journalists in the UK who had been to art schools and universities and who sprinkled articles with references to Futurists, Russian constructivism, German expressionism and Dada. In the 1980s the rise of magazines like *The Face* and *i.D.* not only showcased graphic design but were themselves graphic design statements, and while the bands that they featured were not always cover stars, it was their attitude to commercial design as much as their sound which made them essential content.

There are works here representing post-punk acts from America where, despite the hardcore scene persisting for so long and new wave being more radio friendly, achieved much greater fame than punk acts had managed. It gave the world Pere Ubu and REM, among others, for instance. The inclusion of Blondie in this section is because while they came from the original New York pre-1977 punk scene, their huge worldwide success made millions of people aware that there was such a 'thing' as punk two years after the movement had first flared into being. Yes, they were pop stars too.

By 1986, the idea of sub-genres of music was becoming obsolete as the ever-growing corporate music machine swallowed up the once-thriving indie pioneers of punk, and MTV regurgitated 1950s-style rock 'n' roll revolution via self-consciously 'edgy' videos. The Smiths, arguably the last great independently released post-punk band, broke up in 1987, and before long their record label Rough Trade was no more.

Geologically, aftershocks can be more seismically powerful than the initial earthquake. As readers look at the images across the following pages, perhaps they might agree that a strong case can be made that post-punk produced such an after-effect, in both sonic and graphic design terms.

BLONDIE: *Plastic Letters* LP poster, Chrysalis Records (1978)

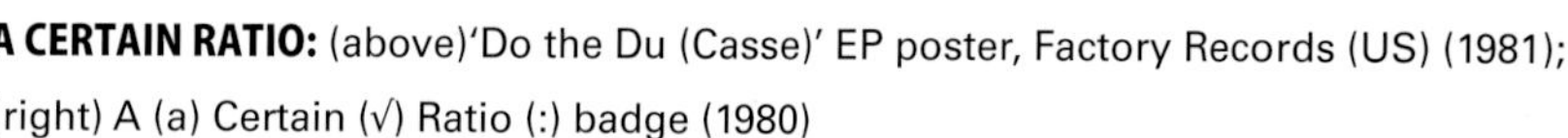

A CERTAIN RATIO: (above)'Do the Du (Casse)' EP poster, Factory Records (US) (1981); (right) A (a) Certain (√) Ratio (:) badge (1980)

1

2

3

1 ATHLETICO SPIZZ 80: *Do A Runner* LP poster, A&M Records (1980), **Rocking Russian** design

2 AU PAIRS: *Playing with a Different Sex* LP poster, Human Records (1981), **Rocking Russian** design; **3** *Sense and Sensuality* LP poster, Kamera Records (1982), **Citizen Bank** design, appropriating a design from El Lissitzky's 1920 'Suprematist Story of Two Squares'

BASEMENT 5: *1965–1980* LP poster, Island Records (1980), **Dennis Morris** photography

This design is one of the strongest photo-collage examples of the period. Basement 5 were the first British punk-informed black rock group (also preceding both Bad Brains and Living Colour), and at various times included former Roxy DJ, filmmaker Don Letts, his B.A.D. co-founder Leo Williams, and photographer/designer Dennis Morris. Some have categorized their sound as 'reggae punk fusion'. Their only LP was produced by Martin Hannett, the legendary producer for Joy Division who also produced U2's first single and Buzzcocks' debut 'Spiral Scratch' EP (under the alias 'Martin Zero').

Andrew Krivine

BLUE ORCHIDS
AGENTS OF CHANGE
THAT IS WHAT I WANT.
EP EP EP EP EP EP EP

BLONDIE: (above) *Parallel Lines* banner poster, Chrysalis Records (1978), **Ramey Communications** design, **Edo** photography

BLUE ORCHIDS: (left) 'Agents of Change' EP poster, Rough Trade Records (1982)

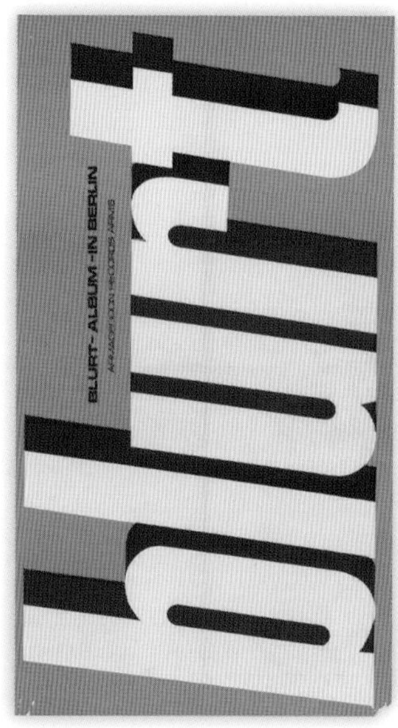

BLURT: (above) *In Berlin* LP poster, Armageddon Records (1981)

1

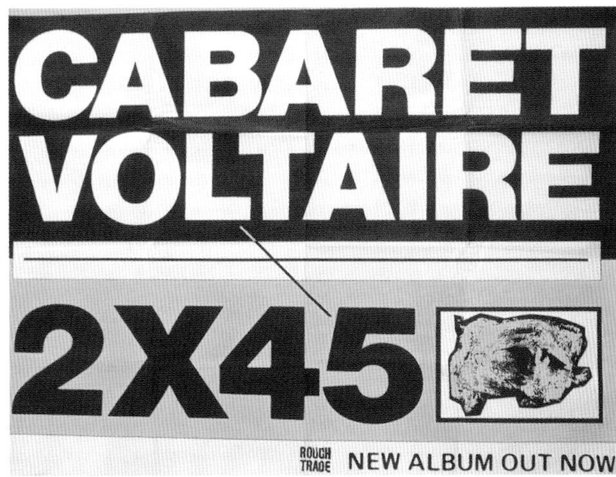

2

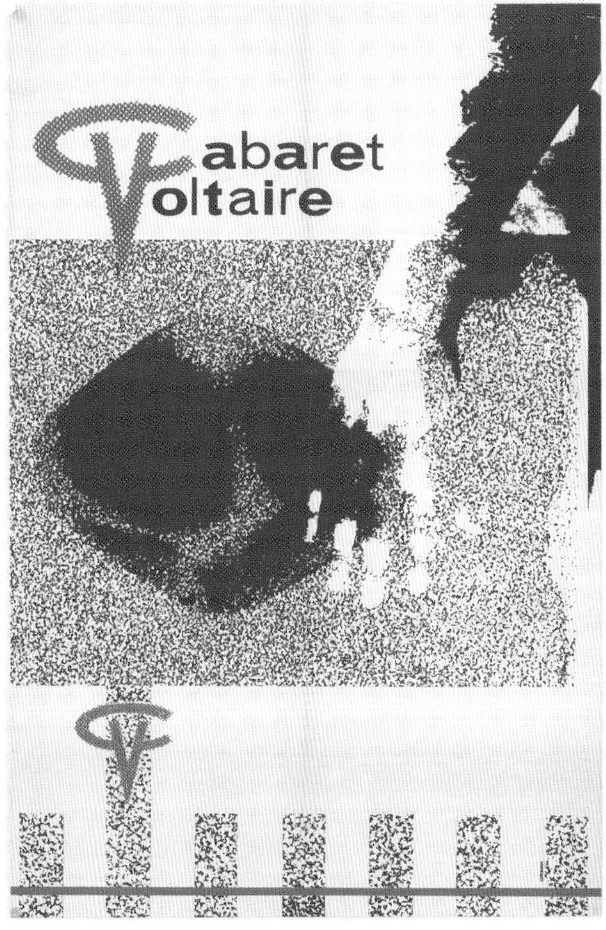

3

CABARET VOLTAIRE: 1 poster for gig at University of London (May 1981); **2 Neville Brody**-designed flyer for the band's fourth album (1982); **3** promotional poster (*c.*1980)

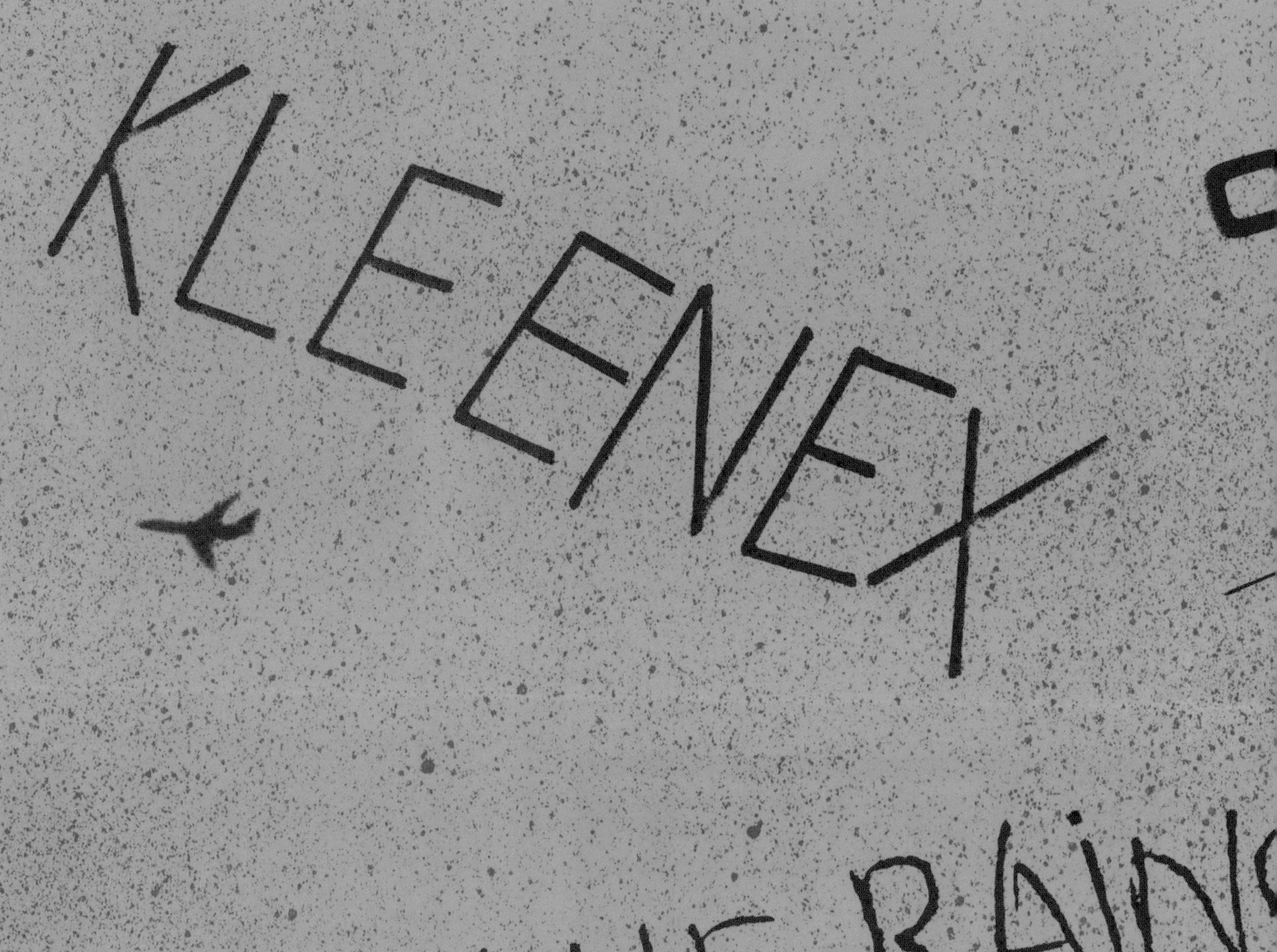
KLEENEX
ROUGH TRADE TOUR
INFORMATION: 01-229-2146

CABARET VOLTAIRE:
Rough Trade Records
package tour flyer (1979)

CHROME: (above, left) *Half Machine Lip Moves* LP advertisement, Siren Records (March 1979)

CLOCK DVA: (above, right) '4 Hours' 45 poster, Fetish Records (1981), **Neville Brody** design

THE COMSAT ANGELS: (above) *Sleep No More* LP poster, Polydor Records (August 1981); (right) *Land* LP poster, Jive Records (1983), **John Sims** design

YOUR COUNTRY NEEDS
YOU

This haunting image of a desiccated hand impaled on barbed wire is a powerful anti-war photograph courtesy of the anarcho-punk band, Crass. The poster lifted the phrase 'Your Country Needs You' from a famous image of Lord Kitchener (Britain's secretary of state for war during World War I), first used on the cover of London *Opinion* magazine *c.*1915. The Crass logo was created by Dave King, the designer also responsible for the Danceteria logo.

Andrew Krivine

CRASS: *The Feeding of the 5,000* LP poster; uncensored reissue of the album, Crass Records (1981), **Gee Vaucher** design

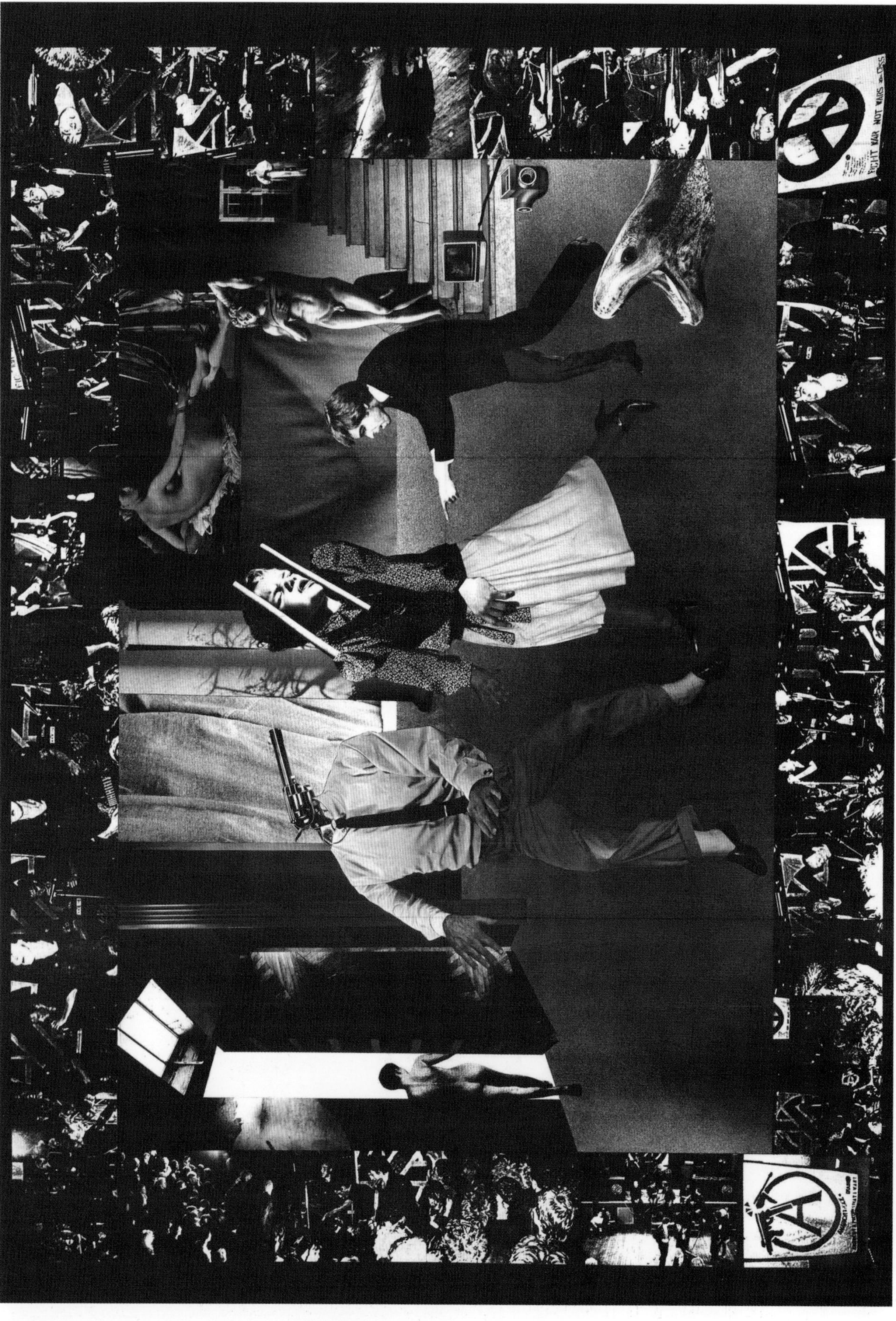

CRASS: *Stations of the Crass* front of LP poster, Crass Records (1979), **Gee Vaucher** design, **Dave King** logo

1

2

3

1 THE CRUCIFUCKS: *Wisconsin* LP poster, Alternative Tentacles Records (1986); **2 CRASS:** 'Nagasaki Nightmare' 45 front cover, Crass Records (1980), **Crass** design (record sleeve colored by previous owner); **3 CRASS LABEL: Sleeping Dogs**, 'Beware' 45 poster, Crass Records (1982)

CRASS: *Christ – The Album/ Well Forked – But Not Dead* LP poster, Crass Records (1982), **Gee Vaucher** (as 'G. Sus') design

IT'S A
MARVELOUS LIFE
NGTHENED SHADOW OF ONE PERSON

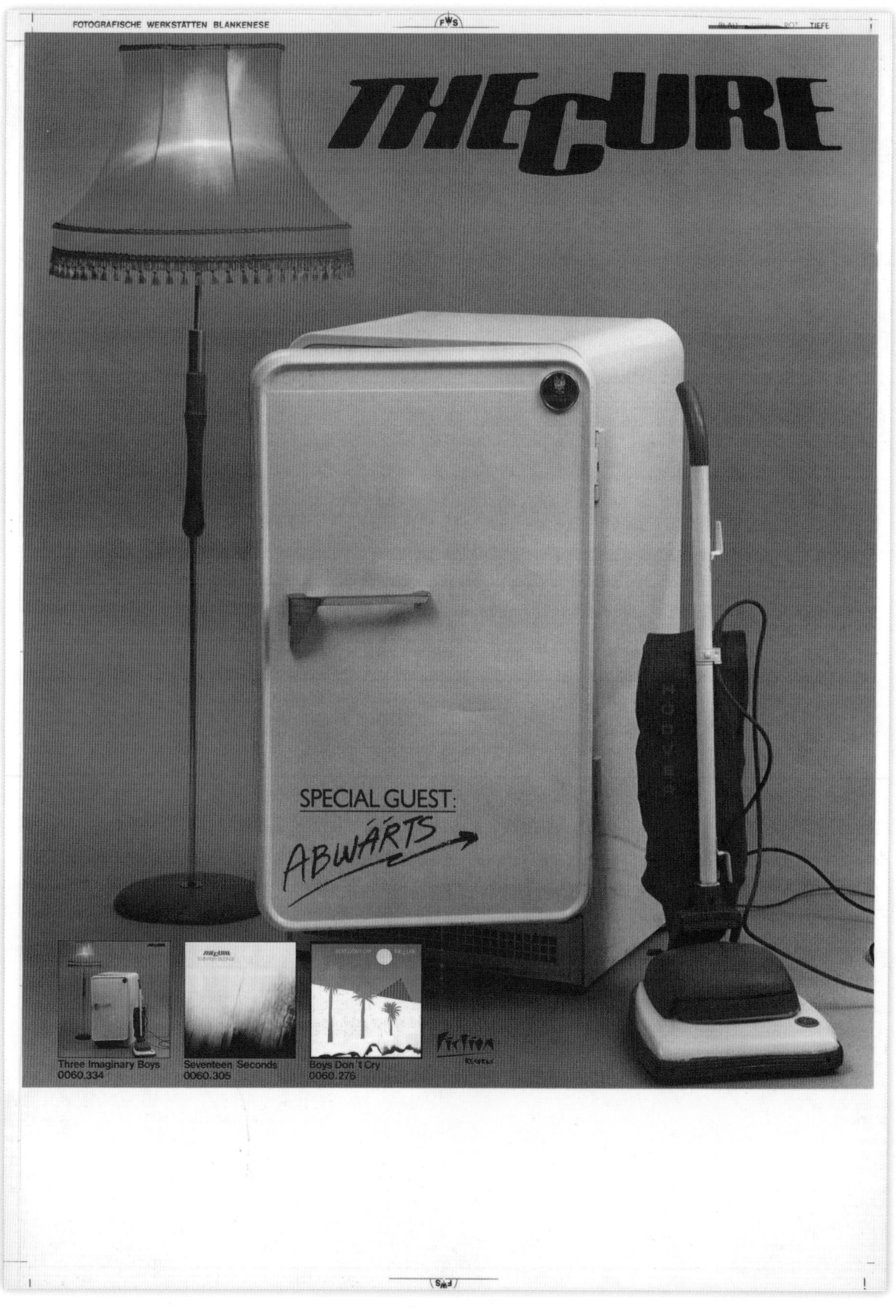

THE CURE: *Three Imaginary Boys* German LP poster, Fiction Records (1979), **Bill Smith** design, **Dave Dragon** artwork, **Bill Smith** and **Martyn Goddard** photography

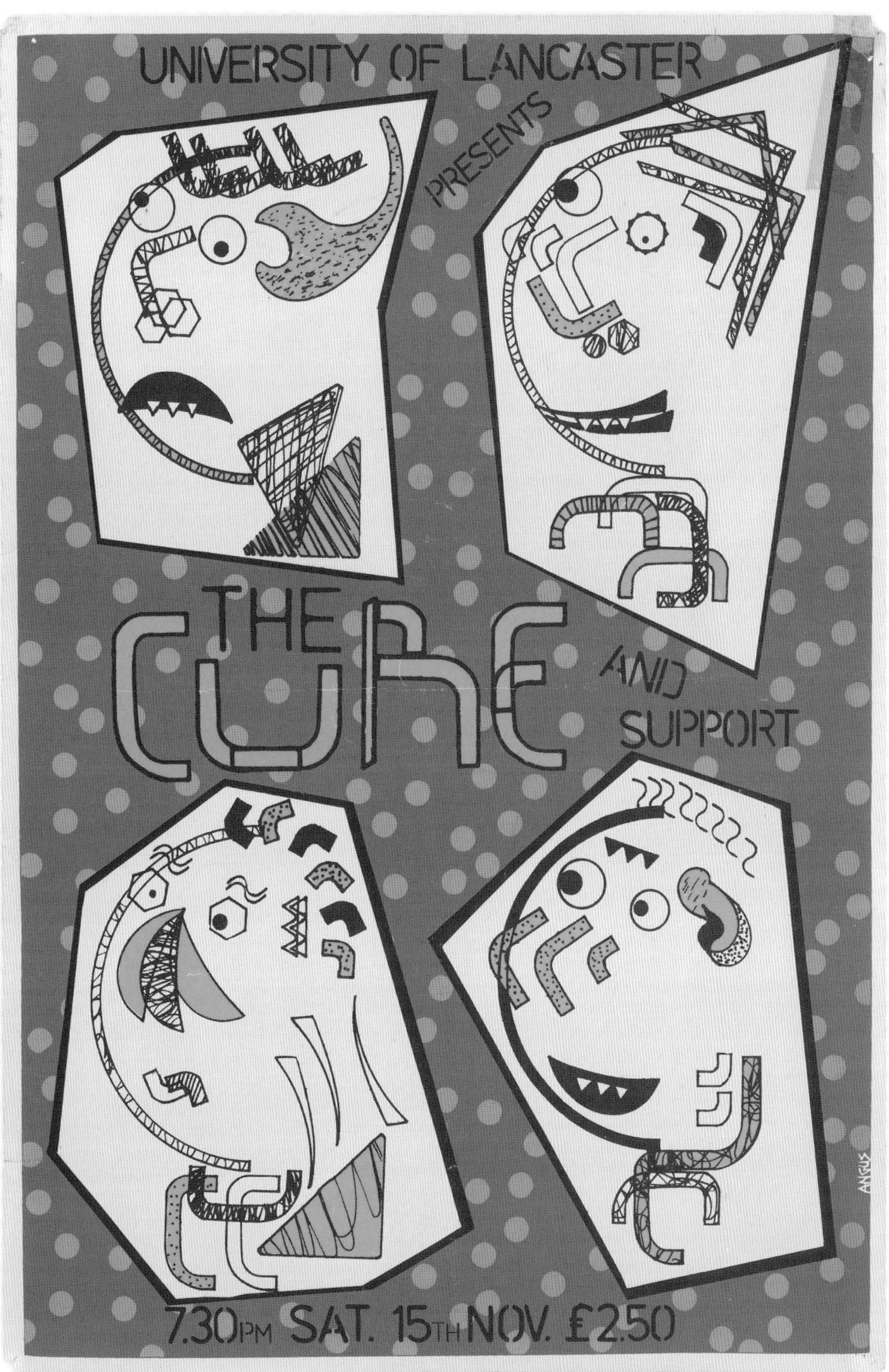

THE CURE: poster for concert atThe University of Lancaster (15 November 1980)

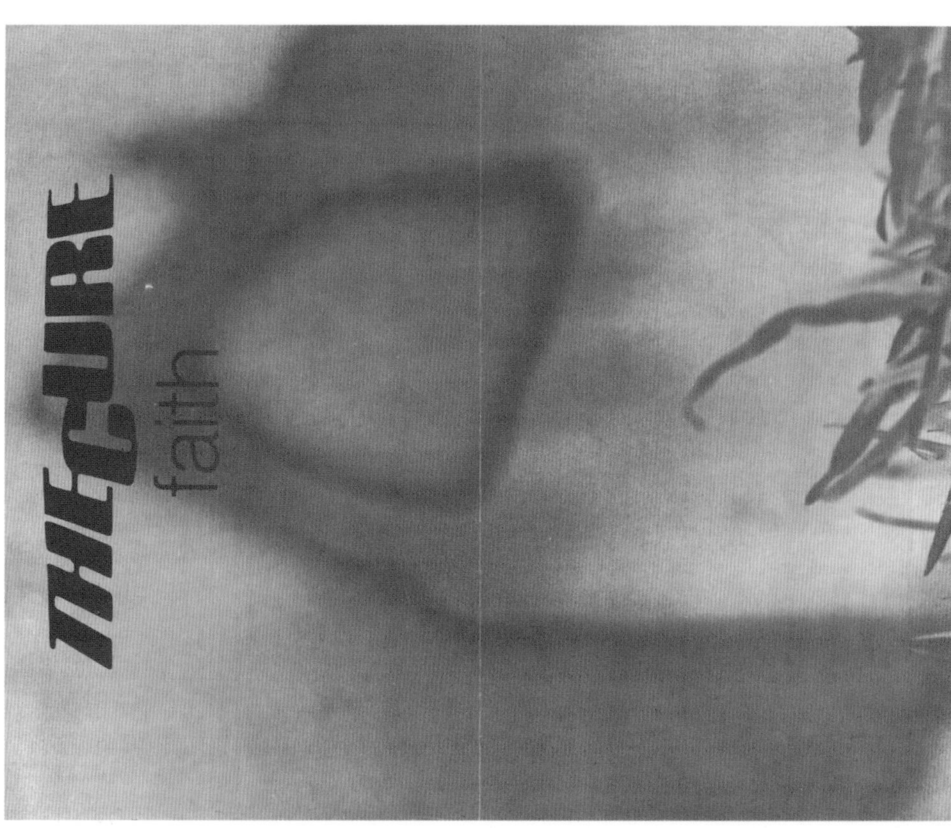

THE CURE: (above) *Faith* LP poster, Fiction Records (1981), **Andy Vella** and **Porl Thompson** artwork; (below) Future Pastimes UK tour poster, Fiction Records (November 1979)

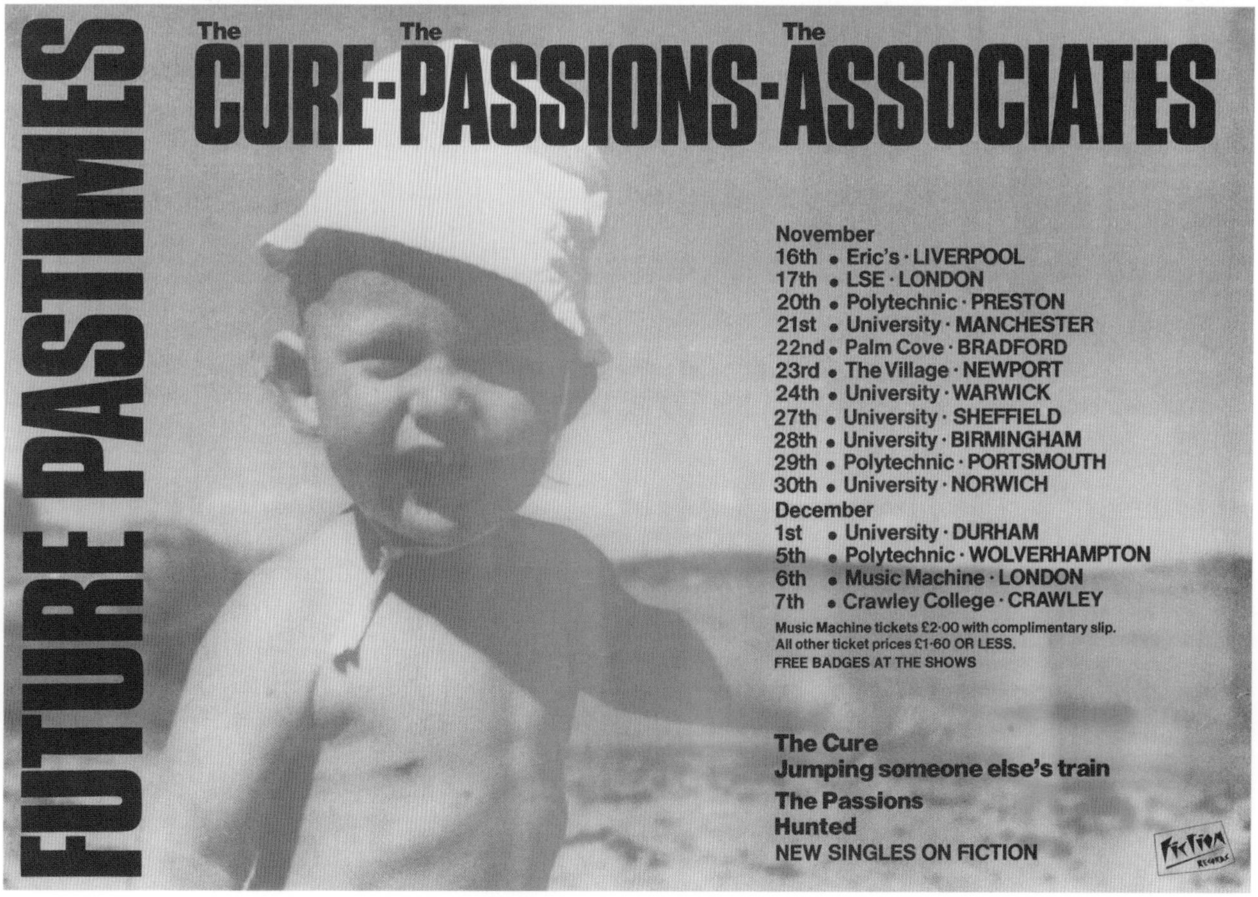

FUTURE PASTIMES

The CURE - The PASSIONS - The ASSOCIATES

November
16th • Eric's · LIVERPOOL
17th • LSE · LONDON
20th • Polytechnic · PRESTON
21st • University · MANCHESTER
22nd • Palm Cove · BRADFORD
23rd • The Village · NEWPORT
24th • University · WARWICK
27th • University · SHEFFIELD
28th • University · BIRMINGHAM
29th • Polytechnic · PORTSMOUTH
30th • University · NORWICH
December
1st • University · DURHAM
5th • Polytechnic · WOLVERHAMPTON
6th • Music Machine · LONDON
7th • Crawley College · CRAWLEY

Music Machine tickets £2·00 with complimentary slip.
All other ticket prices £1·60 OR LESS.
FREE BADGES AT THE SHOWS

The Cure
Jumping someone else's train
The Passions
Hunted
NEW SINGLES ON FICTION

Fiction Records

THE CURE: (below, both) *Pornography* LP poster, Fiction Records (1982), **Ben Kelly** and **The Cure** design, **Michael Kostiff** photography

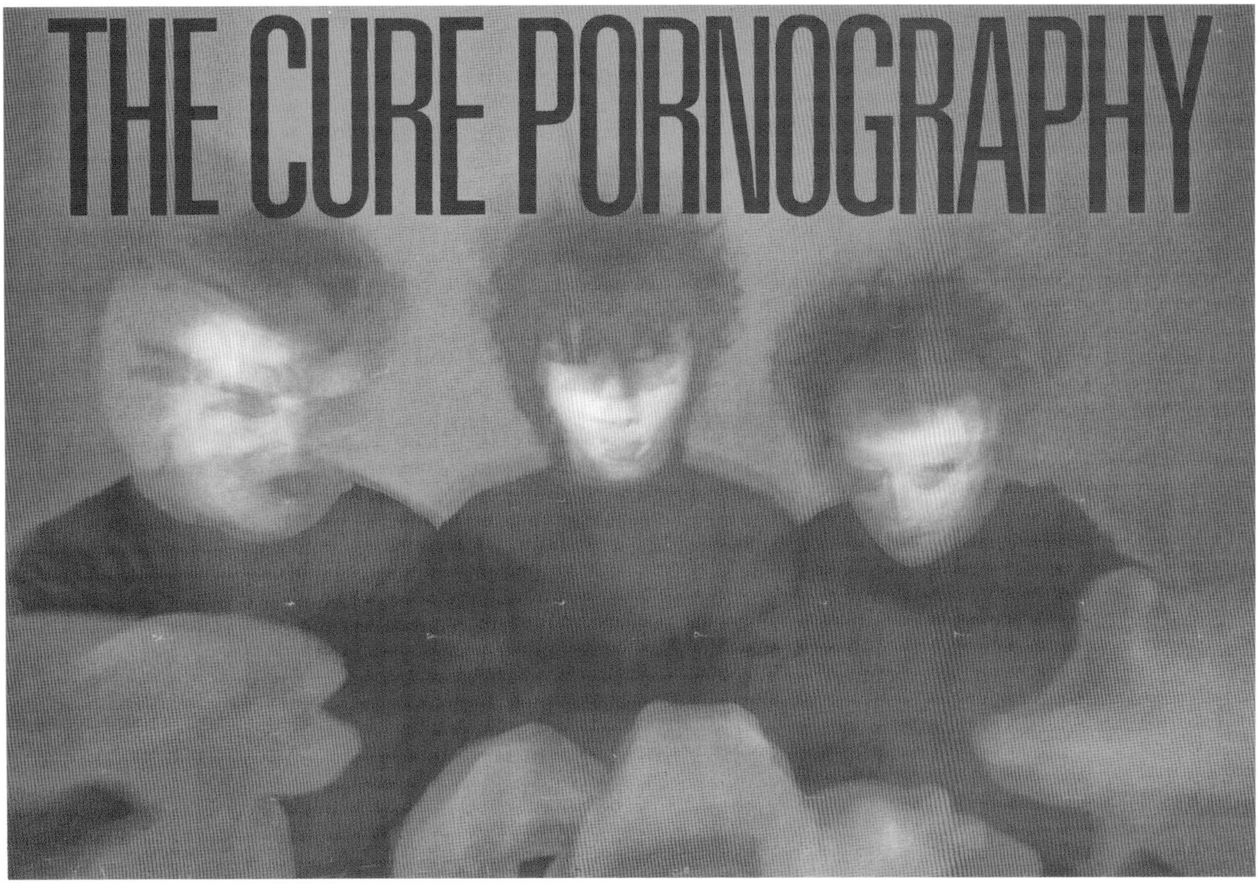

THE CURE PORNOGRAPHY

The Cure's fourth album saw them move into even more complex soundscapes and brooding lyrics, reflecting the development across their previous two albums, *Seventeen Seconds* and *Faith* toward darker, more sombre subjects. The album artwork featured heavily distorted photographs of the group by Michael Kostiff, washed in red, purple and yellow light. The cover and poster were designed and art directed by the band and Ben Kelly, who had worked on a number of record cover designs for Factory Records alongside Peter Saville, but was to make a more significant impact in the field of interior design, notably for his work on The Haçienda nightclub in Manchester, England.

Russ Bestley

1

2

3

THE CURE: 1 *The Top* LP poster, Fiction Records (1984), **Andy Vella** and **Porl Thompson** artwork; **2** *The Head on the Door* US LP poster, Elektra/Asylum Records (1985); **3** *The Head on the Door* UK LP poster, Fiction Records (1985)

DEAD CAN DANCE: (left) poster for concert at Town and Country Club, Kentish Town, London (1984)

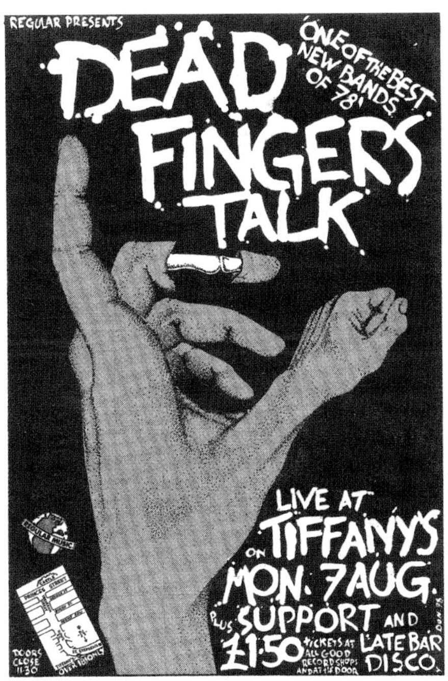

DEAD FINGERS TALK: (above) UK flyer for gig at Tiffany's nightclub, Stockbridge, Scotland (August 1978)

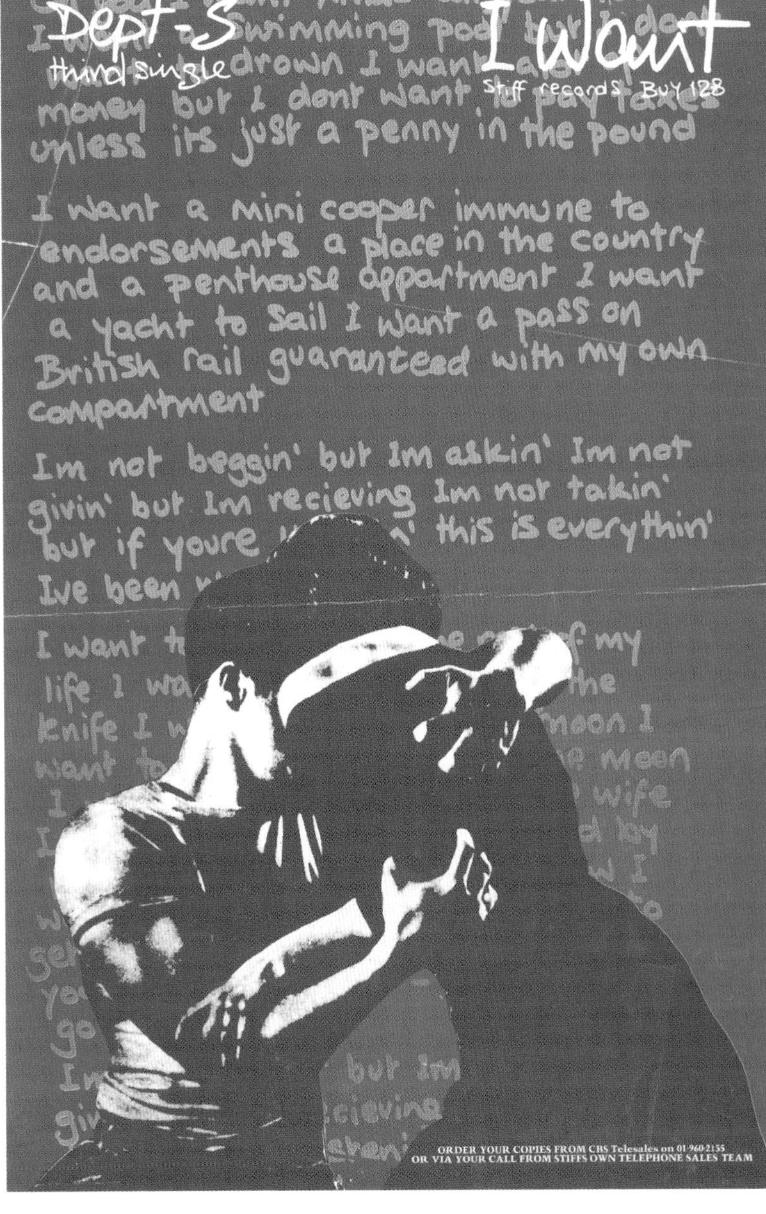

DEPARTMENT S: (right) 'I Want' 45 poster, Stiff Records (1981)

DEVO
LIVE!!
The most outrageous & most talked about group to hit Seattle
Seeing is believing . . . stop into Peaches Records for a special sneak preview!
Paramount Northwest Theatre
Wednesday, January 11, 8 PM
$7.00 advance/$8.00 day-of-show
Tickets available now at Bon Marche (downtown, Northgate, Southcenter & Tacoma Mall), Budget Tapes & Records, The Gob Shoppe in Ballard, Peaches (U-District, Tacoma), Pennylane (Crossroads, West Seattle & Bremerton), Tower Posters & Tickets.

1

A:WE ARE DEVO!
A NEW ALBUM
OUT NOW ON VIRGIN V2106
Q:ARE WE NOT MEN?

2

3

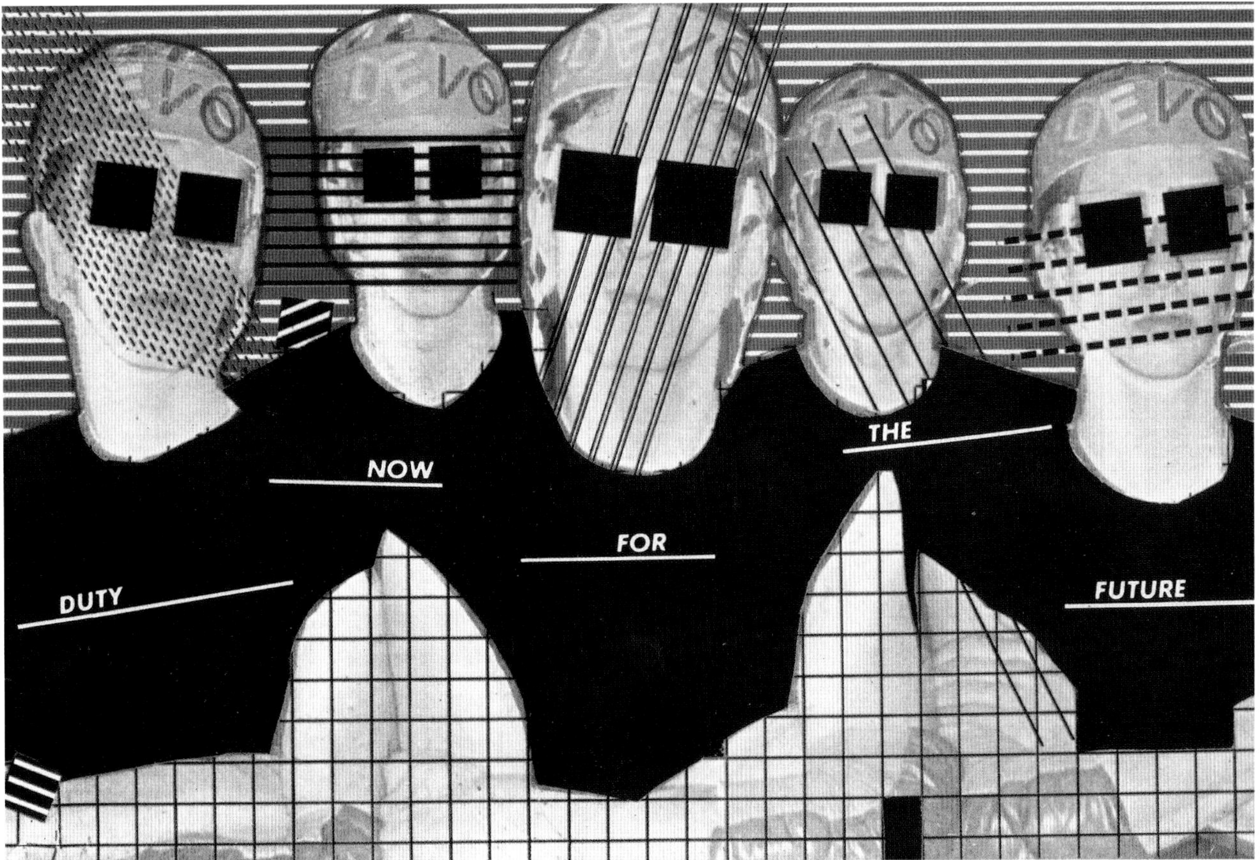

4

DEVO: 1 flyer for concert at Paramount Northwest Theatre, Seattle, WA (11 January 1978); **2** *Q: Are We Not Men? A: We Are Devo!* LP poster, Virgin Records (1978), **Cooke Key** design; **3** *Duty Now for the Future* LP poster, Warner Bros. (1979), **Devo, Inc.** design; **4** *Duty Now for the Future* LP promotional postcard, Warner Bros. Records (1979), **Janet Peir** design, **Yale Greenfield** photography

DOME: *Dome 2* LP poster, Dome Records (1980), **Russell Mills** design

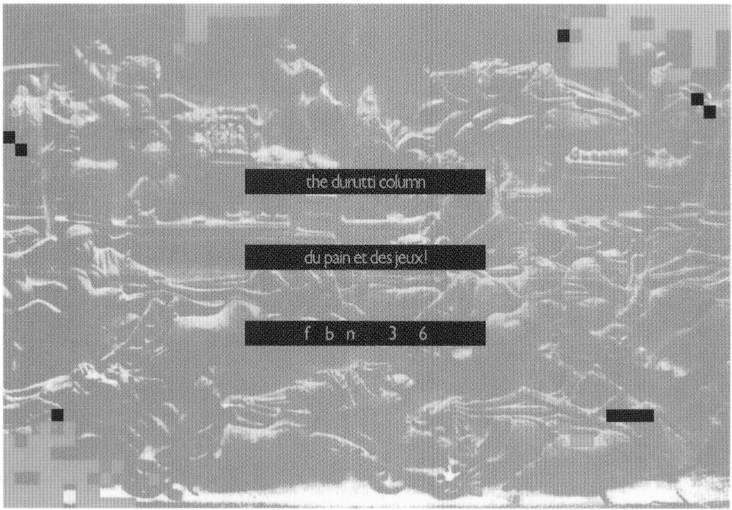

DURUTTI COLUMN: *Circuses and Bread* cassette LP poster, Factory Benelux (1986)

In 1980, after Wire played their last gig for five years, band members Bruce Gilbert and Graham Lewis began a new venture they titled Dome. The poster for their second album is credited to 'Koninck Londyn', otherwise known as Koninck Studios, home of the Quay Brothers, artist and filmmaker twins from Pennsylvania. In the following decade, the Quays would make their name with enigmatic short films heavy with an atmosphere of East European darkness and mystery. In their early years, they produced illustrations, calligraphy and designs for book covers and posters – expressionistic and surreal Polish posters were strong influences. The Quays' printed pieces from this time often feature a single bizarre or monstrous figure placed against an empty background to intensify its strangeness. The *Dome 2* avatar, perhaps wearing a helmet with eye slits, has the presence and strength of a warrior and brandishes four curved blades, although these scimitars, if that's what they are, appear to emerge from apertures in its body, as though they are lacerating their carrier. The entity's material form is both dense and withered, suggesting it could be a supernatural apparition able to change its physical state. The Quays went on to create a similarly disconcerting poster, showing a skeletal winged demon, for Dome's third release, and surreal cover graphics for Gilbert and Lewis' album as Duet Emmo ('Mute Dome'). The imagery is unlike anything else produced for British bands in the post-punk period, and its uncertain provenance gives a mysterious visual dimension to the musicians' avant-garde sound experiments in the studio.

Rick Poynor

EARTHLING: poster for concert at The Underground, New York City, NY (17 August 1981)

Earthling was an electronic/synth trio from Japan, and this concert was promoted by Jim Fouratt and Rudolph Pieper (co-founders of the club Danceteria in 1979). This is quite a striking design, integrating NY skyscrapers with a prominent 'rising sun'.

Andrew Krivine

Heaven Up Here
Ambrosia-Konzerte präsentiert:
ECHO
AND THE BUNNYMEN
in Concert
Neue LP:
Heaven Up Here
KOW 58 320
Heaven Up Here ECHO AND THE BUNNYMEN in Concert
Freitag
12.6.
20 Uhr
BONN,
RHEINTERRASSEN
Estermannstr. 138,
BAB Abfahrt Grau-Rheindorf
VORVERKAUF: KÖLN: Ambrosia, Elsaßstr. 19; Elpi; Theaterkassen: Neumarkt, Rudolfplatz, Kaufhof; DÜSSELDORF: Carmen & ZENSOR, Rock on; DUISBURG: Rock on; ESSEN: Elpi; WUPPERTAL: Elpi; BONN: Elpi, Braun-Peretti; DORTMUND: Elpi, Last chance.
Telefonische Kartenbestellungen:
AMBROSIA, Elsaßstr. 19, 5 Köln 1, 0221 / 31 93 18
Crocodiles
KOW 58 175

1

2

3

ECHO & THE BUNNYMEN: 1 poster for concert in Bonn (June 1981), **Martyn Atkins** design, **Brian Griffin** photography; **2** *The Long Days* UK tour poster (April 1981); **3** 'The Wee Scottish Tour' poster (May 1982)

1

2

ECHO & THE BUNNYMEN:
1 *Porcupine* LP poster, Korova Records (February 1983), **Martyn Atkins** design, **Brian Griffin** photography; **2** 'The Killing Moon' 45 poster, Korova Records (1984)

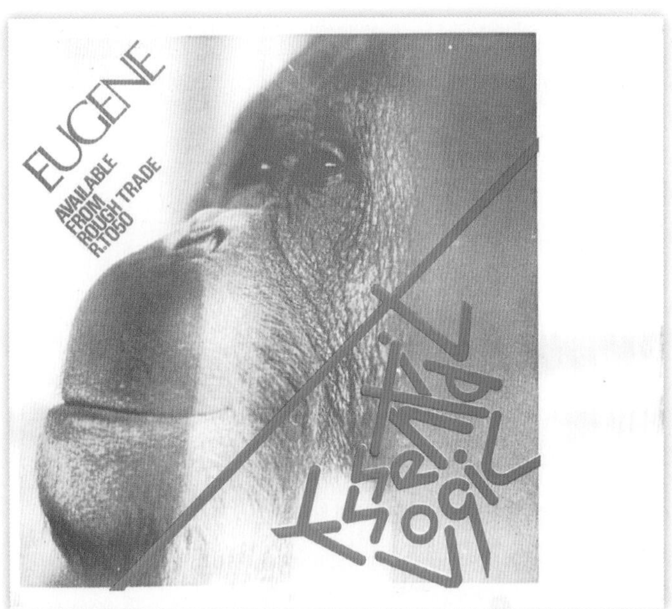

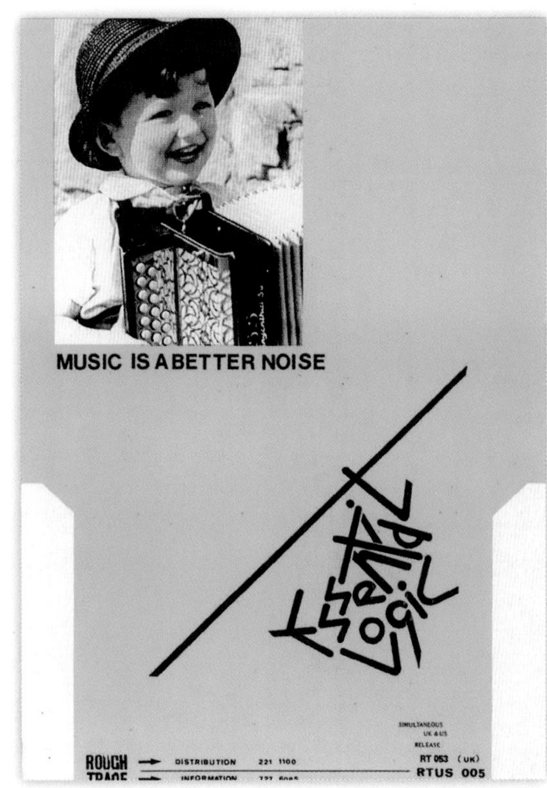

ESSENTIAL LOGIC: (above, left) 'Eugene' 45 poster, Rough Trade Records (1980), **Lora Logic** design; (above, right) 'Music is a Better Noise' 45 poster; Rough Trade Records (1980), **Lora Logic** design

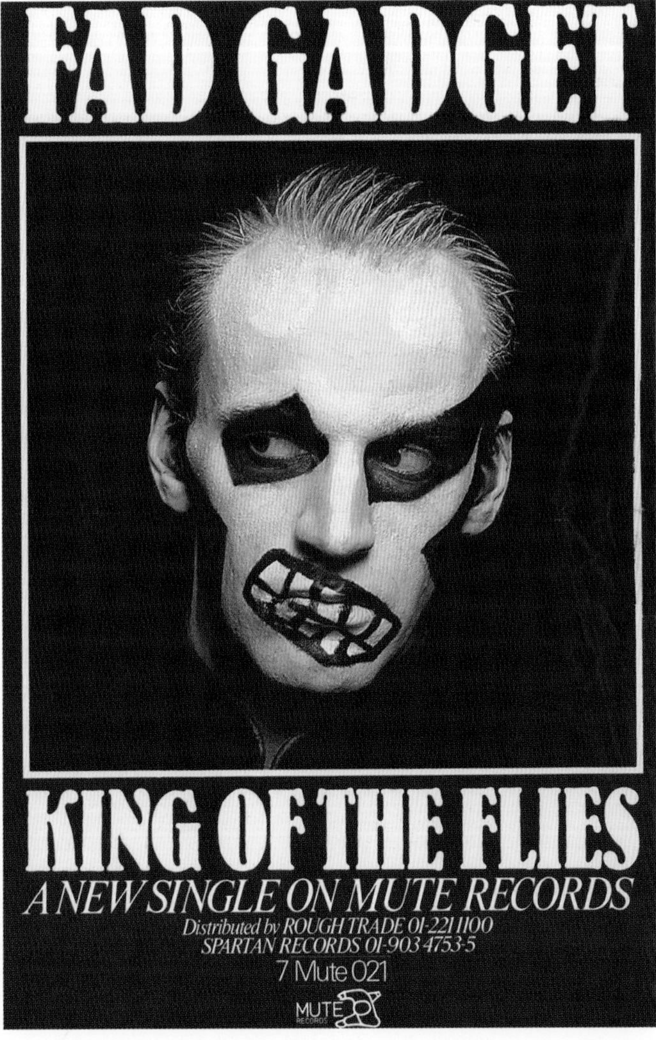

FAD GADGET: 'King of the Flies' 45 poster, Mute Records (1982)

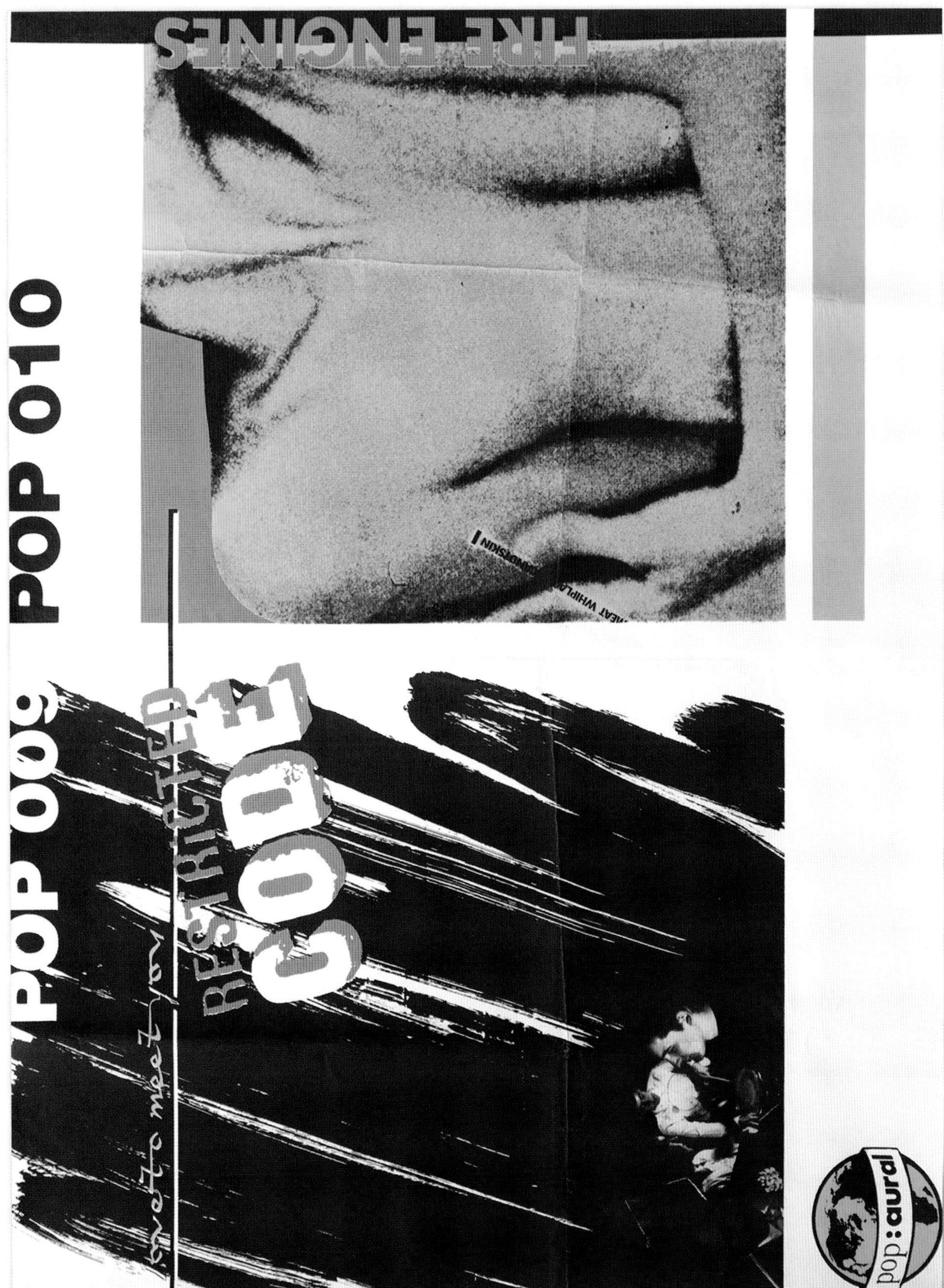

FIRE ENGINES: 'Candyskin' / 'Meat Whiplash' 45 poster, Pop Aural Records (1981)

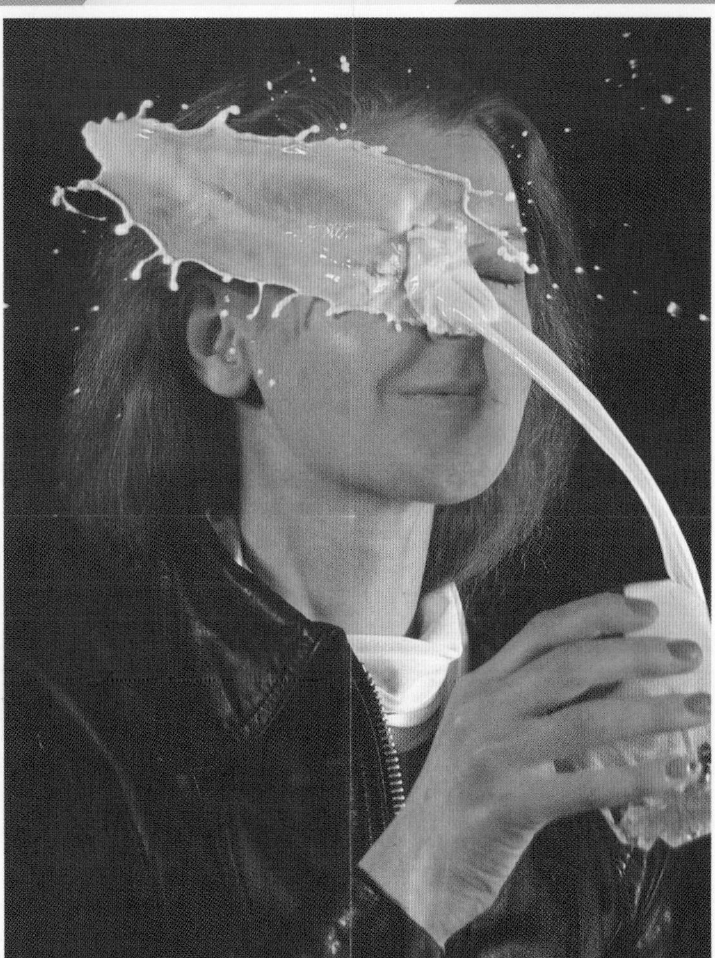

THE FLYING LIZARDS: 'Summertime Blues' debut 45 poster, Virgin Records (1978), **Flying Lizards** design

The Flying Lizards

The Flying Lizards' new album, featuring the hit single "MONEY," is now available on Virgin Records and Tapes

THE FLYING LIZARDS: *The Flying Lizards* LP poster and promo badges, Virgin Records (1979), **Laurie-Rae Chamberlain** xerography

GANG OF FOUR: (right) 'Damaged Goods' 45 promotional sticker, Fast Product (1978); (below) 'At Home He's A Tourist' 45 sticker, EMI Records (1979)

GANG OF FOUR: *Entertainment!* LP and tour blank poster, EMI Records (1979), **Jon King** design, **Cream Group (David Markham)** layout

Gang of Four's *Entertainment!*, released in 1979, ranks among the greatest albums of the punk and post-punk era. Written by a band that knows its Marxist and Situationist theory, songs such as 'Natural's Not in It', 'Damaged Goods' and 'Contract' boast some of the most incisive and politically astute lyrics in the rock canon. Their abrasive power comes from casting a detached and sceptical eye on domestic and emotional behaviour, on the dilemmas of everyday life experienced at the shops, at the disco or in bed, and refusing to reduce political issues to simplistic dogmatic slogans. As is often the case, the tour poster merely reshuffles the essential elements of the front cover, which was designed by the band members Jon King and Andy Gill, who had both studied art. First comes the title with its sardonic exclamation mark. If it's only 'entertainment' the listener wants, then this is a clear signal to look somewhere else. In three Situationist illustrated panels, the band diagrams the relationship between the colonizer (the cowboy) and the colonized (the Indian). The appearance of friendship is merely a prelude to the exploitation of resources, which was the real purpose all along. This was a challenging and frosty enticement to place on the front of a 12-inch LP released not by an independent label but by corporate EMI. On the poster with a red void in the middle, even more so than on the LP, the layout is as sharp-cornered, uncomfortable and commanding as the band's famously jagged sound.

Rick Poynor

GANG OF FOUR: poster for the 'Adieu Party' at the Ancienne Belgique, Brussels (26 June 1982)

JOSEF K: *The Only Fun in Town* LP poster, Postcard Records (1981)

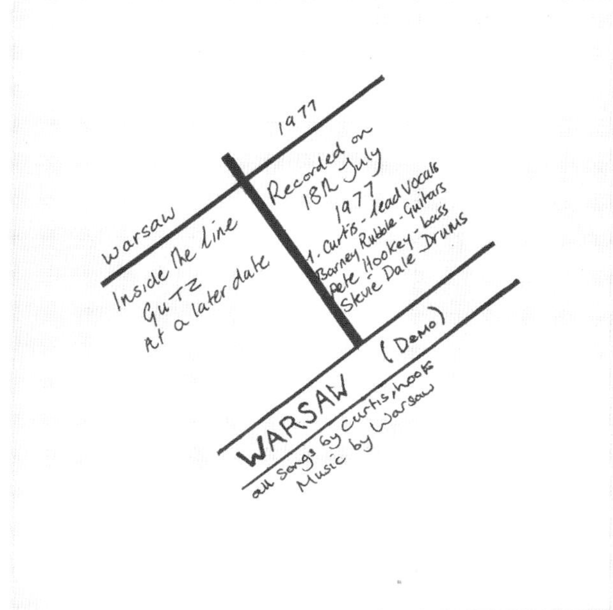

WARSAW: 'The Ideal Beginning' EP front and back cover, and sleeve interior for band who soon became **Joy Division**; unofficial pressing Enigma Records (1981), **Bernard Albrecht (Sumner)** design; **Gareth Davy** photography

JOY DIVISION: 'An Ideal for Living' EP poster, Anonymous Records (1978)

Joy Division's gig at The Factory in Hulme, Manchester on 13 July 1979 was the band's first performance at the club run by their label, following the release of their debut album *Unknown Pleasures*. A few hundred copies of this now rare poster were printed and most of them were flyposted around Manchester. Its designer – a 'js' can be seen in the corner – was the music journalist and critic Jon Savage, who would later write *England's Dreaming: The Sex Pistols and Punk Rock* (1991), one of the crucial histories of the British punk scene. As Savage notes in his essay 'A Punk Aesthetic' (2012), montage was a favourite visual tool and 'the ideal method of dealing with the detritus of consumer culture'. Among the influences on punk's visual language that he cites is Dawn Ades' book *Photomontage*, a survey of work by Alexander Rodchenko, John Heartfield, Raoul Hausmann and other artists, which was published in 1976 at the height of punk. Savage had a sideline making punk photomontages, and in 1978, in collaboration with the collage artist Linder Sterling, he published a fanzine entitled *The Secret Public*, full of bizarre and sexually provocative images. Enigmatic it may be, but the Joy Division poster is a comparatively restrained application of this often confrontational method. What manner of brain juice is being extracted by these disembodied hands, and how does this mental draining relate to the presence of a severe modernist residential block and the conventional housing down the street? More subtly disturbing is the way the 'Y' is insinuating itself on to the 'L'.

Rick Poynor

JOY DIVISION: poster for concert at The Factory, Hulme, Manchester (13 July 1979), **Jon Savage** design

JOY DIVISION: *Unknown Pleasures* Australian LP poster, GAP Records under license from Factory Records (1981), **Peter Saville** design. The image is based on an India-inked image which was included in Harold D. Craft's 1970 PhD thesis. Craft was an astronomy graduate student at Cornell University at the time and his thesis was entitled 'Radio Observations of the Pulse Profiles and Dispersion Measures of Twelve Pulsars'.

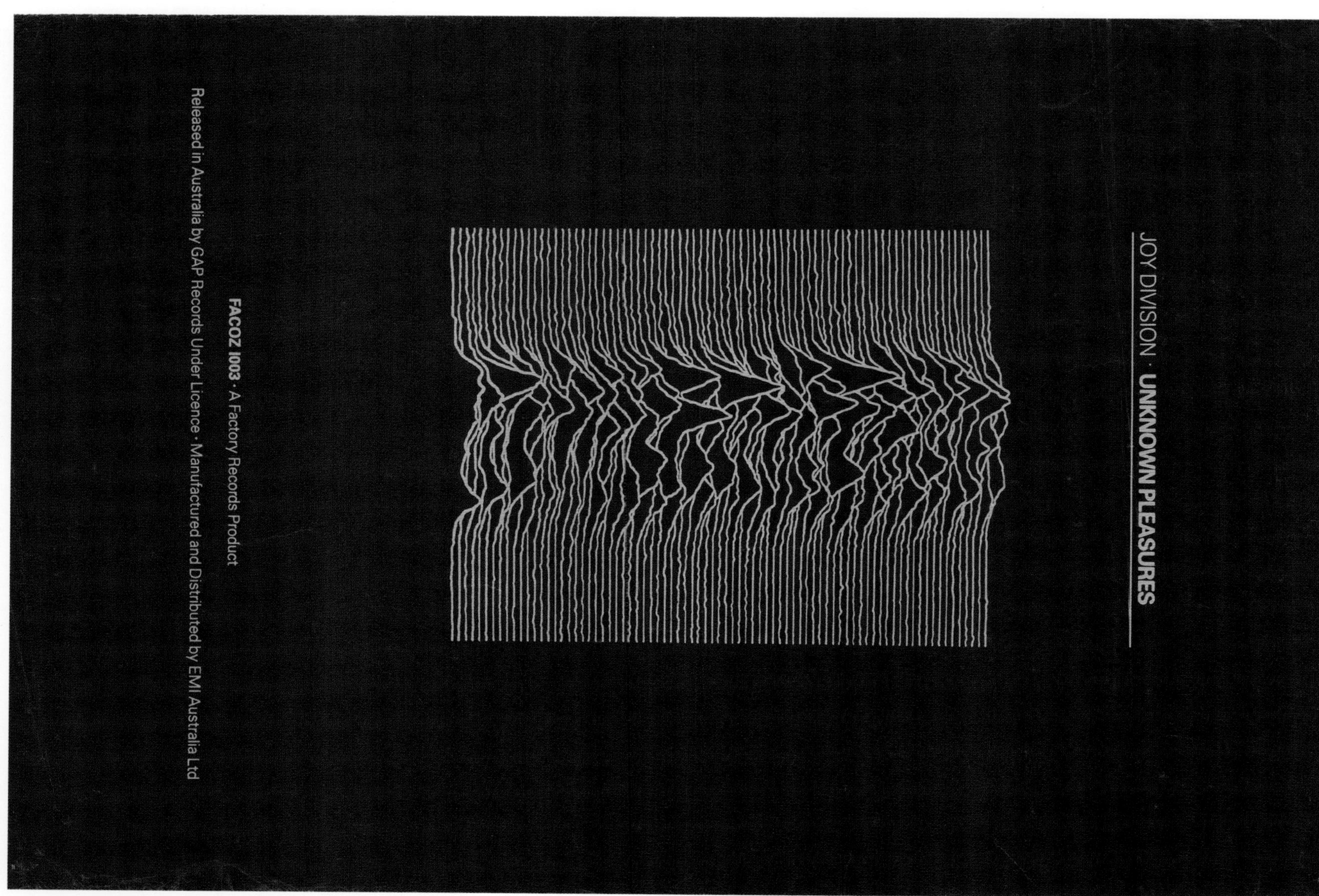

JOY DIVISION: poster reprint (c.1981) for concert at Plan K, Brussels (17 January 1980), **Jocylene Coster** design

This poster was produced to promote a gig during a brief tour of Northern Europe in early 1980, the last the band undertook before Ian Curtis' death in May of that year. Located on the site of a former sugar refinery in Brussels, Plan K was a venue known for introducing Belgian audiences to post-punk bands from Britain. The Brussels based group Digital Dance was the opening act. Several Factory Records acts performed at Plan K during the 1979-82 period, booked by Les Disques Du Crépuscule co-founder, the late Annik Honoré. This poster was designed by Jocelyne Coster and the first printing was on thin newsprint paper stock. I believe the one shown here was printed in the mid-1980s, using the original screen.

Andrew Krivine

JOY DIVISION: *Closer* LP poster, Factory Records (1980), **Peter Saville** and **Martyn Atkins** design, **Bernard Pierre Wolff** photography

This poster was acquired from a former Factory Records employee who salvaged it when the label was in the process of shutting down their offices in the early 90s. It is highly unlikely that more than a handful of this poster variant exist. According to the ex-employee, Factory intended to use this particular design to promote the record in the US but scrapped the idea after Ian Curtis' suicide in May. Given the wave of publicity surrounding his death, there was no need to invest heavily to promote the record. The poster was printed on thick, glossy paper stock and, unlike the record sleeve, the background approximates a light cream yellow, and features a photograph by Bernard Pierre Wolff (previously published in the French edition of *Zoom* magazine).

Andrew Krivine

JOY DIVISION: (above) Italian essay pamphlet *Crepuscules* (*Twilight*) by Sandro Bergamo, De Vittoria printer (c. 1980); (below) *Still* Australian LP poster, Factory Records (1981), based on LP cover design by **Peter Saville**

I WONDER WHO CHOSE THE COLOUR SCHEME, IT'S VERY NICE...

by Russ Bestley

Some punk and post-punk designers became known through their direct connection to a high-profile group or label – Jamie Reid is the most obvious example, for his brilliant work with The Sex Pistols, along with Barney Bubbles (Stiff, Radar, Elvis Costello and The Attractions, Ian Dury and The Blockheads), Peter Saville (Factory, Joy Division, New Order) and Malcolm Garrett (Buzzcocks, Magazine, The Members). Others, including Neville Brody, Russell Mills and Rob O'Connor, expanded their design remit beyond music and shaped the visual styles of the 80s in areas such as typography, magazine design, branding and advertising.

Some designers working professionally behind the scenes did at least garner some acknowledgement from fans as they became more closely associated with a particular group over time. Arturo Vega (Ramones), Bill Smith (The Jam), Peter Christopherson (Throbbing Gristle), Raymond Pettibon (Black Flag), Winston Smith (Dead Kennedys), Gee Vaucher (Crass) and Vaughan Oliver (4AD Records) are obvious examples. Mike Coles is another such designer – an image-maker who developed his own unique aesthetic, inspired hundreds of followers and provided a powerful visual background to the music produced by his collaborators.

In 1976, armed with '£90, a rucksack and a little book of drawings', Coles arrived in London and set out to find work as a commercial artist. He began working freelance in design studios, doing paste-up artwork at a studio that, in his words, '... was one of the last of the old-fashioned, traditional art studios left in London – hot metal type, Cow Gum, Letraset, and a tea lady'. A friend

ABOVE: Malicious Damage clock, **Mike Coles** (1979)

gave him a set of prints by 1930s political photomontage artist John Heartfield, which inspired him to try his own experiments in montage and collage: 'Apart from Heartfield, I loved George Grosz, Gilbert and George and Francis Bacon, plus lots of Victorian freak show stuff. I had always been fascinated by Robert Rauschenberg's work, and that influenced my own approach – I think it was the way his "Combines" of found objects and images showed that you could grab anything you fancy from around you and make art from it.' By contrast, Coles paid little attention to the evolving visual styles associated with the burgeoning punk movement: 'I never took much notice of all the punk stuff; it wasn't until years later that I knew who many of my contemporary designers involved in the scene were, apart from maybe Jamie Reid. I went to lots of gigs and loved all the energy, atmosphere and partying involved, but once back home I was listening to dub, reggae and jazz. I never really felt a part of the punk movement... ever the outsider...'

Asked if he wanted to be involved in setting up a new independent record label based around a new, upcoming band, Coles jumped at the chance. The band turned out to be Killing Joke, the label Malicious

KILLING JOKE: 'Turn to Red' 45/UK tour blank poster, Malicious Damage Records (1979), **Mike Coles** design

KILLING JOKE debut LP cover, **Mike Coles** design for Malicious Damage (1980)

KILLING JOKE: debut LP back cover, **Mike Coles** design and typography for Malicious Damage (1980)

Damage. Killing Joke roadie and future dance music superstar Alex Paterson (AKA The Orb) saw a sign in a bus stop threatening prosecution for malicious damage, and suggested '...that's a good name for a record label', and the designer responded with the classic Malicious Damage visual identity – a smashed clock. 'The idea came from a book about Hiroshima, where I saw a photograph of a watch that had frozen at the moment the bomb dropped. I liked the idea of getting a clock and smashing it, freezing my own little moment in time. Little did I think anyone would care thirty-six years later!' Even this visual device holds a secret – with almost obsessive attention to detail, each Malicious Damage release features a time displayed on the clock face corresponding exactly with the catalogue number of the record.

Coles chose to work with highly charged graphic images for Killing Joke's visual identity, instead of the more traditional approach of including photographs of the band. 'We all shared a similar sense of the absurd. Initially I worked on my own and then showed stuff to the band which they either liked or didn't like. One main point of the early artwork was to try and keep the band totally anonymous and just package the music in weird imagery that made you want to dig further, hence no band photos.' He utilized large blocks of flat colour, as in the stark composition for the cover of the debut Killing Joke 10-inch EP, 'Turn to Red', combining a hand-drawn image of Mr Punch with a photograph of the Centre Point building in central London and two children taken from an old advert for Odol toothpaste: 'Mr Punch was something that fascinated me before Malicious Damage or Killing Joke. That drawing from the first single was done in 1977 after I'd been to the Punch & Judy festival in Covent Garden. I think all the masks, children, war stuff etc., is possibly me reflecting my own childhood. Tall buildings and skyscrapers have always fascinated me, and it's easy to take a dramatic photo of a tall building.'

A similarly stark, high-contrast image treatment led to the creation of one of Killing Joke's most iconic covers, the eponymous debut album in August 1980. The original photograph, by renowned British war photographer Don McCullin, shows Irish youths running away from British troops in Derry, and was taken from *The Sunday Times Magazine* of 16 December 1971 – incidentally just six weeks prior to the notorious Bloody Sunday massacre in the same city. Coles applied white gouache to render the Killing Joke name on a central wall, and then distressed the photograph to create a stark, black-and-white, almost silhouetted image.

The back cover displayed some of the designer's prowess in experimental typography: 'In those days working a lot with typographers and art directors was a bit of a pain, everything had to be perfect and calculated. So when I was doing my own stuff I kicked back against this. The tracklisting on the back of the first KJ album was very Dada-influenced. I also had an old typewriter that I used occasionally, as on the Ski Patrol 'Agent Orange' cover.

'Typesetting was expensive in those days, so Letraset was the preferred option, as most studios had drawers full of it. Sometimes a friendly typographer would sneak something

KILLING JOKE

KILLING JOKE: promo poster using an infamous photo of Nazi brownshirts Sieg Heiling the German abbot, Alban Schachleiter (c. 1934), **Mike Coles** design for Malicious Damage (1980)

onto a job in return for a few beers, but it still had to be smuggled through the system. Often the rough and ready look was because I didn't have large point Letraset, couldn't afford PMTs and used photocopies to enlarge it. These days there's almost too much choice. The funny thing is, I now print type out small, scan it back in and enlarge it, in order to get that rough-edged look from the old days...'

One poster produced for Killing Joke around this time reflects Coles' attitude toward the hypocrisy of organized religion, while at the same time employing his characteristic dark humour: 'I see the humour and the grotesque running parallel. I don't actually try to be funny per se, there's always an element of menace, a threat perhaps. I think a lot of it is ingrained from all that priest/nunnery stuff of my childhood. Lots of smiles and hand-holding but all the while telling you about the horrors of hell and the wrath of God. I remember as a kid, being told the Devil could be hiding everywhere, even inside the nicest of people. I used to go around staring at folk wondering if they were the devil in disguise. I think I'm still doing it.'

Widely known among fans as the 'Pope and the Nazis' image, the poster depicts a Benedictine monk being saluted by a line of Brownshirts in 1930s Germany. Unlike his collage compositions, the irony in the 'Pope' image is clear to see within the original photograph, and no further intervention was necessary: 'Well that image (it's actually the Benedictine monk and musicologist Alban Schachleiter) was brought in by Youth. It was tiny, about two inches square. I couldn't see any point in fiddling with it; what can you do with an image like that, it's already evil, nasty and corrupted, nothing I could do would make it worse. So we just put Killing Joke at the top. I kicked back against religion big-time in my teens, having been brought up as an altar boy and studying for the priesthood. All that Catholic iconography is burned into you from a very early age so I guess that had a profound effect on what I was doing. It finally dawned on me on a visit to Lourdes when I was fifteen that the whole thing was a sick commercial enterprise. It took me years to come to terms with the anger and resentment. Now that I'm over it, I can enjoy visiting churches and cathedrals and stealing the imagery/iconography for my own distorted ends.'

That dark humour had already been at the fore in Coles' sleeve design for the second Killing Joke release, the single 'Wardance' / 'Pssyche' in February 1980. He worked through a number of iterations of dancers placed disconcertingly alongside war photographs, before arriving at a composite montage that 'worked' – Fred Astaire nimbly springing over bodies strewn around First World War trenches, set against a

KILLING JOKE: *What's THIS For...!* LP poster, Malicious Damage Records via EG Records (1981), **Mike Coles** design

blood red sky. Another subtle typographic twist could be seen in the unusual Letraset characters chosen for the song titles, though once again this was driven as much by necessity and the physical materials available as by 'design': 'The oblique/italicized W and A in "Wardance" and the double S in "Pssyche" were done because that was an option on the Letraset sheet, and it looked good. Quite often, before starting a job, I'd have to go through the Letraset to make sure I had sheets with all the requisite characters. Aesthetics came second. It really was a case of using what was available.'

This was a period of dramatic change for the printing industry. While graphic designers found themselves gaining far greater control over the full range of production processes in the realization of their work, it also led to the requirement of a host of highly specialist new skills in order to bring each job to completion. 'I look back at what I did using the old methods with an immense fondness and love the finished results, but it was only using what was available and, more crucially, what was affordable. These days I love using Photoshop and digital photography. Funnily enough, though, although I take a lot of my own photos, I still have and utilize often, the big box of old magazines and printers' samples I had in the 70s. I paid £50 in 1977 for a big box of printing and advertising books and samples, and that along with my ever-growing collection of old magazines constitutes my "stash"... Often I'll assemble a folder of images and scans suitable to the project, then just play with them and see what works. I love the surprise of what can happen this way. I've never really enjoyed the task of chasing a brief, hence my lack of success designing in the corporate world. I still consider myself artist first, designer second.'

(This essay was abridged from an article originally published in Punk & Post Punk 5.3, Autumn 2016.)

KILLING JOKE: 'Wardance' / 'Pssyche' 45 poster, Malicious Damage Records (1980), **Mike Coles** design

MALCOLM MCLAREN: (right) *Duck Rock* LP poster, Charisma/Island Records (1983), **Nick Egan** design, **Dondi White** graffiti, **Keith Haring** artwork; (below) *Duck Rock* LP poster, Island Records (1982), **Nick Egan** design

Duck Rock was a very early 'World Music' record, fusing sounds from Africa, Latin America and, of course, hip-hop into a layered mosaic. Malcolm McLaren identified the two most influential NYC street artists of the early 1980s. In collaboration with Nick Egan, Keith Haring provided the background illustration, graffiti artist Dondi White created the 'Duck Rock' lettering and the customized boom box took centre stage. As an art school student, Nick designed sleeves for two of The Clash's great singles in 1978, '(White Man) In Hammersmith Palais' and 'Tommy Gun'. He went on to design several covers for Malcolm McLaren, including those for Bow Wow Wow and his solo records.

Andrew Krivine

MALCOLM MCLAREN: 'Carmen' 45 poster, Charisma Records (1984), **The Artful Dodgers** design, **Robert Erdmann** photography

The model in the poster was clothed by Vivienne Westwood, possibly from Worlds End, her post-Seditionaries boutique. Worlds End opened in 1980 and created designs for the teenage Annabella Lwin for the launch of Bow Wow Wow by Malcolm McLaren.

Andrew Krivine

MALCOLM MCLAREN: *Fans* LP poster, Island Records (1984), **Nick Egan** design, **Roger Erdmann** photography

MAXIMUM JOY: (above) 'White and Green Place' 45 poster, Y Records (1982)

THE MONOCHROME SET: (above, right) 'The Lighter Side of Dating' 45 poster, Din Disc Records (1980)

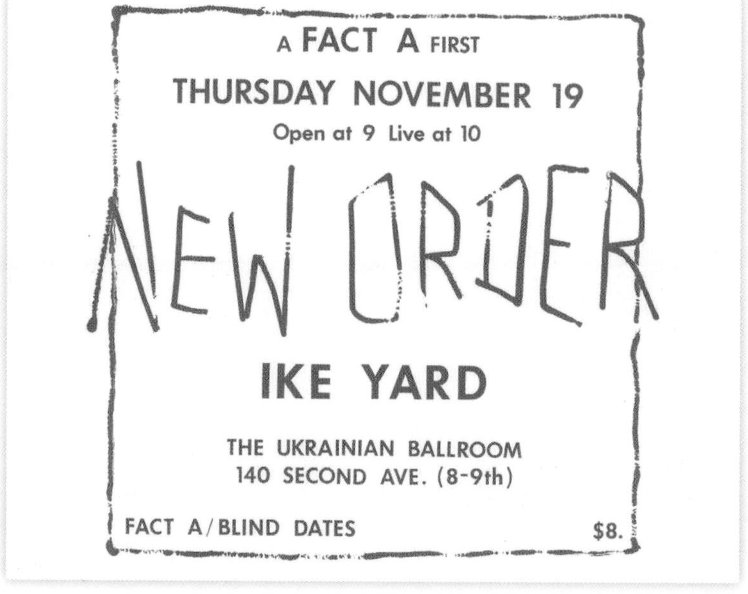

NEW ORDER: poster for the first New Order performance in New York (1981), **Stuart Argabright** and **Michael Shamberg** design

NEW ORDER: (left) poster for gig in Bedford, UK (1981); (below) poster for gig in Berlin, Germany (1981)

This poster features a funereal design with what could be marble heads from a Grecian archaeological site. Of note: at the time that New Order was touring Germany the group had not yet established its post-Joy Division identity – hence the title on the poster. In less than two years, following the release of the monster club hit single 'Blue Monday', New Order would be recognized globally. Club SO36 was one of the finest punk/post-punk venues in Berlin. Located in the Kreuzberg area, the club's name references a local postcode.

Andrew Krivine

1

2

3

NEW ORDER: 1 *Movement* debut LP poster, Factory Records (1981), **Peter Saville** and **Grafica Industria** design, influenced by a poster created for the 1932 'Futurismo Trentino' exhibition by Fortunato Depero; **2** poster for concert at Perkins Palace, Pasadena, CA (6 November 1981); **3** '1981–1982' EP poster, Factory Records (1982), **Peter Saville** design, **Martha Ladly** painting

This was New Order's second LP. Peter Saville found this image on a postcard of the painting 'A Basket of Roses' by French artist Henri Fantin-Latour and then affixed a colour-coded strip to the upper-right corner. Of note: this record cover was issued as a stamp by the Royal Mail in January 2010, as part of a selection based on a 'Top 10 record sleeves of all time' survey conducted in Britain.

Andrew Krivine

NEW ORDER: (above) *Power, Corruption & Lies* LP poster, Factory Records US (1983); (right) UK tour poster (August 1984)

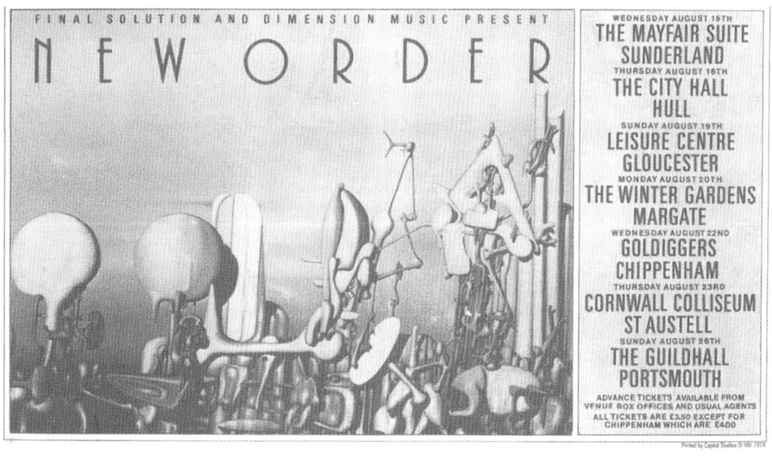

OMD: *Organisation* LP poster, Dindisc Records (1980), **Trevor Key** and **Peter Saville** design, **Richard Nutt** photography

The graphic designer Peter Saville is almost as famous now as many of the post-punk and new wave bands he worked for, and it tends to be his best and most iconic covers, rather than the routine ones, that are shown again and again. The sleeve Saville designed for *Organisation* (1980), the second album by Orchestral Manoeuvres in the Dark (OMD), a synth-pop band founded by Andy McCluskey and Paul Humphreys, doesn't feature in his monograph, published in 2003. It might not be a classic cover but in the context of new wave music it was still distinctive, adopting a restrained style of presentation more usually found on contemporary jazz albums released by a label such as ECM. The poster follows the same format, except there are extra words to accommodate at the bottom. The photograph by Richard Nutt shows Marsco, said to be the finest of the Red Hills on the Isle of Skye in Scotland. The brooding picture suits the album's melancholic tone, although the wild outdoor imagery is intriguingly at odds with the band's technological futurism. Some additional conceptual tension arises from Saville's use of sans serif typography, which is not the obvious choice to support such a romantic picture (the album title is set in a more traditional serif face). There is no integration of text and image. Instead, the designer presents the photograph as a complete image in itself, like an exhibit on a gallery wall. This was an early example of Saville's tendency to milk his selections as art director for every scintilla of stylistic meaning. Everything rested on how something was framed.

Rick Poynor

OMD: (above) *Orchestral Manoeuvres in the Dark* debut LP poster, CBS Records (1981), **Peter Saville** design; (right) tour poster for concert at Trinity Hall, Bristol, Dindisc Records (February 1980), **Peter Saville** design

OMD: *Architecture & Morality* LP/tour poster for concert at Cornwall Coliseum, St Austell, Dindisc Records (28 November 1981)

1

OMD: 1 'Souvenir' 45 poster, Dindisc Records (1981); **2** German tour poster (1983); **3** *Dazzle Ships* LP poster, Virgin Records (1983), based on an original design by **Peter Saville** for the single, 'Telegraph'

modern Sounds presents
Orchestral
O
M
Manœuvres
D
In The Dark
CONCERT '83

22. 3. MÜNCHEN Deutsches Museum
23. 3. FRANKFURT Jahrhunderthalle
24. 3. HANNOVER Kuppelsaal
25. 3. HAMBURG CCH
26. 3. DÜSSELDORF Philipshalle
28. 3. BERLIN Eissporthalle
29. 3. NÜRNBERG Meistersingerhalle
30. 3. MANNHEIM Mozartsaal
31. 3. DORTMUND Westfalenhalle II
Der Vorverkauf hat begonnen!

2

3

THE PASSIONS: 'The Swimmer' 45 poster, Polydor Records (1980)

PERE UBU: (below) *Dub Housing* LP/tour blank poster, Chrysalis Records (1978), **John Thompson** design, **Mike Mellen** photography

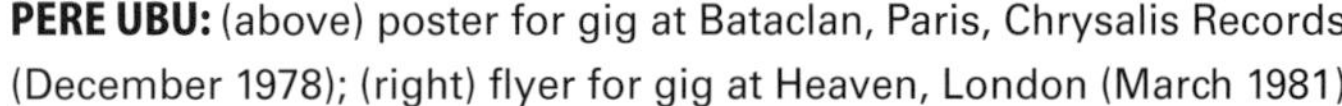

PERE UBU: (above) poster for gig at Bataclan, Paris, Chrysalis Records (December 1978); (right) flyer for gig at Heaven, London (March 1981)

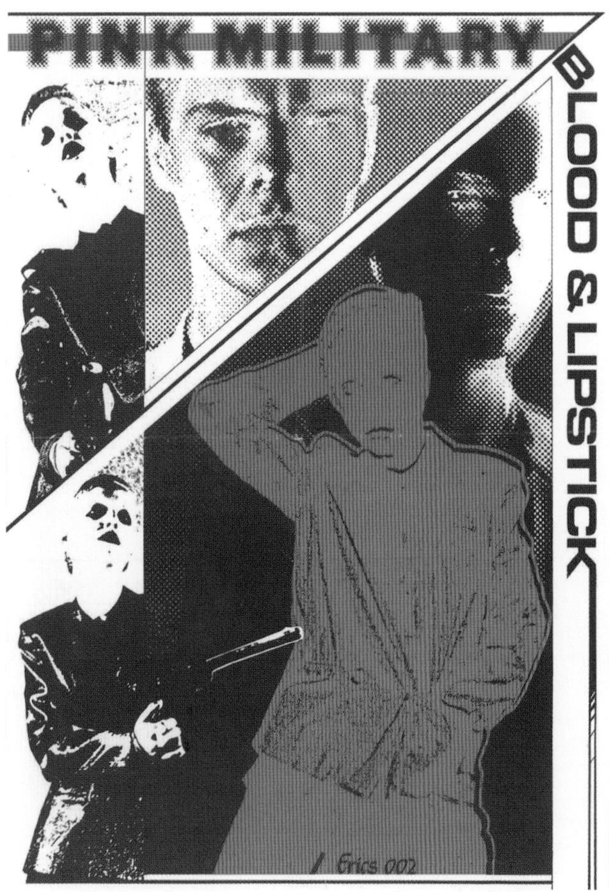

PINK MILITARY: (left) 'Blood & Lipstick 12-inch single poster, Eric's Records (1979)
POISON GIRLS: (right) 'All Systems Go' poster, Crass Records (1981), **Lance D'Boyle** design

THE POP GROUP: (below) poster for concert in Cardiff (February 1978); (right) *For How Much Longer Must We Tolerate Mass Murder?* LP poster, Y Records (1980)

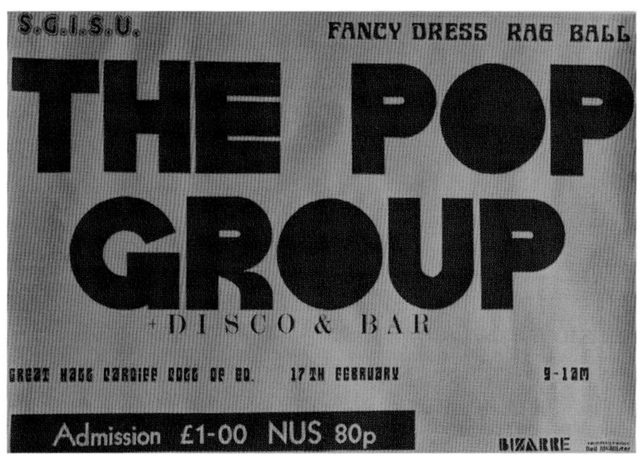

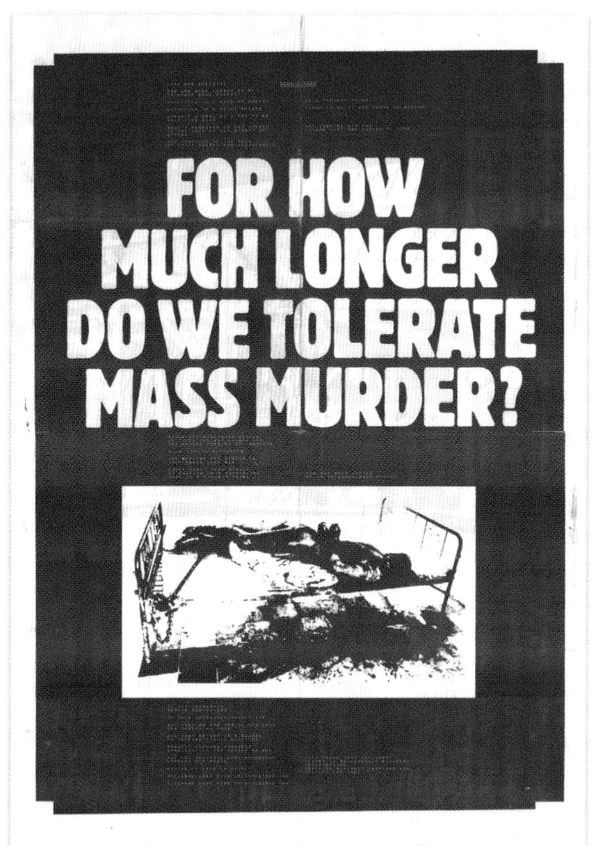

THE POP GROUP / THE SLITS: 'In the Beginning There Was Rhythm' 45 poster, Y Records (March 1980)

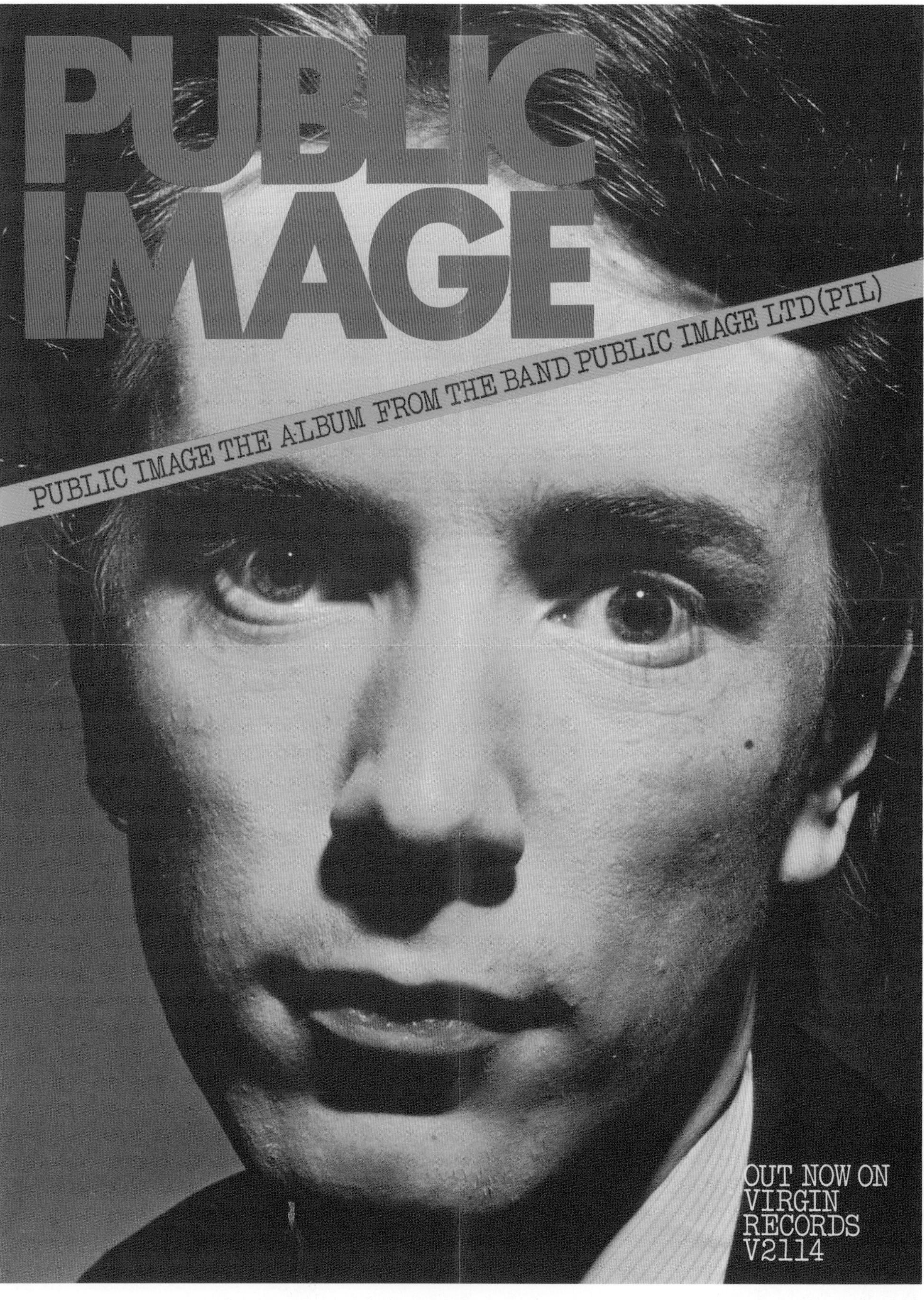

PUBLIC IMAGE LTD: *Public Image* debut LP poster, Virgin Records (1978), **Zebulon** design, **Dennis Morris** photography

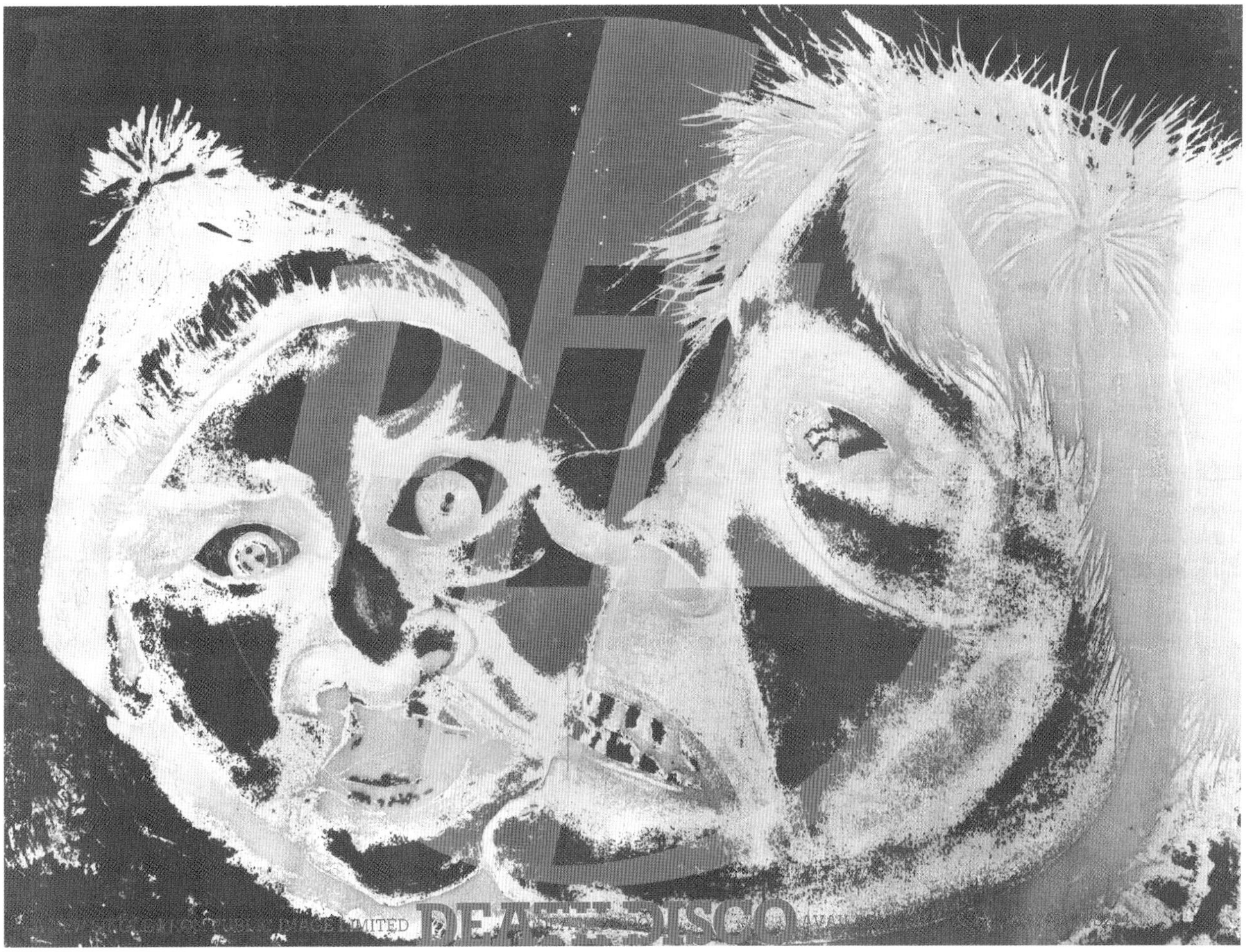

PUBLIC IMAGE LTD: 'Death Disco' 45 poster, Virgin Records (1979), **John Lydon** artwork

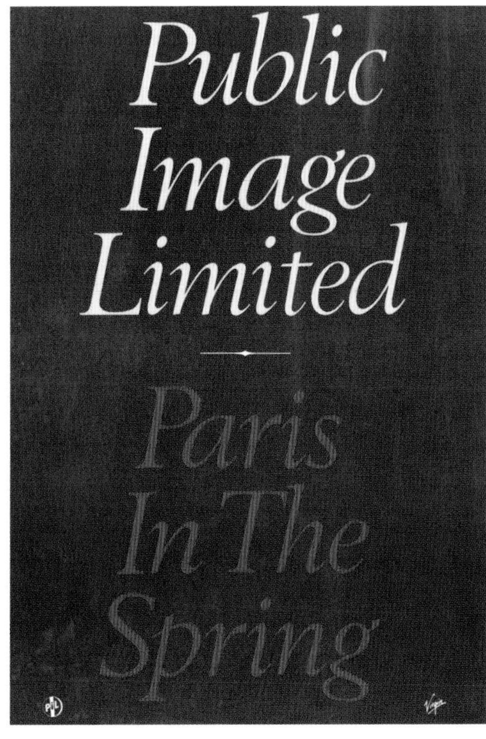

PUBLIC IMAGE LTD: (left) 'Memories' 45 poster, Virgin Records (1979); (right) *Paris Au Printemps* LP poster; Virgin Records (1980), **Image Publique S.A.** design

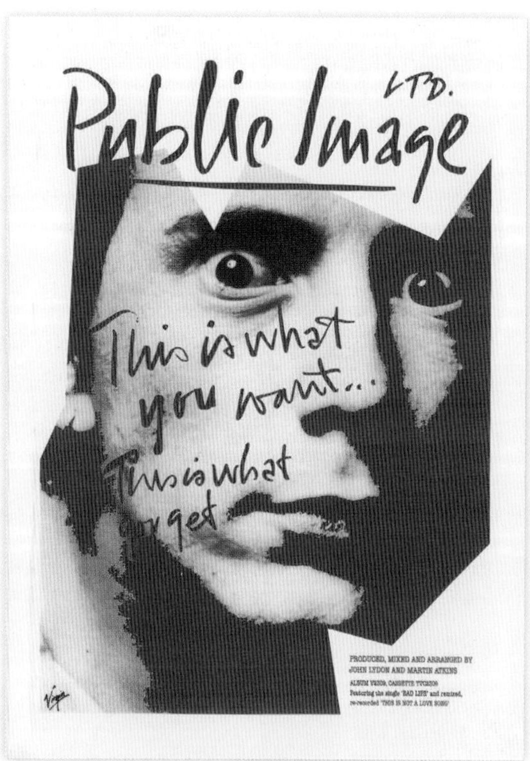

PUBLIC IMAGE LTD: *Metal Box* LP poster (above), Virgin Records (1979); (left) *That is What You Want... This Is What You Get* LP poster, Virgin Records (1984)

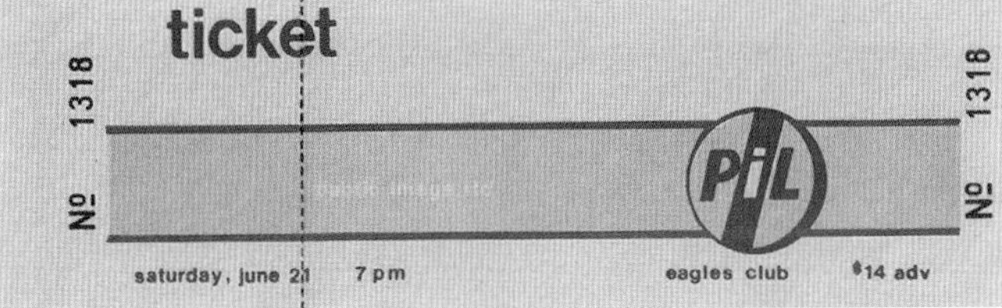

PUBLIC IMAGE LTD: (top) *Album* LP poster, Virgin Records (1986); (bottom) US tour ticket (1986)

In 1978, the cover of XTC's album *Go 2* presented buyers with a text. 'This is a RECORD COVER. This writing is the DESIGN upon the record cover.' And so the text continued, deconstructing the entire design process. For a while it seemed like the last word on the mechanics of promotion and sales. But eight years later, Public Image Ltd's *Album* pushed the process of demystification as far as it can go without eliminating the design entirely and presenting the merchandise in a wordless plain wrapper. The idea came from the standardized generic packaging used by Ralphs supermarket in Southern California, which makes an appearance in the cult film *Repo Man* (1984). The vinyl disc simply bore the word 'Album' on the cover, along with two blue rules and the PiL logo. Every other piece of printed material connected with the release was treated in the same way: Compact Disc, Cassette, Single, 12-inch Single, Video and Poster to hang on the wall. There was no other information. The playwright Bertolt Brecht called this kind of spectacle-revealing manoeuvre the 'alienation effect'. No matter what the image on a cover might be, as a rule we take its presence for granted. Only by removing it and then stating the obvious – this is an Album and that's all there is – can buyers be encouraged to think about what the process of promoting and consuming the music ordinarily involves. Paradoxically, the effect of breaking the spell is most likely to pique interest and renew the consumer's commitment to the experience. So long as it remains a rarity, the album that eschews the usual promotional paraphernalia has a great deal of cachet, and the cover succeeds by sleight of hand in encouraging the act of purchase that everybody wants, even diehard punks.

Rick Poynor

R.E.M.: (opposite) **1** flyer mock-up for concert at First Avenue, Minneapolis, MN (26 April 1982); **2** 'Chronic Town' EP poster, IRS Records (1982); **3** *Murmur* LP poster, IRS Records (April 1983); **4** tour poster (with The Three O'Clock), IRS Records (1983)

PUNISHMENT OF LUXURY: (above) poster for concert in Cologne, UA Records (March 1980)

PYLON: (right) *Gyrate* US tour blank poster, DB Records (1980), **Sean Bourne** design

r.e.m.
From Athens,GA.
Mon. APRIL 26th
1

R.E.M.
chronic town
a five song, twelve inch $5.98 list ep
produced by mitch easter + r.e.m.
© 1982 International Record Syndicate, Inc. Manufactured and distributed by A&M Records, Inc.
2

3

R.E.M.
MURMUR
$6.98 list

4
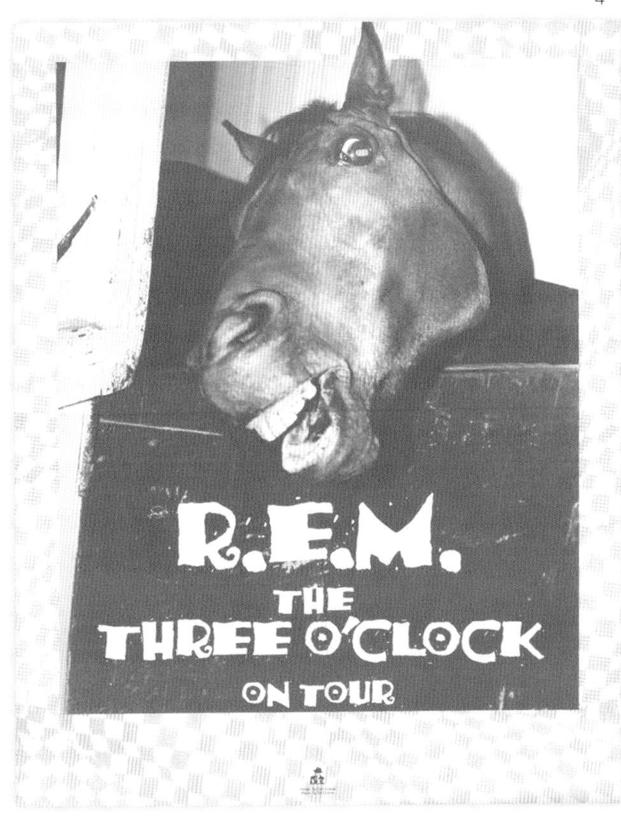
R.E.M.
THE
THREE O'CLOCK
ON TOUR

1

2

3

REMA-REMA: 1 flyer for gig at Moonlight Club, West Hampstead, London (6 February 1979); **2** flyer for gig at Screen On The Green cinema, Islington, London (30 March 1979); **3** flyer for gig at Acklam Hall, Notting Hill, London (26 April 1979), all **Gary Asquith** design

1

2

RICH KIDS: 1 front cover of promotional book (1978), **Rocking Russian** design; **2** 'Ghosts of Princes in Towers' 45 flyer, EMI Records (1978); **3** UK tour poster, EMI Records (1978), **Rocking Russian** design, signed by the band

3

SCARS: (left) *Author! Author!* LP poster, Pre Records (1981), **Rocking Russian** design

PETE SHELLEY: (above, right) *Homosapien* LP poster, Genetic Records (1981), **Paul Henry** sleeve design, **Bruno Christian Tilley** graphics, **Trevor Rogers** photography; (below) UK tour blank poster (1982)

SKI PATROL: 'Cut' 45 poster, Malicious Damage Records (1981), **Mike Coles** design, **Francis Cook** background photograph, foreground image from Todd Browning's 1932 film *Freaks*

1

2

3

FINAL SOLUTION
PRESENTS —
The SLITS,
VINCENT UNITS
MOA AMBASSA
DOORS OPEN 8.00 P.M
FRIDAY 18 JAN 1980 The UNIVERSITY of LONDON,
MALET ST, W.C.1.
TICKETS £2.00, AVAILABLE
FROM — ROUGH TRADE, SMALL WONDER RECORDS, HONKY TONK RECORDS,
BOYS, or ON THE DOOR.

THE SLITS: 1 'Man Next Door' 45 poster, Y Records (1980); **2** 'Earthbeat' 45 poster; CBS Records (1981), **Neville Brody** design; **3** poster for concert at The University of London (18 January 1980)

THE SLITS: *Return of the Giant Slits* LP poster, CBS Records (1981), **Neville Brody** design

THE SMITHS

MEAT IS MURDER

FEATURING HOW SOON IS NOW?

THE SMITHS: *Meat Is Murder* US LP poster, Sire Records (1985), image from *In The Year of the Pig* d. Emile de Antonio (1968), **Morrissey** design, **Caryn Gough** layout

1

2

3

THE SMITHS: 1 'Panic' 45 poster, Rough Trade Records (1986), **Morrissey** design, **Caryn Gough** layout, Richard Bradford cover star; **2** front of US tour programme (June 1985), **Caryn Gough** layout; Viv Nicholson cover star (courtesy of Syndication International); **3** *The Smiths* US LP poster; Sire Records/Rough Trade Records (1984). The Smiths never allowed their likeness to be used in any materials to promote records in the UK.

1

2

STOCKHOLM MONSTERS: 1 'How Corrupt Is Rough Trade?' 45 poster, Factory Benelux Records (1985); **2** 'Happy Ever After' 45 front cover, Factory Records (1982), **Mark Farrow** design

VIC GODARD & THE SUBWAY SECT: 3 flyer for gig at The Forum, London (1981) referencing Magritte's 1964 work, 'Son of Man'; **4** 'Stop That Girl' 45 poster, Oddball Records (1981)

3

4

Suicide. Four decades later the band name still alarms. What kind of nihilism is this? Are Alan Vega and Martin Rev proposing there is something desirable about self-elimination, something to be applauded? Like many punk gestures, what the name 'means' is the outrage, offence, confusion and dissonance it provokes. Vega and Timothy Jackson's visual interpretation celebrates the horror with an image that could be blood trails from a slit wrist, or the mess on the wall from a gunshot to the head. The album cover artwork's more complex colour splurge becomes, in the promotional poster, a uniformly gore-red silhouette, a kind of logo, into which the band picture, harshly outlined in black, can be plugged. The photo anticipates the looser sonic experiments of post-punk, which Suicide's rhythmic electronics prefigure, and looks back to Warhol and the Factory, and the psychedelic solarizations of 1960s album covers. There is nothing remotely punk about the close-set typography, which gives the lurid crimson bouquet a firm base. The red star moves from its central position at the apex on the album cover to a corner spot calculated to disrupt the symmetry. These graphic details are all signs that a professional designer's hand is at work. This poster is far from being a semi-articulate howl of disgust. By placing the elements with a precision that borders on being tasteful, the designer has made the band's attitude even more disquieting and harder to fathom for those not in the know. For Suicide fans tuned into its brutal iconoclasm, the cold, alienating aesthetic is abominably cool.

Rick Poynor

SUICIDE: *Suicide* debut LP poster, Cherry Red Records (1977), **Timothy Jackson** artwork

THE TEARDROP EXPLODES: 1 'Reward' 45 front cover; Phonogram Records (1981), **Martyn Atkins** design; **2** Out of the Culture Bunker UK tour poster (June 1981); **3** *Wilder* Australian LP tour poster, Mercury Records (1981), **Martyn Atkins** typography and photography

1

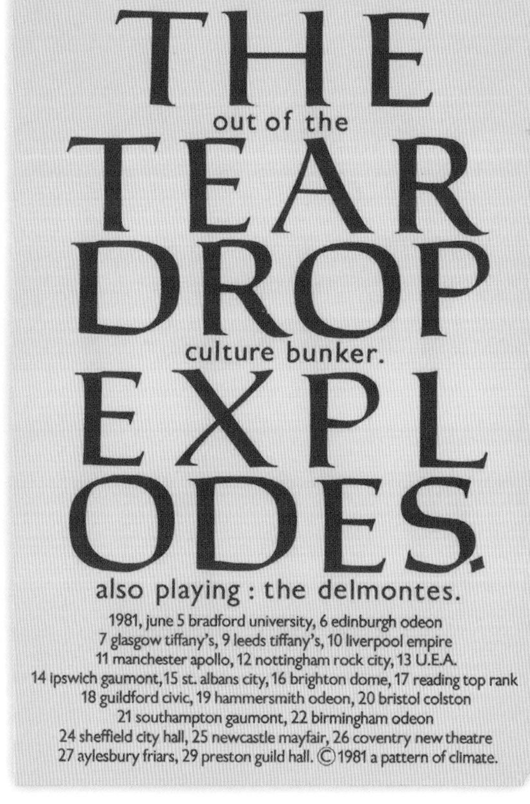

2

3

THEATRE OF HATE: flyer for concert at University of London (May 1981)

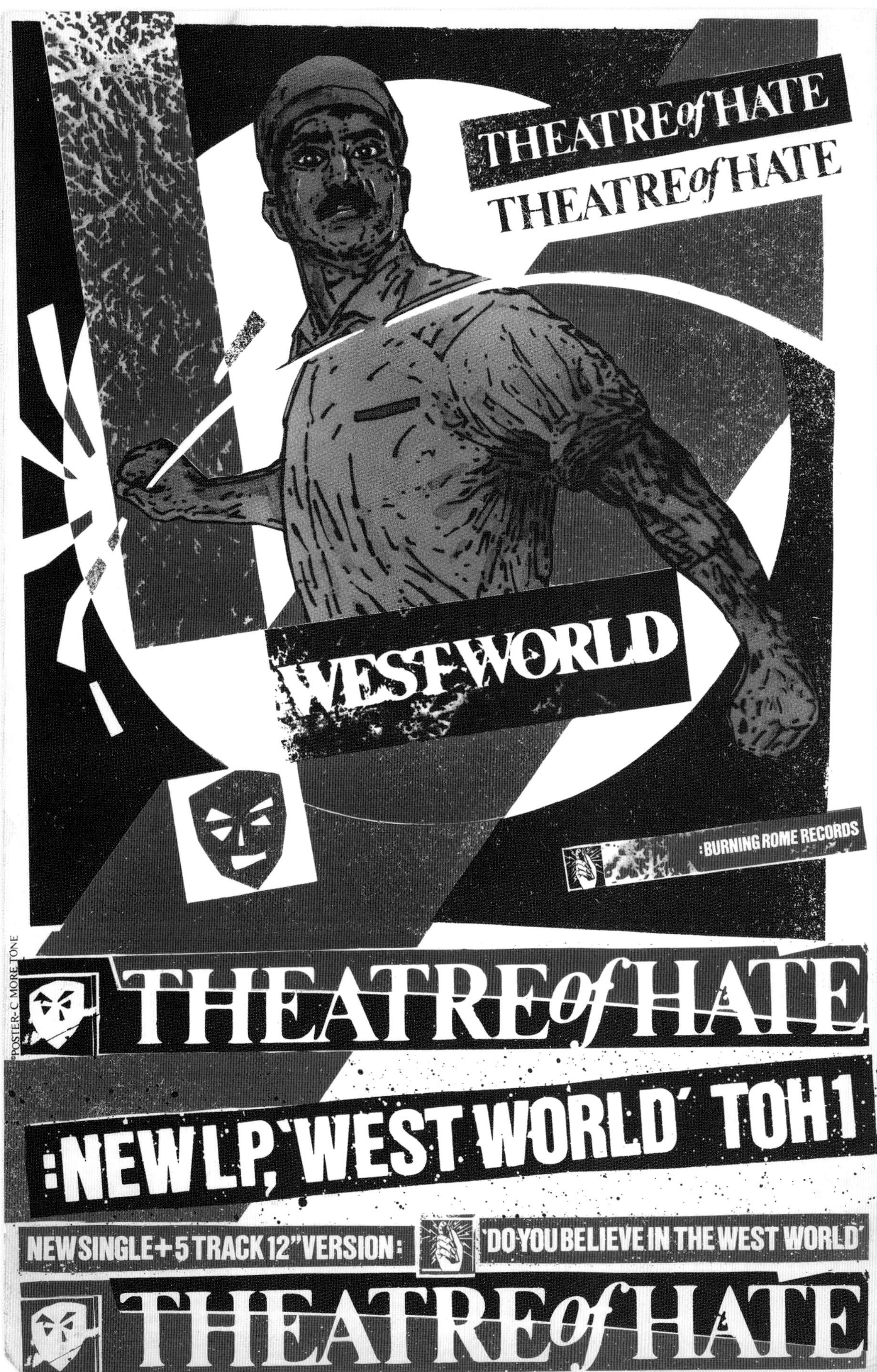

THEATRE OF HATE: *West World* LP poster, Burning Rome Records (1982), **Chris Morton** (aka C. More Tone) design

1

2

3

344

THROBBING GRISTLE: 1 *D.o.A.* LP advertisement from *ZigZag* magazine (November 1978); **2** Recording Heathen Earth VHS insert (1983); **3** 'We Hate You' 45 double-gatefold A4 sleeve front image, Sordide Sentimental (1979), **Yves von Bontee** collage artwork, **Loulou Picasso** pochette

ULTRAVOX: (left) *Ha Ha Ha!* LP tour blank poster, Island Records (1977), **Bloomfield-Travis** design, **Dennis Leigh** sleeve concept; (below, both) *Rage in Eden* LP posters, Chrysalis Records (1981), **Peter Saville Associates** design, based on original works by **Claus Hansmann** and **Herve Moran**

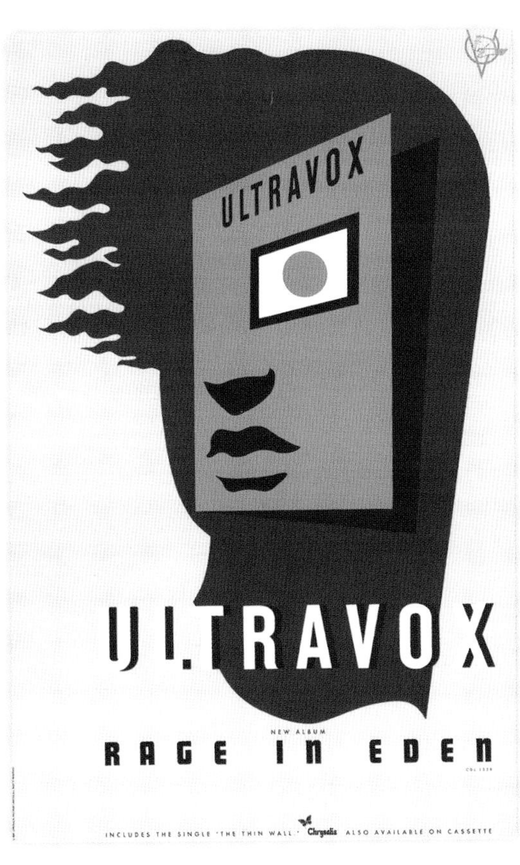

VIOLENT FEMMES: *Violent Femmes* LP poster, Slash Records (1983), **Jeff Price** design, **Ron Hugo** photography

VIRGIN PRUNES: 'Twenty Tens' EP posters, Baby Records (1980)

VIRGIN PRUNES: *...If I Die, I Die* LP poster, Rough Trade Records (1982)

1

2

3

WAH! HEAT: 1 'Better Scream' 45 front and back cover, Inevitable Records (1979); **2** '7 Minutes to Midnight' 45 poster, Inevitable Records (1980); **3** *Nah=Poo-The Art of Bluff* LP poster, Eternal Records (1981)

WALL OF VOODOO: (right) 'Wall of Voodoo' EP poster, IRS Records (1980), **Index Images** design

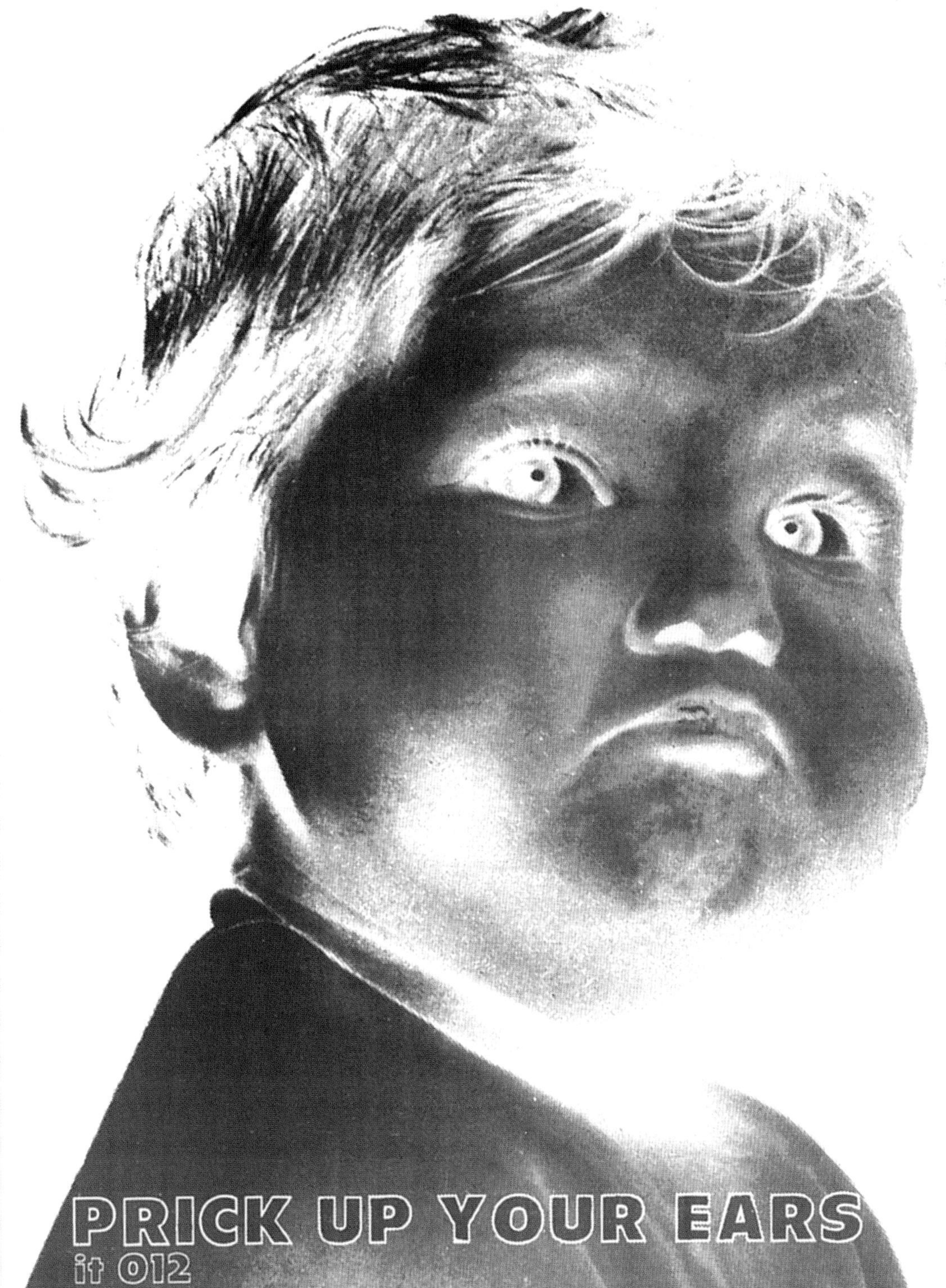

YEAH YEAH NOH: 'Prick Up Your Ears' 45 poster, In-Tape Records (1984)

CONTRIBUTORS

Dr Russ Bestley is reader in graphic design at the London College of Communication. His areas of specialist interest include graphic design and popular music, particularly punk rock. He co-authored and designed a number of books with Ian Noble, including *Visual Research* (AVA Bloomsbury, 2004, 2011, 2015), *Up Against the Wall: International Poster Design* (RotoVision, 2002) and *Experimental Layout* (RotoVision, 2001). Russ has designed books, posters, programmes and music graphics for the Punk Scholars Network, Active Distribution, Viral Age Records, PM Press and other DIY and independent labels, publishers and producers. He is editor of the journal *Punk & Post Punk*, and a member of the international Punk Scholars Network.

Art Chantry has worked in graphic design in Seattle for more than three decades. During that time, he produced a body of work that rivals some of the best graphic design in the world. An architect of the original grunge style through his work on *The Rocket* (1984–94) and with the Sub Pop label, he has won hundreds of design and advertising awards, including a bronze lion at Cannes, and the Poster Laureate of the Colorado International Invitational Poster Exposition. His work has been collected and exhibited by some of the most prestigious museums and galleries in the world, including the Louvre, the Smithsonian, the Library of Congress and the Rock and Roll Hall of Fame. In April 2017, Art was one of seven designers to receive the AIGA Medal. To this day, his hard-edge scrappy look can be seen everywhere from punk rock record covers to corporate annual reports.

Sebastian Conran is a leading international industrial designer. He is a 'closet inventor' and keen advocate of design process. His approach is both playful and pragmatic, enhancing life via the thoughtful transformation of science, technology and engineering into user experience, consumer lifestyle and social culture.

Glen Cummings is founding principal and creative director of MTWTF. His work has been widely exhibited and published. From 2002–13, Glen acted as a design critic at the Yale University School of Art, where he received his M.F.A. in graphic design. He is vice president of AIGA/NY, a fellow for the Design Trust for Public Space, and the founder of GDNYC, a consortium of designers and educators that promotes design research. Prior to his work as a designer, Glen was the guitarist of NYHC / crossover bands Ludichrist and Scatterbrain.

Malcolm Garrett RDI FISTD is the creative director of Images&Co, a partnership with writer Kasper de Graaf dating to 1981. Malcolm has a global reputation for his influence on graphic design and popular culture, through his landmark designs for bands including Buzzcocks, Magazine, Duran Duran, Simple Minds and Peter Gabriel, and his pioneering role in championing interaction design since the early 90s. An official ambassador for Manchester School of Art, he is joint artistic director of Design Manchester, which he co-founded in 2013. Malcolm has lectured extensively, and his work has been widely exhibited around the world. He holds several honorary doctorates and professorships and was among the first ten designers to be inducted into the Design Week Hall of Fame in 2015.

Steven Heller is co-chair of the School of Visual Arts MFA Design/Designer as Author + Entrepreneur programme. He was art director of the *New York Times Book Review* and its Visuals columnist. The author or editor of over 170 books on design and popular art, he writes the Daily Heller for *Print* magazine and is a contributing writer for the Atlantic online. In 2011 he received the Smithsonian's National Design Award for 'Design Mind'.

Adam Michaels is a designer, editor and publisher. He is principal of inventory form and content and publisher of Inventory Press. Previously, he was founding principal of internationally renowned design studio Project Projects (2004–17), recipient of the 2015 Cooper-Hewitt National Design Award for Communication Design. His work is in the permanent collection of the Art Institute of Chicago and the New York Museum of Modern Art Library.

Ian Noble (b. 15 October 1960, d. 30 January 2013) was a graphic designer, writer and educator. A head of the undergraduate graphic design programme at the London College of Printing (now London College of Communication, LCC) in 1996, he went on to lead the postgraduate graphic design programme at LCC, before becoming academic director in communication design at Kingston University. Ian co-authored *Visual Research* (AVA Bloomsbury, 2004, 2011, 2015), *Up Against the Wall: International Poster Design* (RotoVision, 2002) and *Experimental Layout* (RotoVision, 2001) with Russ Bestley, and wrote *Picture Perfect: Fusions of Illustration and Design* (RotoVision, 2003).

Rick Poynor writes about design, photography and visual culture. He was founding editor of *Eye* magazine and co-founder of *Design Observer*, where he contributes a weekly column on photography. In 1986, he contributed to the cult book *More Dark Than Shark* (Faber) about Brian Eno. Other books include *Vaughan Oliver: Visceral Pleasures* (Booth-Clibborn Editions, 2000); *No More Rules: Graphic Design and Postmodernism* (Laurence King, 2003); and *Sergei Sviatchenko: Collages* (Schlebrugge, 2014).

Michael Wilde is a Pulitzer Prize- and National Book Award-winning editor, sometimes author, painter, songwriter, poet and on-again/off-again DJ for hands-on community radio, who loved to see The Cramps in their heyday. He still has the ticket for their cancelled Ritz concert the night John Lennon was shot.

INDEX OF ARTISTIC CONTRIBUTORS

AD=art direction | AW=artwork | D=design | G=graphics | P=photography | T=typography

D=design | P=photography | AW=artwork | T=typography | G=graphics